The
Treatment
of
Alcoholism

The
Treatment
of
Alcoholism

By

Edgar P. Nace, M.D.

BRUNNER/MAZEL *Publishers* • NEW YORK

Library of Congress Cataloging-in-Publication Data

Nace, Edgar P., 1939–
    The treatment of alcoholism.

    Bibliography: p. 251.
    Includes index.
    1. Alcoholism—Treatment. 2. Alcoholics—
Rehabilitation. I. Title. [DNLM: 1. Alcoholism—
therapy.   WM 274 N118t]
RC565.N32   1987   616.86'106   87-11691
ISBN 0-87630-468-4

Copyright © 1987 by Edgar P. Nace

Published by
BRUNNER/MAZEL, INC.
19 Union Square
New York, New York 10003

MANUFACTURED IN THE UNITED STATES OF AMERICA

10 9 8 7 6 5 4 3 2 1

To my wife, Carol,
and my sons, Bradford and Randolph

Acknowledgments

I am indebted to Jerry M. Lewis, M.D., who unselfishly offered support, encouragement, and attention. The time he gave enabled this project to attain a maturity which would not have been obtained otherwise. Dr. Lewis's careful consideration of each issue was a generous application of scholarship. His praise was heartening. Criticisms, suggestions, and elaborations sent me back to the drawing board with the confidence that more effort would produce a better result.

Virginia Austin Phillips read each sentence. She kindly endured split infinitives, dangling participles, and less precise assaults on the language. Her editing skills far exceeded the grammatical as she grasped the author's purpose and sharpened the contours of intent. I am grateful to her for her invaluable assistance in the preparation of this book.

Gene Usdin, M.D., offered skilled consultation and was always encouraging.

Mary Smaczniak, my secretary, was uncomplaining and unflinching as more and more demands were put on her. She prepared each revision, tracked down material, and made corrections. I very much appreciate her skill and diligence.

Along the way, other secretaries at Timberlawn Psychiatric Hospital provided substantial assistance. In particular, Ms. Pam Sandlin and Ms. Lori Buller provided excellent technical support in the early days of the project.

Finally, I would like to thank Doyle Carson, M.D., Medical Director of Timberlawn Psychiatric Hospital. Dr. Carson's encouragement of his staff and his interest in their endeavors create an atmosphere where each individual physician enjoys the opportunity to excel in his or her own way. This book represents, in part, the fruition of Doyle's leadership and I am grateful to him for the role he has played in this effort.

Contents

List of Tables and Figures

Introduction

This text is directed to psychiatrists, psychiatry residents, and medical students. Emphasis is placed on reaching physicians because of the neglect of training programs, including medical schools, to teach about alcoholism.

The intent of this text is to encourage interest in alcoholism and alcoholic patients. My experience is that if alcoholism is approached from a fresh perspective, that is from a vantage point free of the prejudices acquired during training years, a sympathetic chord will be struck as a deeper appreciation of the disease process is gained. The dreadful underlying seriousness of this illness will no longer be masked by the pathological defenses of the patient, or by physicians' biases.

All who make use of this text will not wish to undertake the clinical management of alcoholic patients. Hopefully, readers will gain an appreciation of the power of a chemical dependence on the human psyche as well as the subtleties of this dependence. The physician who has developed the ability to recognize the manifestations of the dependence and who has acquired the conviction and skill to initiate a treatment plan has the potential to arrest the destructive process of alcoholism.

If clinicians gain the skill and courage to face and directly confront the alcoholic patient with the facts of his or her illness, this step and this step alone may have a major impact on the patient's health care and, possibly, his or her well-being. Some may not wish to treat over the long term each alcoholic patient they encounter. But, if they are able to make the diagnosis, share the facts which determine the diagnosis, make a proper referral, and do so in a concerned, caring, and persistent manner, a "seed" will have been planted in the mind of the alcoholic patient. To the extent that we do not cooperate with the pathological defenses of the patient by ignoring or denying manifestations of the disease or by subtly rejecting the patient, we will be countering a destructive process. Often we will not see the end result, but the process of recovery can be initiated by any physician as a patient with alcohol dependence becomes recognized in his or her clinical work.

This text is focused on treatment and, therefore, does not attempt to cover all of the many facets of alcoholism, for example, cellular membrane physiology or anthropological considerations. References are provided in this text for the interested reader. All of the various schools of thought, theories, or points of view are not presented. The research and clinical literature are drawn upon only to the extent that they may aid in clinical management. The text is based on clinical experience in treating alcoholic patients; the experience gained from working with many excellent physicians and teachers; and, in particular, the insights shared by recovered (as well as nonrecovered) alcoholics. Attending Alcoholics Anonymous (AA) meetings and friendships with many AA members have been invaluable to me in further understanding the disease of alcoholism.

The necessary skill to undertake treatment of alcoholics will not be acquired through textbooks or scientific literature, but rather through clinical experience which allows long-term work with a sufficient variety of alcoholic patients. Then, and only then, a deeper understanding of alcoholism, an understanding that is not approached by the usual process of medical education, is obtained.

Many counselors in alcoholism treatment centers bring a strong sense of dedication and conviction to their work as a result of their own successful recovery. Few physicians will have such personal experience to motivate them. The physician's conviction of the importance of providing appropriate treatment, the belief in a positive outcome, and the dedication to the task, if not derived from a personal recovery from alcoholism, can emerge from a deeper understanding of the phenomenon of alcoholism and from an appreciation of its many consequences. However, even initial efforts to better understand this illness will falter unless the physician is willing to learn more about himself or herself. This requires an exploration of one's attitude toward, resistances against, and avoidance of alcoholic patients.

Psychiatrists who are effective with alcoholic patients strongly believe that their efforts are worthwhile. They anticipate a good outcome. They are hopeful and, therefore, instill hope. The effective psychiatrist is convinced that the alcoholic is out of control of his life and that all resources and skills must be brought to reverse the situation. Not to respond is to forward the destructive process of alcoholism, akin to offering only symptomatic treatment for a potentially curable cancer.

Initially, it will be necessary to confront the fact that alcoholism is often considered difficult to treat. The opening chapter addresses the issue of "A Difficult Task?" It is argued that the idea of treatment difficulty is derived partly from a lack of appreciation for the heterogeneity of the illness. Alcoholism is exceedingly variable in its presenting symptoms, whether one considers patterns of alcohol use or consequences of use. Patterns vary from the weekend binge, where over a fifth of whiskey a day is drunk for two to three days in a row, to the more polite daily sipping of sherry from late afternoon into evening. The presenting symptoms of alcoholism can be varied, ranging from acute medical complaints to encounters with the law. Such a range of presenting symptoms may obscure the diagnosis of alcoholism in favor of other diagnoses, for example, "anemia of undetermined etiology" or "antisocial personality disorder." Alcoholism, therefore, is protean in its association with other medical conditions. It commonly is associated with, disguised by, determined by, or contributes to other psychiatric disorders, leaving the clinician with difficult questions: How many diagnoses are there? What do I treat first? and, If alcohol is part of the picture, how?

The etiology of alcoholism is essentially unknown but is best thought of as multidetermined. Thus, another form of heterogeneity is introduced. The factors that seem to influence the development of alcoholism in one patient may not be apparent in the next. Some patients have families with extensive histories of alcoholism, others none at all. Some patients drank heavily in the face of losses, while others developed alcoholism after reaching pinnacles of success. Finally, choosing a course of treatment is a highly variable and often idiosyncratic process. Treatment planning is built upon the sands of bias and not on the bedrock of a methodologically sound data base.

In spite of the heterogeneous nature of alcoholism (and its treatment), the hurdles initially encountered can be overcome. The clinician will be able to proceed with a rationally determined course of treatment as alcoholism and the alcoholic patient are better understood. This text will discuss treatment approaches and priorities which will minimize much of the confusion surrounding the heterogeneity of alcoholism.

In the first chapter a process of getting involved will be presented. Then, overviews of epidemiology, medical consequences, and costs of alcoholism are presented in Chapter 2.

The third chapter examines "barriers" which can impede the treatment of alcoholism. These barriers are not the pathological defenses and resistances of the alcoholic patient. The latter will be discussed subsequently. Rather, the reference is to an amalgam of ignorance, pessimism, and hostility shared by many. Perhaps these barriers are inherent in and derived from society's attitudes regarding alcoholism and, unfortunately, the physician is likely to have such negativism reinforced by medical training. A closer look at these barriers will be necessary in order to remove their obstructive effect.

Next, in Chapter 4, definitions of alcoholism and alcohol abuse are presented, and the process of making a diagnosis is described. Apart from the obvious practical value of establishing a diagnosis, it is important that both patient and doctor recognize that alcoholism is an entity capable of medical verification. In part, this approach helps to negate feelings that being alcoholic is "bad" and a "label." The doctor must feel comfortable making this diagnosis and not feel that diagnosing someone as alcoholic is stigmatizing.

Why is alcoholism a disease? What phenomena provide the structure for a disease concept of alcoholism? "Lip service" is paid to the disease concept, but it is questionable how many physicians accept or understand the nature of this disease. Chapter 5 describes the phenomena which underlie the disease of alcoholism. The concept of psychological dependence is emphasized as the central experience of the alcoholic patient. The constructs of denial, craving, loss-of-control, personality regression, and conflicted behavior round out the disease concept and are related to the essential feature—psychological dependence.

Chapter 6 describes the impact of alcoholism on marriage and the family. The problems of spouse psychopathology, spouse abuse, and child abuse are presented. Dynamics operating in the marriage and family as a result of alcoholism are described. An understanding of the magnitude of alcoholism's impact on the individual, family, and society will spur most physicians to prepare themselves for the task at hand. The need to provide conscientious service will be stimulated.

In Chapter 7, "Beginning Treatment," the role of the psychiatrist in initiating treatment is reviewed, including a discussion of the doctor-patient relationship. The importance of intervention and the constructive use of crises are discussed.

The next two chapters address optimal inpatient and outpatient treatment programs and the "ingredients" which make up such programs.

Chapter 10 on "Psychodynamic Considerations" reviews psychodynamic theories as applied to alcoholism, emphasizing the varying role psychodynamics play in individual patients. For example, in some alcoholics dynamic factors may be predisposing. In other alcoholics, psychodynamics seem relevant as a precipitating factor. In most, if not all alcoholics, dynamics can modify the course of treatment and its outcome.

Chapter 11, "Specific Therapies," reviews individual, group, and family therapies. The role of psychotherapy, the timing of psychotherapy, and how therapy with an alcoholic differs from the nonalcoholic patient are discussed. This chapter presents the controversial issue of pharmacotherapy with alcoholics. Antidepressants, lithium, tranquilizers, and sedatives have often been misused in the treatment of alcoholism. A perspective on the role of psychopharmacologic agents is necessary for effective clinical management. The utilization of disulfiram will be discussed; it can be a valuable adjunct to treatment if used with a full understanding of its potential and limitations.

Chapter 12 reviews alcoholism as it relates to, or coexists with, other psychiatric disorders. Organic brain syndromes associated with alcoholism are presented and treatment described. Particular attention is given to the treatment of alcohol withdrawal syndromes. The diagnosis and treatment of depression, anxiety, and psychosis in alcoholics are discussed. The relationship between personality disorders and alcoholism requires clarification. Recovery from an addictive disorder is seen to facilitate personality growth and possibly to attenuate certain malignant features of character pathology. Finally, the relationship between drug abuse and alcoholism is reviewed.

The final chapter, on Alcoholics Anonymous (AA), reviews the background and development of the organization, with current data on AA attendance. The wisdom, support, and "healing" provided to an alcoholic by the fellowship of AA should be appreciated by physicians. The sometimes ambivalent relationship between AA and psychiatry is recognized. It is vitally important that the psychiatrist encourage and support a patient's involvement with AA. There is a need for mutual respect, but initiative on the part of the psychiatrist may be necessary to overcome distrust and to gain confidence.

Before concluding this introduction, the emphasis on abstinence needs explanation. Better health, improved vocational functioning, and more satisfying family and personal relationships are major therapeutic goals. However, the latter depend on abstinence from alcohol (Saxon, Nace, & Cammarota, 1983).

Abstinence, rather than attempts at controlled drinking, is put forth as a major treatment goal. In the late 1960s and early 1970s experimental efforts were made to teach alcoholics to drink in a controlled or restricted manner. A spate of studies utilizing behavior modification techniques, such as aversive conditioning, contingency contracting, and blood alcohol level discrimination, demonstrated that alcoholics could modify their use of alcohol and that these techniques yielded results equal or superior to controls given "traditional" treatment which emphasized abstinence (Litman & Topham, 1983). Enthusiasm for the approach was short-lived. Why? In part, the idea of controlled drinking was antithetical to the disease concept of alcoholism and resisted by traditional workers in the field. More important, however, was the recognition by many recovered alcoholics working in the field that the offer of continued use of alcohol to many if not most alcoholics was a deadly snare—a snare which might delay the alcoholic's efforts to face giving up alcohol or which might encourage some already abstinent alcoholics again to attempt to drink.

Also, results from controlled-drinking studies revealed that the major advantage of behavioral approaches was to retain patients in treatment for longer periods than controls (Litman et al., 1983). This might well be due to the increased interest which a behavioral treatment team would have in those subjects (patients) to whom the newer approaches were being applied. In addition, the early enthusiasm for controlled drinking waned as data accumulated. Ewing and Rouse (1976) found the attempt to inculcate controlled drinking as not worth the effort. Their subjects either relapsed or turned to the abstinence model. Seixas (1977), in a critical review of treatment outcome as reported in the Rand Report (Armor, Polich, & Stanbul, 1976), points out that alcoholics who were abstinent 6 months after treatment had a 3 : 2 chance of also being abstinent 18 months after treatment. Alcoholics who were drinking normally when followed up 6 months after treatment only had a 1 : 3 chance of being normal drinkers at 18 months. Those alcoholics who were drinking pathologically at 6 months after treatment only had a 1 : 6 chance they would not be drinking pathologically at the 18 month follow up. Since the Rand Report, a large long-term follow-up study of alcoholics from Washington University found stable moderate drinking to occur in only 1.6% of alcoholic subjects (Helzer et al., 1985). These data clearly show the tenuous nature of "normal drinking" in alcoholics.

Recently, controlled drinking strategies have been confounded by the finding that one of the seminal studies on the success of controlled drinking has been refuted (Sobell & Sobell, 1973). The initial positive results of this widely referenced study were found to be specious by an independent research team (Pendery, Maltzman, & West, 1982).

Most clinicians have known some alcoholics who restricted their drinking rather than strive for abstinence. Some were successful for months or years, but remained vulnerable to a return to pathological drinking. Occasionally the patient with a recent history of alcohol dependence, that is, of less than six months duration and whose life is socially and emotionally stable, may gain control over alcohol use. It is unusual, however, to see a patient in this early stage of alcoholism. By contrast, I have seen scores of alcoholics who had from time to time attempted futilely to restrict their drinking. Abstinence, therefore, is the recommended goal for the alcoholic. It is unambiguous, effective, and safe.

With this introduction, we can proceed to the more specific tasks of clinical work, the first of which is to overcome pessimism and to arm the clinician with a greater appreciation of the magnitude and spectrum of the alcoholic's defenses of denial and minimalization. Change in the clinician's attitude about alcoholism and an understanding of alcoholism as a disease are the first steps in promoting change in the alcoholic patient. We can then proceed to an understanding of psychodynamic factors, treatment settings, specific therapies, and interrelationships between alcoholism and other psychiatric disorders. The intended result is to prepare the clinician to use his or her relationship with the alcoholic to better advantage, to apply specific therapies, and to foster involvement in Alcoholics Anonymous, all in a manner which meets the unique needs of each alcoholic patient.

The
Treatment
of
Alcoholism

CHAPTER 1

A Difficult Task?

I would be inclined, if one of my relatives had to have either schizophrenia or addiction to alcohol, to believe that his chances for getting back into normal life would be greater if he had schizophrenia.—Karl Menninger, *JAMA*, 111: 1447, 1938

Dr. Menninger's discouraging tone would ring true for many physicians. Alcoholism is usually seen as a difficult clinical undertaking, often hopeless.

This chapter briefly addresses some aspects of alcoholism that contribute to the clinician's apprehension regarding alcoholic patients. Most professionals have not obtained their views regarding treatability from long-term experience with a variety of alcoholic patients. Their views are more likely to have been shaped by treating alcoholics in acute, high-pressure medical settings, by biases passed on in clinical training programs, by passive acceptance of prevailing negative stereotypes of the alcoholic, or by searing family experiences with an alcoholic relative.

Clinicians who have treated a large number and variety of alcoholic patients over time would find such pessimism quite puzzling in light of today's experience. The question posed in the chapter heading would appear to be simplistic. Qualifying questions would immediately come to mind: Which alcoholic? At what stage of the illness? What kind of treatment? By whom?

Nevertheless, the treatment of alcoholism is often difficult and immediately brings the psychological defense of denial to mind. The alcoholic patient has years of experience in denying the organizing principle of his behavior: his dependence on alcohol. This pivotal fact—psychological dependence on alcohol coupled with denial of the dependence—is threatened by the physician's authoritarian diagnosis.

Whether in the office or at the bedside, the physician's initial encounter with an alcoholic patient may prompt a litany of perplexity, protest, or apology. The physician is at a disadvantage and can be thrown off guard. Unlike most patients, who readily seek an understanding of their condition and the steps necessary to restore health, the alcoholic patient often leaves one feeling foolish or unnecessary. "I don't know what this is all about." "My wife and I had some differences. They're patched up now."

Both unconscious forces and learned behaviors are brought to the fore by the alcoholic patient, to avoid the awful truth of alcohol dependence. "I've learned my lesson, I just have to quit." "I won't go in the hospital."

A mosaic of defense mechanisms thwarts, frustrates, or diverts the attention of the physician. The ubiquity of the alcoholic's denial is a well-known, cardinal feature of the disease of alcoholism and is discussed further in Chapter 5.

A second contribution to the notion that treatment is difficult may be less apparent. Destructive attitudes and biases of physicians regarding alcoholism present "barriers" to effective care. These barriers are intrinsic to the physician and may be just as formidable as the denial of the patient. Medical training, early clinical experience, and skepticism from the scientific literature nourish the notion of treatment difficulty and foster negative attitudes. Barriers to effective clinical care will be further addressed in Chapter 3.

Finally, a third factor influences the clinical care of alcoholic patients— a factor which, if not understood, can undermine therapeutic efforts. This factor is the heterogeneity of alcoholism—a diversity which spans the association of alcoholism with other psychiatric disorders, the presenting symptoms of alcoholism, the etiology of alcoholism, and treatment planning for the alcoholic patient.

The *diversity of psychiatric disorders* with which alcoholism may be associated has confounded the clinical efforts of many skilled mental health professionals. Commonly in the past, but perhaps less so today, alcoholism was treated as a symptom of an underlying disorder. This has been a classic error, because the alcoholism was often unrecognized or expected to remit spontaneously when the primary disorder subsided. It is essential to recognize the coexistence of disorders.

In some instances, the disorders are interdependent, that is, reciprocal. This is seen occasionally in panic disorders, which are attenuated or prevented by the patient's reliance on increasing amounts of alcohol.

A 29-year-old married woman found alcohol shortened severe bouts of anxiety and, if drunk steadily during the day, provided relief from anticipatory anxiety. The chores of child care and house-keeping were also lightened. She was able to discontinue alcohol use only when supplied with increasing amounts of benzodiaze-pines. Inpatient treatment was necessary in order to establish an effective treatment regimen.

Alcoholism may exacerbate another disorder, and vice versa. Depression provides a common example:

A middle-aged male successfully abstained from alcohol for 10 years. A series of deaths in his family resulted in depression and he returned to alcohol use. His drinking rapidly became out of control, and the loss of his sobriety deepened the depression. The alcoholism and affective disorder needed to be treated in tandem.

Some psychiatric disorders such as organic brain syndromes may derive from alcoholism. Seven such syndromes are recognized and will be discussed in Chapter 12.

Similarly, alcohol dependence may derive from another psychiatric disorder. This has commonly been referred to as "secondary alcoholism." The development of alcoholism in the absence of a preceding psychiatric disorder may be considered "primary alcoholism." An example of "secondary alcoholism" is provided by the next vignette. It illustrates how alcohol use progressed from a medication for mania (symptomatic use of alcohol) to the development of a full-blown dependence (disease of alcoholism).

A man in his early 30s presented for treatment of alcoholism following an 8-year history of bipolar affective disorder. His manic episodes had led to heavy drinking, which provided some degree of tranquilization. Lithium was initiated and controlled the manic episodes, but by that time a dependence on alcohol had been established, and the patient was unable to control his drinking. Admitted to an inpatient alcoholism program in a psychiatric hospital, effective management of his manic episodes was reinforced, while he gained an understanding of the disease of alcoholism. Lithium, supportive psychotherapy, and AA involvement proved effective in sustaining this patient's health following hospitalization.

Viewing alcohol use as a symptom was nearly fatal for the following:

A young, married professional woman was admitted for the second time to a medical floor for the treatment of pancreatitis. This time, she and her internist shared their concern over her use of alcohol. Seen in psychiatric consultation, the patient willingly accepted referral to an alcoholism treatment program. A disturbing feature of this case was the fact that the patient had been in intensive psychotherapy with a psychiatrist who was unable to provide any guidance regarding alcoholism and intervention occurred only after an acute medical crisis. The patient responded very favorably to the combination of an intensive alcoholism program, AA, and individual therapy.

Treatment of alcoholism in a psychotic patient can begin when the acute psychosis has resolved, then continuing, concomitant treatment of the psychosis and alcoholism are necessary.

A postal employee in his 40s was first admitted for a psychosis characterized by religious delusions that included the belief that he was "the second son of God." In addition to the psychotic process, the patient was alcoholic and had been referred to the postal department's alcoholism recovery program. Satisfactory psychiatric treatment of the psychosis allowed this man to participate in a psychiatrically based alcoholism treatment program. He took his treatment of alcoholism very seriously, since he valued his job, which depended on his eliminating alcohol from his lifestyle. Phenothiazines and supportive psychotherapy kept the psychosis within manageable limits.

Even the patient who presents a combination of problems suggestive of a poor prognosis may respond favorably:

A middle-aged disabled seaman, who was partially paralyzed by a stroke, was suspicious and easily angered, and he displayed behaviors and attitudes compatible with a long-standing personality disorder. With no remaining ties to family or trade, his unstructured life accelerated the process of chronic alcoholism. He agreed to an inpatient alcoholism treatment program after having nearly set fire to his rooming house during a bout of drunkenness. When he thought the staff weren't attending adequately to his medical needs he promptly signed out. Following a grand mal seizure he was persuaded to reenter the program. On this occasion he formed an attachment to his alcoholism counselor. This relationship provided a pivot for which an appreciation of AA developed. Eventually, he found part-time employment grounds-keeping at a home for juveniles. The informal relationships he formed with troubled young people and the opportunity it provided to "steer them right" added a dimension of meaning and renewal to his life and sustained his pride in sobriety.

Not all persons with alcoholism have an additional psychiatric disorder or pronounced psychopathology. Many demonstrate excellent ego strengths as soon as their addiction is arrested. Following are examples of "primary" alcoholism:

A successful young executive in his 30s, who was second in command of a prestigious company, sought consultation after his wife locked him out of their suburban home. For several months, he had promised to be home in time for dinner, but would arrive drunk 4 to 6 hours later. The patient was chagrined and perplexed by his behavior. He had a fine wife and valued his marriage. Individual counseling that explained the phenomenon of alcoholism and the concepts of "loss of control" and "craving" proved sufficient to assist the man in becoming abstinent. He came for appointments every 2 to 3 weeks, had a "slip" one night about 9 months after starting therapy, then resumed regular appointments for several more months. He did not avail himself of AA and did not require inpatient treatment.

A semiretired attorney, head of a foundation, was seen in hospital consultation with the findings of weight loss, anemia, and alcohol withdrawal symptoms. His wife was threatening separation unless he did something about his drinking. He agreed to individual psychiatric appointments and disulfiram. He refused an alcoholism rehabilitation program, tried AA briefly, but decided that "all alcoholics need is a kick in the ass and to follow directions." This homespun philosophy extended to a prolonged and successful recovery.

A 53-year-old man, employed by his father-in-law, sought consultation regarding his use of alcohol. After witnessing a deteriorating course of alcoholism in a family member he was concerned that he might have a problem. Although impatient and skeptical, he accepted an invitation to meet a friend who was active in AA. He immediately became engaged in AA, felt that he should have been there 10 years earlier, and, after two additional therapy sessions, felt no necessity for further appointments. He has continued with AA and is aware that his therapist serves as a back-up should he ever need disulfiram, hospitalization, or psychotherapy.

In many instances, despite favorable prognostic factors, as well as competent treatment efforts, a deteriorating course ensues.

The wife of a physician, in her late 30s and the mother of two adolescent children, was admitted to an inpatient alcoholism program. Some narcissistic and histrionic personality traits were apparent, but did not cause significant conflict with other patients or staff. Within days after discharge from the inpatient phase of treatment, she began drinking. She then contacted an older male patient whom she had met in the hospital, left her family, moved in with him, and continued to drink. Efforts by her husband, AA friends, counselors, and psychiatrists failed to reestablish sufficient sobriety to allow further therapy. When the older man died of a heart condition, the wife began to wander among inner city neighborhoods, and her personal deterioration matched her social decline. Her family was humiliated and angry, and they broke off contact.

The psychiatrist is faced with the fact that a dependence on alcohol may accompany any other psychiatric disorder and, indeed, may even be disguised by the disorder. By the same token, alcoholism may mask a psychiatric disorder, which becomes apparent only when alcohol use is terminated. In either case, it is necessary to treat the alcoholism as a disease and establish a course of treatment specific to it. Psychiatric disorders coexisting with alcoholism require specific and parallel plans of treatment.

In addition to the heterogeneity of the diagnostic context in which alcoholism exists, the clinician faces a second area of diversity: *symptom presentation*. The presenting symptoms of alcoholism vary markedly from individual to individual. Social manifestations such as marital separation, threat of job loss, or financial problems can point the way to an underlying dependence on alcohol. Or the disorder can be brought into focus only after intervention of the judicial system, which may occur in cases of child abuse, driving while intoxicated (DWI) arrests, or acts of belligerence. Physicians, in particular, have an excellent opportunity to detect alcoholism either through complaints about drinking from a family member or through recognition of the many associated medical signs and symptoms. The history, physical examination, and laboratory studies, provide ample clues for the diagnosis. Signs or symptoms from any area upon which alcoholism may have an impact should alert the clinician to look further.

Table 1-1 lists alcohol-related problems for the drinker, the family, and the community. The clinician may encounter problems in any one of these areas or across the entire spectrum. Again, the diagnosis depends more on the number of signs and symptoms than on a specific category of symptoms.

A recent study by Vaillant (1983a) documents that the common problems of alcohol abuse—accidents, job loss, medical problems, and marital strife—have nearly equal diagnostic import. The number of symptoms of abuse determine the diagnosis, rather than any specific category of symptoms. For example, Vaillant's (1983b) study of 400 males reports that criteria for physiological dependence on alcohol, as defined by the American Psychiatric Association's *Diagnostic and Statistical Manual of Mental Disorders (3rd edition)* or *DSM-III* (1980), correlated at a level of $r = .87$ with a scale measuring social consequences of drinking.

Although the variety of presenting symptoms of alcoholism is extensive, a hierarchy of presenting symptoms was described as early as 1946

TABLE 1-1
Alcohol-Related Problems*

For the drinker
• Accidents
• Aggressiveness
• Arrests
• Climatic exposure
• Withdrawal symptoms
• Associated medical illnesses (e.g., cirrhosis, pancreatitis, anemia)
• Impaired working capacity
• Malnutrition
• Loss of friends
• Loss of family
• Loss of job
For the drinker's family
• Marital discord
• Child abuse
• Spouse abuse
• Mental disorders (especially depression, anxiety)
• Fetal damage from maternal drinking
• Child neglect
• Child development problems
• School dropout
• Delinquency
• Poverty
For the community
• Victims of drinker-caused accidents
• Property damage
• Violence
• Output losses (e.g., in factory, on farm, administrative inefficiency)
• Economic costs of services (health, welfare, law enforcement)
• Loss of skilled manpower (premature death)

---

*Modified by permission from Moser J: Prevention of Alcohol-Related Problems, 1980. Toronto, Alcohol and Drug Addiction Research Foundation.

by Jellinek (1946). Jellinek's (1952) original chart of alcohol addiction, which describes a progression—prealcoholic, prodromal, crucial, and chronic phases—is reproduced in Table 1-2. A 1973 replication of Jellinek's work by Pokorny and Kanas (1980), using a structured interview with both alcoholic and control samples, correlated .74 with Jellinek's study. A comparison of the Pokorny and Kanas progression with the Jellinek system is presented in Table 1-3. Awareness of a typical succession of symptoms is useful, especially in estimating chronicity of the illness. Although these two studies list a wide range of signs and symptoms, which may appear in various phases, each patient need not have most of them nor follow such an exact order. On the other hand, Mandell

TABLE 1-2
Jellinek Chart of Alcohol Addiction*

Prealcoholic Phase
  a. Occasional relief drinking
  b. Constant relief drinking
  c. Increase in alcohol tolerance
Prodromal Phase
  1. Onset of blackouts
  2. Surreptitious drinking
  3. Anticipatory drinking
  4. Gulping drinks
  5. Guilt feelings
  6. Avoiding reference to alcohol
  7. Frequent blackouts
Crucial Phase
  8. Loss of control
  9. Rationalized drinking
  10. Social pressures
  11. Grandiose behavior
  12. Aggressive behavior
  13. Persistent remorse
  14. Periods of total abstinence
  15. Changing drinking pattern
  16. Dropping friends
  17. Quitting jobs
  18. Behavior becomes alcohol-centered
  19. Loss of outside interests
  20. Reinterpretation of interpersonal relations
  21. Marked self-pity
  22. Geographic escape
  23. Change in family habits
  24. Unreasonable resentments
  25. Protecting supply
  26. Nutritional neglect
  27. First hospitalization (alcoholism)
  28. Decreased sexual drive
  29. Alcoholic jealousy
  30. Regular morning drinking
Chronic Phase
  31. Onset of benders
  32. Marked ethical deterioration
  33. Impairment of thinking
  34. Alcoholic psychoses
  35. Drinking down (socially)
  36. Drinking technical products
  37. Loss of alcohol tolerance
  38. Indefinable fears
  39. Tremors
  40. Psychomotor inhibition
  41. Obsessive drinking
  42. Religious needs
  43. Admitting defeat

*Reproduced by permission from Pokorny and Kanas (1980).

TABLE 1-3
Chronological Order and Phasing of 27 Alcoholism Experiences:
Comparison with Jellinek Order and Phasing*

Variable	Mean age of onset in Alcoholic Sample (N = 102)	Pokorny and Kanas Phase	Order of Onset in Jellinek System (43 items in all)	Jellinek Phase
First blackouts	30.8	Early	1	Prodromal
Frequent anticipatory drinking	31.0	Early	3	Prodromal
Frequent grandiose behavior	31.0	Early	11	Crucial
Frequent aggressive behavior	31.2	Early	12	Crucial
Jealousy	33.2	Early	29	Crucial
Evasion	34.3	Early	6	Prodromal
Sneak drinks	35.1	Early	2	Prodromal
Frequent blackouts	35.3	Early	7	Prodromal
Rationalization	35.9	Early	9	Crucial
Frequently avoids friends	35.9	Early	16	Crucial
Loss of control	36.2	Middle	8	Crucial
Frequently quit jobs	36.2	Middle	17	Crucial
Frequent benders	37.0	Late	31	Chronic
Frequent technical products	37.6	Late	36	Chronic
Protect supply	37.7	Late	25	Crucial
Control attempts	38.0	Late	14	Crucial
Frequent morning drinking	38.3	Late	30	Crucial
Remorse	38.4	Late	13	Crucial
Geographical escape	38.4	Late	22	Crucial
Loss of interest	39.0	Late	19	Crucial
Frequent tremors	39.5	Late	39	Chronic
Frequent neglect	40.4	Late	26	Crucial
Religious need	41.4	Late	42	Chronic
Tolerance decline	41.7	Late	37	Chronic
Admitting defeat	42.7	Late	43	Chronic
Hospitalization	43.4	Late	27	Crucial
Sexual decline	43.6	Late	28	Crucial

Note. Rank order correlation between Pokorny and Kanas' study order and Jellinek's = .74.
*Reprinted by permission, from Pokorny and Kanas: Phenomenology and Treatment of Alcoholism, 1980. New York, SP Medical and Scientific Books.

(1983), in a review of phases of alcohol dependence, points out that individuals who have an alcohol-related problem at Time 1 tend to have alcohol-related problems when queried at Time 2. Commonly, the problems differ at the two points in time.

The heterogeneity of alcoholism is further expressed in the mystery of its *etiology*. Alcoholism is best considered a disease of multiple causality. This lacuna in our knowledge may even be useful in discussing alcoholism with patients or their families because the patients are relieved of their assumption that they had brought the illness on themselves, and the families are relieved to know that they did not cause it.

It is reasonable to think of alcoholism as having multiple determinants; for example, social, psychological, and genetic factors all seem to contribute to the development of alcoholism. Among social factors, the availability of alcohol is of major importance. It has been documented that changes in the quantities of alcoholic beverages available influence per capita consumption rates (Moser, 1980). Government policies such as increasing the number of distribution outlets, lowering tax rates, or subsidizing production each result in greater per capita consumption.

As alcohol consumption increases, some indices of health deteriorate. Cirrhosis rates vary with level of alcohol consumption in the general population (Pophan, Schmidt, & deLint, 1978). Admission rates for alcoholism and alcoholic psychosis, as well as the incidence of laryngeal and esophageal cancers, are associated with per capita alcohol consumption. The price of alcoholic beverages relative to spendable income has been documented to relate both to consumption within a society and an increase in liver cirrhosis rates (Pophan, Schmidt, & deLint, 1978). For a detailed description of the relationships between production of alcoholic beverages, consumption, and subsequent health problems see Moser's (1980) monograph.

Psychological factors such as stress, depression, anxiety, and characterological disturbances have been associated with alcohol abuse. Weissman, Myers, and Harding (1980) report that 71% of individuals diagnosed as alcoholic had at least one other psychiatric diagnosis over the course of their lifetimes. Kernberg (1975) links alcoholism with borderline personality disturbances, and Nace, Saxon, and Shore (1983), using a standardized diagnostic instrument, describe the presence of borderline personality disorder in hospitalized alcoholics. Disorders more commonly found in alcoholics and in their family members include anxiety, depression, antisocial personality disorder, anorexia nervosa, hypertension, drug abuse, and hyperactivity (Andreasen & Winokur, 1979; Eckert, Goldberg, Halmi, Casper, & Davis, 1979; Goodwin & Guze, 1979; Goodwin, Schulsinger, Hermansen, Guze, & Winokur, 1975; Morrison & Stewart, 1971; Munjack & Moss, 1981; Overall, Brown, Williams, &

Neill, 1973; Tarter, McBride, Buonpane, & Schneider, 1977; Wood, Wender, & Reimherr, 1983).

Studies of psychological factors that reinforce use of alcohol include McClelland, Davis, Kalin, and Wanner's (1972) work with both social drinkers and alcoholics. These studies indicate that heavy drinking promotes a feeling of "personalized power" and serves as an escape from inner conflict, particularly in males who have doubts about their masculine adequacy. Also, alcoholic patients are highly susceptible to relapse when experiencing frustration and anger, social pressure, or negative emotional states (Marlatt, 1978).

Khantzian (1981) describes how earlier concepts such as oral dependency, fixations, and instinctual drives that contribute to alcohol use have been replaced by a more modern concept of disturbances in ego structures. Khantzian emphasizes that defects in self-care and affect regulation are operative in alcoholic patients. In addition, pathological self-formations are noted to occur commonly in alcoholic patients (Kernberg, 1975).

The association between alcoholism and preexisting psychiatric disorders, stressful events, or particular dynamic formulations does not establish any of them as a sufficient or necessary cause. Nevertheless, the relevance of such psychological factors in the clinical care of alcoholic patients must be emphasized.

The possibility of a genetic predisposition to alcoholism receives support in Goodwin, Schulsinger, Hermansen, Guze, and Winokur's (1973) report of a Danish study of 55 adopted-out sons of alcoholic parents and a control group of 78 adopted-out sons of nonalcoholics. The adoptions took place in early infancy. Alcoholism was defined as heavy drinking leading to problems in three of four areas. The adopted-out sons of alcoholics were three times as likely to be alcoholic as the controls. Further, the siblings who grew up in the home with their alcoholic biologic parents had no higher rate of alcoholism than those who had been adopted (Goodwin, Schulsinger, Moller, Hermansen, Winokur, & Guze, 1974).

A second, larger study (Cloninger, Bohman, & Sigvardsson, 1981), conducted in Sweden, examined the effect of both genetic and environmental variables. Adopted sons whose biological fathers were alcoholics were alcohol abusers in 22.8% of cases compared to 14.7% for adopted sons whose biological fathers were not alcoholics. This study is unique among genetic studies for its effort to examine both genetic and environmental variables. When the 862 adopted men were rated as mild, moderate, or severe on a scale of alcohol abuse and characteristics of both the biological parents and postnatal environment were determined, statistical analyses identified two types of alcoholism that seemed to be heritable: Type 1 ("milieu limited") occurred more commonly and was characterized by "mild alcohol abuse" in both biological parents. The parents' alcohol abuse was not severe enough to lead to treatment. The sons of these parents were predisposed to alcoholism only when environmental factors were provocative of alcohol abuse. The sons with such environmental provocation were twice as likely to develop alcohol abuse as the general population. Type II ("male-limited") alcohol abuse was found in males whose biological fathers were rated as "severe" alcohol abusers. The sons, in this instance, developed alcohol abuse independent of the postnatal environment and at a rate nine times that of the general population.

The issue of inheritance is less clear for females. Goodwin et al.'s (1974) study found no evidence for a genetic cause in women, but the sample size was small. In a Swedish study (Bohman, Sigvardsson, & Cloninger, 1981), adopted daughters whose biological mothers were alcoholic had an incidence of alcoholism three times greater than adopted daughters from nonalcoholic parents (9.8% vs. 2.8%). No excess of alcoholism in adopted daughters was found when all alcoholic biological fathers were contrasted with nonalcoholic biological fathers. When the data were examined from the point of severity of alcohol abuse in the biological fathers, however, a two-fold increase in alcoholism was noted in the adopted daughters whose biological fathers were mild alcohol abusers without a history of criminality. Yet, daughters of severely alcoholic fathers with a history of criminality showed no increase in alcoholism over controls.

If, in fact, genetic factors play an essential role in the development of alcoholism, it remains unclear how the genetic influence is expressed. Schuckit (1985) and Schuckit, Li, Cloninger, and Deitrich (1985) outline the possibilities:

- Altered metabolism of ethanol or acetaldehyde
- Increased risk of ethanol-related organ damage
- Increased capacity to develop tolerance or physical dependence
- Altered reaction to ethanol ingestion
- Personality variables
- Increased risk as a result of other psychiatric disorders

Of all the above, a genetic predisposition seems most clearly established in the metabolism of alcoholism. Li describes (in Schuckit et al., 1985) three classes of alcohol dehydrogenase (ADH) isoenzymes which have been identified in the human liver. It is estimated that five different human ADH genes exist. There is variability in the distribution of isoenzymes of ADH among different racial populations. For example, "atypical" ADH phenotypes occur in about 85% of Asians, but in only 5% to 20% of Europeans or black Americans. Another enzyme of major importance in the metabolism of alcohol is acetaldehyde dehydrogenase (ALDH). It has been noted that many Orientals develop a flush, tachycardia, nausea, and vomiting after alcohol ingestion. A mitochondrial form of ALDH has been found to be missing in individuals who are "flush reactive." As a result, acetaldehyde is not efficiently metabolized and produces an unpleasant effect. This genetic enzyme defect in ALDH may serve, therefore, as a protection against the ingestion of alcohol and the development of alcoholism.

Tantalizing findings have emerged that suggest that males with a family history positive for alcoholism (and therefore at higher risk themselves) may have a less intensive reaction to the acute effects of alcohol (Schuckit et al., 1985). As a result, they may be less aware of the amount drunk. Similarly, men at high risk for alcoholism produce more alpha rhythm (an indication of relaxation) in EEG studies (Pollock, Volavka, Goodwin, Mednick, Gabrielli, Knop, & Schulsinger, 1983) and differ in the latency and amplitude of the P300 brain wave (Begleiter, 1984; Elmasian, Neville, Woods, Schuckit, & Bloom, 1982). The P300 evoked brain wave reflects a capacity to pay attention to a particular stimulus in the environment. Individuals at possible risk for alcoholism seem less able or less willing to attend to this task.

Any association between genetic factors and personality variables remains clouded (Schuckit et al., 1985). Evidence linking genetic factors for the development of alcoholism with genetic factors influencing the expression of other major psychiatric disorders also is generally lacking (Schuckit et al., 1985).

An extensive review (Cotton, 1979) of the familial incidence of alcoholism notes that 45% to 80% of alcoholics did not have an alcoholic relative. By the same token, 60% of the males in the Swedish study (Cloninger et al., 1981)—regardless of severity of alcoholism—did not have a family history of alcoholism. It would seem that as important as genetic factors may eventually prove to be, such factors do not seem to be necessary, nor are they sufficient, for the development of alcoholism in most patients.

Finally, we face not only the problems of heterogeneity in associated psychiatric disorders, symptom presentation, and etiologic factors, but also considerable variation in treatment planning.

How does one determine what treatment to offer which patient? For the most part, treatment planning is determined largely by what the patient believes is necessary or is willing to accept. Some patients will accept an out-of-state, freestanding, AA-oriented rehabilitation program rather than suffer the "stigma" of entering a competent alcoholism program in a local psychiatric hospital. Others turn toward the psychiatric hospital because they prefer to think of themselves as "depressed," rather than "alcoholic." Many patients refuse residential treatment, balk at attending AA meetings, but come back to the psychiatrist for individual or family treatment. Others take refuge in AA as a welcome respite from a psychiatrist's probing.

Physicians must accept how limited is the influence they have on compliance with their treatment plans but do everything they can to get something started. With time, therapeutic influence may grow, and the patient may accept what the physician feels to be optimal. The man or woman who refuses hospitalization may, when outpatient approaches fail, then agree to an inpatient program. The alcoholic who seems too comfortable with repeated bouts of inpatient rehabilitation may accept "no" to yet another inpatient stay, if it is pointed out gently that he or she did not follow through previously with aftercare plans. Use of outpatient treatment may illustrate to such a patient that progress is a function of consistent effort over a long term.

The patient's financial resources are a second major determinant of treatment selection. It may be unfortunate that financial status or insurance coverage influences treatment selection, but to think otherwise is to be naive. Given financial resources, however, other patient characteristics play a major role in treatment planning. The educated patient or the patient who seems introspective and verbally skilled may be directed toward a treatment program that utilizes psychotherapy; an unsophisticated patient may need only paraprofessional counseling and to go to AA. Unfortunately, there are remarkably few data either to support or to contradict these biases.

A related factor is any bias of the physician recommending treatment. The medical director of a large corporation explained that he referred "uncomplicated" alcoholic employees to a nonhospital alcoholism rehabilitation center and the "complicated" alcoholics to an alcoholism program in a psychiatric hospital. I was familiar with patients in both programs, but was never able to determine the basis for his categorization of "complicated" and "uncomplicated." The decision did not seem to be based on age, marital status, occupational level, or medical or psychiatric considerations.

Some physicians rarely recommend anything other than AA, while others refer an alcoholic only to a psychiatrist. All physicians' referral repertoires are shaped by their experiences with alcoholic patients, their experiences with particular types of treatment, the personnel involved, and their conceptualization of alcoholism. In addition, each physician, through training and experience, develops a subjective impression of what treatment will suit which patient.

Matching of patient to treatment appears to transcend any rational process derived from a methodologically sound data base. Solomon (1981) summarizes the issue as follows:

> The concept of enhancing outcomes by tailoring therapeutic technique to fit the type of client has widespread acceptance, but this view is supported more by opinion than by research evidence. There appears to be a selective bias in which type of client is exposed to which form of treatment. However, the assignment of treatment tends to be guided by considerations other than differential efficacy, perhaps because clear indicators for appropriate treatment matching have yet to emerge from the research.

Similarly, Pattison (1982), a consistent advocate of careful treatment planning for alcoholic patients, acknowledges "only modest" research evidence for the efficacy of matching. The clinicians must act on the basis of their best judgment and the data in hand. The physician's determination to deal with the patient's addiction, to put forth a treatment plan, and to follow through with a continuing evaluation of results may prove to be as powerful in influencing outcome as the specific treatment recommended. This statement does not imply that a constant search for the most effective approach for any given patient be minimized; it requires constant attention. Rather, our search need not obscure our commitment to delivering clinical care.

The literature regarding treatment planning lacks clarity, which may contribute to the widespread attitude that treatment of alcoholism is difficult. A 1977 study (Edwards et al., 1977) reports that alcoholics given one-half hour of "advice" do as well as alcoholics provided a substantial and intensive treatment program. Subsequent analysis (Orford, Oppenheimer, & Edwards, 1976) revealed, however, that the more severely addicted alcoholics actually do better with the intensive treatment program. Sixty-nine percent of the addicted ("gamma" alcoholics) who had intensive treatment were rated as "good" outcome, while 0% who had minimal treatment had "good" outcome. Most clinicians would likely seek a more intensive type of therapy for the more severely ill on the basis of clinical common sense—a decision which would be verified by this research effort.

Encountering difficulty is common to all areas of medicine that treat chronic illnesses of uncertain etiology. With patience, each clinician develops, slowly and painfully, skills to meet these challenges and can contribute to the data base of his specialty.

These several aspects of alcoholism, which contribute to its reputation as "difficult to treat," are put forth to indicate that the author does not deny the nature of the task, but proposes that the difficulties are not insurmountable and that the treatment of alcoholism shares the vicissitudes of the larger context of chronic illnesses.

CHAPTER 2

The Magnitude of Alcoholism

This chapter presents, in abbreviated form, data on the economic cost of alcoholism to society, information about the epidemiology of alcoholism, and a summary of the major medical complications of alcoholism. It will not be comprehensive as a text on any of these topics, but is put forth with the following objectives:

1) To outline the mammoth impact of alcohol abuse and dependence on our society
2) To provide basic facts so that patients and families can be knowledgeable about the implications of alcoholism
3) To direct the interested reader to resources for further information

As one appreciates the seriousness of alcoholism, it is likely that preconceived notions and attitudes about alcoholism will change. Through an increase in knowledge and understanding of the impact of alcoholism on the individual, the family, and society one becomes less likely to be misled by the defenses of the patient into minimizing, denying, or ignoring the alcohol problem. In other words, as we become better informed of the facts of alcoholism, we are less likely to cooperate mistakenly with the unhealthy denial and resistances of the patient which retard recovery. The clinician will be able to take seriously what his patient, tragically, may not take seriously. Ambivalence about worthwhileness of trying to work with alcoholic patients will be minimized and confidence in the importance of this task bolstered as further understanding of the personal and social cost of alcoholism is gained. Treatment for the alcoholic is seen best as a life or death matter.

ECONOMIC COSTS

The National Institute on Alcohol Abuse and Alcoholism (NIAAA) estimates that in 1983 alcohol abuse and alcoholism cost the United States over $116 billion dollars. (For a comparison with costs related to drug abuse and mental illness, see Table 2-1, Harwood et al., 1984.)

TABLE 2-1
Updated Costs to Society of Alcohol Abuse/Drug Abuse,
and Mental Illness, 1983 (dollars in millions)

	Alcohol Abuse	Drug Abuse	Mental Illness	Total
Core Costs				
Direct				
Treatment and Support	$ 14,865	$ 2,049	$33,445	$ 50,359
Indirect				
Mortality[a]	18,151	2,486	9,036	29,673
Reduced Productivity	65,582	33,346	4,048	102,976
Lost Employment	5,323	405	24,044	29,772
Other Related Costs				
Direct				
Motor Vehicle Crashes	2,667	[c]	—	2,667
Crime	2,607	6,565	966	10,139
Social Welfare Programs	49	3	259	311
Other	3,673	677	831	5,181
Indirect				
Victims of Crime	192	945	—	1,137
Crime Careers	0	10,846	—	10,846
Incarceration	2,979	2,425	146	5,549
Motor Vehicle Crash (time loss)	583	[c]	—	583
Total	$116,674[b]	$59,747[b]	$72,775[b]	$249,196

Totals may not add due to rounding
[a]At 6 percent discount rate
[b]The total costs to society for each of the three ADM disorders are not comparable since the completeness of data available for each cost category varied significantly. For example, the estimate of reduced productivity is relatively complete for alcohol abuse, only partially complete for drug abuse, and incomplete for mental illness.
[c]Although costs are hypothesized to occur in this category, sufficient data are not available to develop a reliable estimate.
Source: Harwood et al., 1984

The largest item—lost employment and productivity—includes losses from the excess mortality and morbidity associated with alcoholism. This figure has been estimated at $89 billion in 1983. Seventy-five percent of the nation's alcoholics are employed, but their productivity, absenteeism, tardiness, and work conflicts cost an estimated $70.9 billion, and future productivity lost because of mortality is about $18.1 billion (Harwood et al., 1984). More recently, direct treatment and support costs were estimated at $10.5 billion in 1980 and $14.9 billion by 1983. These expenditures were for hospitalization, professional services, outpatient care, terminal care for alcohol-related illness and traumas, and support services (DeLuca, 1981).

Other related costs include those associated with motor vehicle accidents, fires, and proportionate shares of the costs associated with the administration of the criminal justice system, social welfare, and highway safety. Also included is the lost productivity resulting from imprisonment for crimes related to alcohol abuse.

For the year 1977, it was estimated that nearly 12,000 deaths and 300,000 injuries occurred from traffic accidents where alcohol was implicated. Nearly one-half of highway fatalities are associated with alcohol use. Among these, one-half of the fatalities implicate a person with alcoholism, while the rest are due to social drinkers or young drinkers with a high blood alcohol level at the time of the accident (Cahalan, 1982).

A strong relationship between violent crime and alcohol abuse is apparent; for example, 67% of homicide offenders had a blood alcohol concentration above 0.01%, and 37% of aggravated assault cases and up to 50% of rape cases were committed while the offender was drinking. The victim had been drinking in nearly one-third of cases. In addition, one-third of suicides are alcohol-related, and at least 50% of fatalities from burns are alcoholics. The latter account for nearly one out of four burn victims (Cahalan, 1982).

The profound cost of alcohol abuse and alcoholism both in economic terms and in human suffering is apparent even from a brief review of available statistics. Today, the economic figures would, of course, be higher than those calculated from 1977. The human cost is not quantifiable. Our knowledge of the number of people affected by alcohol abuse in the United States has improved considerably, however, as data from recent well-designed studies have become available.

EPIDEMIOLOGY

Approximately 68% of Americans age 21 or over consume alcoholic beverages (Cahalan, Cisin, & Crossley, 1969). Thus, nearly one-third of the population does not drink, that is, has less than one alcoholic drink per year. This point is worth noting as the newly diagnosed alcoholic commonly fears being conspicuous by virtue of not using alcohol.

A review of the population surveys of American drinking practices and associated drinking problems suggests that nearly 8% of drinkers develop alcohol dependence (Robins et al., 1984). The recently conducted Epidemiologic Catchment Area Studies of the National Institute of Mental Health found that alcohol abuse/dependence was among the three most prevalent disorders in the three urban areas studied. For men, it was the most prevalent disorder. Findings from the three urban areas—St. Louis, Baltimore, and New Haven—indicate lifetime prevalence rates for alcohol abuse/dependence at 15.7%, 13.7%, and 11.5%, respectively. A marked difference between males and females in all three sites was found. The male to female prevalence rates in St. Louis were 28.9% to 4.3%; in Baltimore, 24.9% to 4.2%; and in New Haven, 19.1% to 4.8%. Rates of alcohol abuse/dependence did not differ between blacks and nonblacks at the three sites. In New Haven, college graduates had a statistically significant lower rate of alcohol abuse/dependence than those with less education, but no differences by educational level were found in the other two urban sites (Robins et al., 1984).

A survey of private psychiatric hospitals in 1970 found that 11% of admissions were given a primary diagnosis of alcoholism. By 1980, this figure had increased to 15% (Moore, 1982). These figures are likely to be on the low side as one private facility (Moore, 1972) found that 50% of male admissions and 22% of female admissions scored in the alcoholic range on the Michigan Alcoholism Screening Test (MAST) (Selzer, 1971).

A 1977 survey of Veterans Administration hospitals found that 27% of the patients in psychiatric facilities and 19.6% in the general hospitals were "defined alcoholics" (Freed, 1982). Undiagnosed substance abuse, especially alcohol, is a common problem in psychiatric facilities, and often complicates or dilutes treatment efforts (Alterman & Erdlen, 1983).

Despite the high prevalence of alcoholism in the general population, utilization of sources of help is low. Only 1% of those surveyed by the NIAAA had ever sought help from physicians, clergy, Alcoholics Anonymous, or alcoholism treatment programs (Clark & Midanik, 1982). Even when admitted to hospitals, the diagnosis is seldom made. For example, in one study from a psychiatric hospital, 25% of the men and 60% of the women who met the criteria for alcoholism on the MAST received neither a primary nor secondary diagnosis of alcoholism (Moore, 1972).

Epidemiologic studies have shed light on the relationship between patterns of alcohol use and the likelihood of alcohol-related problems. Frequency of use (e.g., number of days alcohol is used per month) is associated with the amount of alcohol used per drinking occasion. In other words, the more often one drinks, the more one drinks per occasion. The 1979 NIAAA Study (Clark & Midanik, 1982) found that of males who had 60 to 120 drinks per month, 9% met criteria for alcohol dependence. Of males who drank more than 120 drinks per month, 39% were alcohol dependent. For women, the 60 to 120 drinks per month group had an incidence of 11% qualifying for alcohol dependence, whereas the figure leaped to 52% in women drinking more than 120 drinks per month. A "drink" is considered $1^1/2$ ounces of 80-proof liquor, a 4-ounce glass of wine, or a 12-ounce bottle of beer.

Binge drinking—being intoxicated for several days in a row at least once in the past 12 months—in 100% of cases for both men and women has been associated with other alcohol-related problems (e.g., marital problems, job problems, health problems). Respondents who report "never" or "infrequently" getting drunk have very few, if any, symptoms of alcohol dependence. Reporting drunkenness "at least once a month" is associated with symptoms of dependence in 79% of cases (Clark & Midanik, 1982).

Frequency of drinking and amount consumed per occasion seem to be components of a general preoccupation with alcohol. Quantity and frequency of use are related to frequency of drunkenness, which in turn is highly associated with alcohol-related problems.

MAJOR MEDICAL COMPLICATIONS

This section reviews the impact of alcohol use on the various organ systems of the body. Although this material may be very familiar to physicians, nonmedical professionals and the public in general usually are not aware of the scope of potential health problems secondary to alcohol abuse. Alcoholic patients are usually painfully naive in this regard. Part of the treatment of alcoholism involves informing the patient of the medical complications that are in evidence as well as those with a potential for development. Such information is not provided as a scare tactic, but is offered with respect for the individual's need to make choices: For example, to choose whether or not to continue to drink. The more information each patient has relative to his or her condition, the more informed the decision can be.

Alcoholic Liver Disease

The organ most commonly thought to be affected by alcohol is the liver. Alcohol is not stored in the tissues, and less than 10% is eliminated through the kidneys, lungs, or skin. The liver bears the brunt of ridding the body of alcohol. Within the past 10 to 15 years research has demonstrated that the ethyl alcohol molecule is hepatoxic even in the presence of adequate dietary intake (Lieber, 1984). This is of importance, not only for an understanding of the pathogenesis of alcoholic liver disease, but to counter the common rationalization that "alcohol won't hurt me if I eat well." Ethanol has been shown to produce fatty liver, damage hepatic cells, alter liver cell regeneration, and promote collagen deposition (Mezey, 1982).

Ethanol increases oxygen consumption in the liver. Because of the increased consumption of oxygen, a relative hypoxia may occur in the perivenular area of the liver, the site where fibrosis commonly occurs. Considerable evidence over the past 10 years supports a hypermetabolic condition induced in the liver. This change in state has also been associated with energy wastage, that is, the observation that animals given their calories in the form of alcohol lose weight in contrast to the situation when they are fed a similar amount of calories in the form of carbohydrates (Lieber, 1984).

Alcohol is metabolized principally by alcohol dehydrogenase (ADH). With chronic exposure to alcohol, a second system, the microsomal ethanol-oxidizing system (MEOS) plays a role. The latter system generates only heat without storable forms of energy. This probably accounts for the failure to gain weight noted above, as calories from alcohol are "wasted calories." On the other hand, the ADH metabolism route produces storable energy in the form of increased amounts of acetyl coenzyme A. The increase in the latter compound produces an increase in the ratio of the pyridine nucleotide cofactors NADH to NAD+. The increased NADH/NAD+ ratio has the following clinically relevant effects:

1) Decreased oxidation of fatty acids resulting in *fatty liver*.
2) Production of ketones and lactic acid which, in turn, produce hyperuricemia. The presence of an *increased serum uric acid* level can be a clue to the presence of alcoholism and may result in secondary gout.
3) Decreased glucogeogenesis and resultant *hypoglycemia*. This can be especially important if glycogen stores have been depleted by poor dietary intake. Therefore, the intoxicated individual is at risk for the development of hypoglycemia, and blood glucose monitoring may be necessary.

In addition to the altered metabolism induced by alcohol, excess acetaldehyde may be produced. Acetaldehyde, like its precursor ethanol, has an adverse effect on liver cells. Protein secretion can be inhibited, and the ability to oxidize fatty acids can be depressed by acetaldehyde (Alterman & Erdlen, 1983).

The profound biochemical alterations that follow from excessive alcohol use set the stage for alcoholic liver disease, the first manifestation of which is *fatty liver*. Triglycerides accumulate intracellularly in the liver in obesity, malnutrition, poorly controlled diabetes, and toxins. Ethanol, the most common toxin in North America, accounts for the majority of cases of fatty liver. Clinically, the liver is substantially enlarged, and the spleen normal in size. The patient usually does not feel ill. The most pronounced laboratory abnormality is the elevation of gamma glutamyl transpeptidase (GGTP)—an enzyme whose hepatic synthesis is stimulated by alcohol. The serum glutonic oxaloacatic transaminase (SGOT) and alkaline phosphatase may be slightly elevated. Bilirubin and prothrombin time are normal. This condition is reversible and is common in drinkers whose alcohol consumption exceeds 5 drinks per day.

The second stage of alcoholic liver disease is *alcoholic hepatitis* (in contrast to viral hepatitis which takes months or years to develop), a slow, smoldering process which may proceed or coexist with cirrhosis. Not all chronic alcoholics develop hepatitis, and it does not necessarily lead to cirrhosis. Liver biopsy is the only certain means of diagnosis. However, hepatitis is likely in the presence of low grade fever, malaise, jaundice, enlarged *tender* liver, and dark urine (bilirubin). Laboratory studies commonly show an elevated SGOT and serum glutonic pyruvic transaminase (SGPT), with the ratio of SGOT/SGPT being greater than 1. With viral hepatitis this ratio is usually less than one. Bilirubin, alkaline phosphatase, and GGTP are markedly elevated. Treatment is usually straightforward: Abstinence from alcohol, rest, good nutrition, folic acid, and multivitamins. The use of steroids or propylthiouracil is uncertain, but may benefit certain patients.

The development of alcoholic hepatitis has been considered as possibly due to an autoimmune reaction against hyaline. Liver damage has also been postulated as being secondary to the "hypermetabolic" state of the liver after chronic alcohol abuse, hence the use of propylthiouracil.

The outcome of alcoholic hepatitis is significantly influenced by abstinence. Nearly 80% will recover if alcohol use is avoided. Twenty percent may progress to cirrhosis. If alcohol use continues, 50% to 80% develop cirrhosis, and the remainder have chronic hepatitis.

The most severe expression of alcoholic liver disease is cirrhosis ("scar tissue"). Cirrhosis is the sixth leading cause of death in the United States. It is believed that alcoholic hepatitis precedes cirrhosis, but this has not been established conclusively. A wedge section biopsy is the surest means to make the diagnosis. The usual liver tests are not conclusive. Clinical signs include the following: hard, nodular liver, usually enlarged early in the course of the illness, but later shrunken; enlarged spleen, gynecomastia, testicular atrophy, "spider" angiomas, ascites, peripheral edema, red palms, Dupuytren's contracture, tremor, jaundice, confusion. Favorable prognosis depends on:

1) Abstinence from alcohol
2) Absence of ascites, esophageal varices, jaundice, or renal insufficiency.

A study of 278 documented cirrhotics found that abstainers had a 63% 4-year survival rate while continuing drinkers had a 40% survival rate. Five-year survival rate for abstainers without the complications mentioned above was 89% (Powell & Klatshim, 1968).

The most common and severe complications of cirrhosis are:

1) *Portal Hypertension*—leads to gastro-intestinal bleeding from esophageal varices and hemorrhoids, porto-systemic encephalopathy, and hypersplenism.
2) *Sodium and Water Retention*—results in ascites, edema, and renal failure.
3) *Hepatoma*—the development of primary liver cancer has been associated with the presence of cirrhosis in 64% to 90% of cases. Depending on the study, 5% to 30% of those with cirrhosis develop hepatocarcinoma. As cirrhotic patients are managed more effectively and survive longer, the incidence of hepatoma may increase. An average time of 8 years between onset of cirrhosis and primary cancer of the liver has been reported (Purtilo & Gottlieb, 1973).

In addition, there may be defects in immune functions, coagulation, and glucose tolerance (similar to diabetes). Peptic ulcer, gall stones, and renal tubular acidosis are possible further complications.

Alcoholic Pancreatitis

The first attack of acute alcoholic pancreatitis usually occurs after 10 to 15 years of heavy drinking. In some patients chronic pancreatic insufficiency, characterized by malabsorption and secondary diabetes, develops without any acute episodes (Korsten & Lieber, 1982).

Pancreatitis in the United States is caused in one out of three instances by alcohol. Another one-third is caused by gall stones, but in this case chronic pancreatitis is rare. The other third of cases may be due to trauma, viral infection, or metabolic and drug-induced causes.

The two theories most favored for the mechanism of alcoholic pancreatitis are precipitation of protein in the peripheral ducts of the pancreas with subsequent obstruction, inflammation, and calcification; and ethanol-induced hypertriglyceridemia, which stimulates lipase breakdown of triglycerides to free fatty acids. The latter are injurious to the pancreatic cells with subsequent release of more lipase (Dreiling & Bordalo, 1977).

The clinical features of acute pancreatitis consist of *epigastric pain* lasting for hours to days with a sensation of boring pain straight through the back. A history of recent ethanol intake, aggravation of the pain by eating, and a family history of elevated serum triglycerides should be sought. Epigastric tenderness and a low grade fever are typical. Laboratory studies indicate an elevated lipase, amylase, and GGTP (Bonkowsky & Anderson, 1981).

Intravenous fluids, nothing by mouth, and pain relief (Demerol, not morphine), are the standard initial treatment steps.

With continued drinking severe complications of chronic pancreatitis develop including pancreatic insufficiency, pseudocysts (danger of rupture, abcess or obstructive jaundice) and pancreatic ascites (fluid contains high amylase and protein concentrations). The prognosis is most influenced by abstinence from alcohol. For example, patients treated surgically for pain had a 10-year survival rate of 80%, if abstinent. Those continuing to drink had a 10-year survival rate in the 25% to 50% range (Korsten & Lieber, 1982).

Gastrointestinal Tract

Esophagus. Alcohol consumption commonly leads to reflux esophagitis as a result of decreased peristalsis and decreased tone of the lower esophageal sphincter.

In 30% to 65% of cases squamous cell carcinoma of the esophagus occurs in alcoholics. The latter malignancy has been associated with alcohol abuse, but is likely to be enhanced by concurrent cigarette smoking (Mezey, 1982).

Esophageal varices are a life-threatening complication of cirrhosis and occur secondarily to portal hypertension.

Stomach. Alcohol disrupts the mucosal barrier of the gastrium, allowing hydrogen ions to seep back into the mucosa, which causes release of histamine and hemorrhage from capillaries. Acute hemorrhagic gastritis is five times more common in the alcoholic population. Vomiting (with or without hematemesis), anorexia, and epigastric pain are the common symptoms (Bonkowsky & Anderson, 1981).

Another cause of gastric bleeding in the alcoholic is the laceration of the gastric mucosa at the gastroesophageal junction. This condition, the Mallory-Weiss syndrome, is caused by increased gastric pressure resulting from retching and vomiting.

Gastric emptying is delayed with heavy ethanol intake, but oral use of alcohol does not increase gastric secretion. Peptic ulcer disease is found with the same frequency in both alcoholic and nonalcoholic populations.

Small intestine. Histological changes in the walls of the small intestine of alcoholics have been documented even with adequate nutritional intake. Malabsorption is a common complication and is characterized by diarrhea, weakness, and weight loss. Folate, Vitamin B-12, Thiamine, and Vitamin A are commonly malabsorbed. Decreased uptake of nutrients such as the amino acids, L-methionine, and D-xylose have been documented (Mezey, 1982).

Cardiovascular System

Moderate use of alcohol mobilizes high density lipoproteins, which are believed to prevent or reverse coronary artery atherogenesis. The enthusiasm for the evidence that alcohol may have a protective effect against coronary artery disease should be tempered by the better established effect of alcohol on the myocardium. Damage to small intramyocardial arteries is believed to underlie alcohol cardiomyopathy, a long-recognized cause of congestive heart failure. Regular, heavy drinking (80 grams of alcohol/day, i.e., approximately six drinks/day) for perhaps 10 or more years may be necessary to produce this condition. Occasional episodes of heavy drinking in nonalcoholics without organic heart disease can produce transient, possibly fatal arrhythmias (Knott & Beard, 1982).

During alcohol withdrawal, hypertension is common up to two to three weeks after the last drink. Increased sodium retention and an increase in circulatory catecholamines may be responsible. More recently, a link between regular alcohol use and elevated blood pressure has been demonstrated (Gruchow, Sobocinski, & Barboriak, 1985). Epidemiologic studies are finding significantly elevated systolic and diastolic pressures in individuals consuming three or more drinks per day. No differences are noted between nondrinkers and those drinking two or fewer drinks daily (Knott & Beard, 1982).

At this stage of our knowledge, it would seem that alcohol should not be recommended for those with heart disease, and that heavy, chronic consumption of alcohol is deleterious to the myocardium and its vasculature and may be implicated in hypertension.

Hematologic System

Ethanol induces thrombocytopenia ($100,000/mm^3$) independent of liver disease or folate deficiency. This defect, present in about 25% of alcoholics, begins to correct itself within several days after cessation of alcohol use (Chanarin, 1982; Cornwell, 1981).

Red blood cell formation is directly suppressed in the presence of alcohol. In addition, folic acid deficiency is a common finding and leads to large red blood cells and an increased mean corpuscular volume (mcv). The increased mcv is an excellent screening test for the presence of alcohol dependence in hospitalized populations.

Anemia is common in alcoholic patients and may result from decreased red blood cell formation, folic acid deficiency, decreased heme-synthesis, liver disease, hypersplenism, or gastrointestinal bleeding.

Clotting mechanisms may be impaired as a result of fewer platelets, decreased platelet survival, or decreased production of Vitamin K-dependent clotting factors in the liver.

Immune Systems

Bacterial pneumonia is more than twice as common in alcoholics than in nonalcoholics, and mortality from pneumonia is at least three times greater among alcoholics than nonalcoholics (MacGregor, 1985). Other life-threatening infections, such as peritonitis, septicemia, meningitis, and septic arthritis, also occur with an increased incidence over that of the general population.

The four major immune defense systems are adversely affected by chronic alcohol use. *Antibody* production is affected in that new antigens do not stimulate an antibody response in the presence of alcohol. However, antigens to which the organism previously had been exposed retain the capacity to induce antibody production. *Polymorphonuclear leukocytes* are bacteria-devouring cells. Their production in the bone marrow is decreased by chronic drinking and their movement toward inflamed tissues inhibited by alcohol intoxication. These effects are reversed by withdrawal from alcohol. The *reticulo-endothelial system* which produces macrophages used for the removal of bacteria is impaired in that the macrophage's ability to recognize a foreign cell is impaired. Finally, *T-cells*, specialized lymphocytes which destroy viruses, fungi, and tumor cells, do not undergo necessary morphologic transformations and are reduced in the circulation (MacGregor, 1985).

Peripheral and Autonomic Nervous System

Peripheral neuropathy, characterized by decreased reflexes, sensory loss, parethesia, and pain, has been reported in 10% of alcoholics seen in a city hospital. It is typically bilaterial, symmetrical, and affects the distal lower extremities first (Bernat & Victor, 1982). Although not commonly noted, the autonomic nervous system may be affected also. Symptoms include lack of sweating, hoarseness, dysphagia, hypotension, hypothermia, impotence, and urinary retention or incontinence (Mayer & Khurana, 1982).

Vitamin B deficiencies secondary to poor nutrition are considered the major etiologic factor.

Musculoskeletal System

Acute alcoholic myopathy is an alcohol-induced disorder (not the result of a nutritional deficiency). Muscle swelling, tenderness, and cramps, usually proximal, are characteristic. The syndrome resembles thrombophlebitis. Creatine kinase is elevated, and myoglobulinemia can result in renal failure. A chronic alcoholic myopathy, with proximal muscle weakness and wasting, is difficult to distinguish from the effects of a poly-neuropathy (Rubin, 1979).

The incidence of fractures is considerably increased in the alcoholic population (Bliven, 1982). In addition to the trauma common to the alcoholic patient, osteopemia (atrophy of bone) is also prevalent. This is likely due to nutritional and disuse factors, but does increase fracture vulnerability, especially in the neck of the femur.

Another condition—more common in alcoholics—is nontraumatic idiopathic osteonecrosis of the femoral head. This is an ischemic condition characterized by hip pain. The mechanism is undetermined.

Finally, compression syndromes leading to muscle, nerve, or bone damage warrant mention. These result from prolonged pressure on tissue secondary to a recumbent position assumed while intoxicated. For example, "Saturday night palsy" refers to compression of the ulnar nerve, with resultant paresis, parathesias, and muscle wasting.

Endocrine

The hypothalamic-pituitary-adrenal system is stimulated by large doses of alcohol in normal subjects and by alcohol withdrawal in most alcoholics. The elevated serum cortisol level is the result of a "stress" response (Fazekas, 1966). Although uncommon, a pseudo-Cushing's syndrome may occur in alcoholics. With abstinence, the physical findings (rounded face, purple striae, obesity, thin extremities, buffalo hump) disappear and cortisol levels return to normal.

The dexamethasone suppression test (DST) is often abnormal in detoxified alcoholics. A recent study (Swartz & Dunner, 1982) reported that one-third of detoxified alcoholic males had elevated cortisol levels at a 4:00 p.m. testing (17 hours after administration of dexamethasone). However, the 8:00 a.m. cortisol level (9 hours after dexamethasone) was elevated in only 5%.

Abou-Saleh, Merny, and Coppen (1984), investigating only the 4:00 p.m. DST level, found that alcoholics abstinent from 3 to 6 weeks had abnormally elevated DST results in 28% of cases compared to 11% for normal controls. Of eight alcoholics undergoing detoxification, six had an abnormal DST. The DST was not considered diagnostic of depression in this sample of recently detoxified alcoholics. The Beck Depression Inventory scores and Severity of Alcohol Dependence scores (Stockwell, Hodgson, Edwards, Taylor, & Rankin, 1979) were similar in those with normal and abnormal DST results.

In a larger sample, 7 of 38 alcoholics tested 3 weeks after alcohol withdrawal failed to suppress. Three of these seven were determined to be persistently depressed, but the other four represented false positive DSTs (Kroll, Palmer, & Greden, 1983). In a study of 31 alcoholics, the DST was significantly correlated with age and not with the presence of major depression, abnormal liver function, or length of sobriety prior to the test (Nelson, Sullivan, Khan, & Tamragouri, 1986). The utility of the DST in diagnosing depression in hospitalized alcoholics is very questionable at this time.

The effect of alcohol on thyroid hormones, prolactin, and growth hormone is uncertain. There seems to be little effect on thyroid function (Stokes, 1982). An increased incidence of breast and thyroid cancer and malignant melanoma in alcoholics has been reported (Dixon, Exon, & Malins, 1975). It is undetermined whether increased secretion of pituitary hormones in response to alcohol may account for these findings.

The effect of alcohol on the hypothalamic-pituitary-gonadal system is better determined. Alcohol has been found to decrease testosterone synthesis in the testes as well as increase its peripheral clearance. As a result hypogonadism, infertility, decreased libido, and impotence are common in alcoholic males. It is also likely that alcohol decreases luteinizing hormone (LH) and follicle-stimulating hormone (FHS) and formation at the hypothalamic or pituitary level (Van Thiel et al., 1981).

Increased plasma estrogen is found in cirrhotic males and accounts for the findings of gynecomastia, female fat and hair distribution, spider angiomata, and palmar erythema.

The hypothalamic-pituitary-gonadal system has not been well studied in women. Amenorrhea, infrequent periods, and decreased fertility have been described (Gavaler, 1985).

Fetal Alcohol Syndrome (FAS)

Alcohol crosses the placenta. A continuum of fetal abnormalities, possibly contingent on the amount of alcohol consumed during pregnancy, has been observed. No safe dose of alcohol during pregnancy has been established (Lundberg, 1984). At least one feature from each of the following three categories must be present for the diagnosis of FAS (Rosett, Weiner, & Edelin, 1981):

1) Growth retardation before or after birth in weight, length, or head circumference (below the 10th percentile)
2) Abnormal features of the face or head (microcephaly, short palpebral fissures, thin upper lip, or poorly developed philtrum)
3) Central nervous system abnormality including mental retardation, abnormal neonatal behavior, or developmental delay

Alcohol use in the first trimester is implicated in morphologic abnormalities (especially facial features such as a short nose, thin upper lips, indistinct philtrum, microcephaly, epicanthus folds, low nasal bridge). The second trimester carries an increased risk of spontaneous abortion, and the third trimester is affected by alcohol through decreased fetal growth (Rosett, Weiner, Zuckerman, McKinley, & Edelin, 1980).

Lowered birth weight is the most reliable effect resulting from intrauterine exposure to alcohol. In a study of 300 cases of FAS, the average birth weight was 2,000 grams compared with a median birth weight in the United States of 3,300 grams (Abel, 1982).

Effects on behavioral development have been described by decreased sleep or increased restlessness during sleep (Rosett, Snyder, Sander, Lee, Cook, Weiner, & Gould, 1979); hyperactivity characterized by distractibility, restlessness, and short attention spans (Shaywitz, Cohen, & Shaywitz, 1980); and mental retardation. In the United States average IQ scores of 65 were found in a group of patients with FAS (Streissguth, Herman, & Smith, 1978) and children in Sweden with signs of FAS had an average IQ under 70 (Olegard et al., 1979). Streissguth recently described a French study wherein one in every 690 births was a full FAS, and one in every 212 births had findings of partial FAS. In yet another culture with heavy alcohol consumption, the Indian tribes of the Southwest Plains, a full FAS was found in one of every 102 births and a partial FAS in one of every 56 births (Streissguth, 1985).

Taking into consideration the wide range of samples studied, the incidence of fetal alcohol syndrome has been estimated to occur in 1 or 2 of every 1,000 live births. This is an incidence comparable to spina bifida and Down's Syndrome. Moderate to heavy drinking in early pregnancy carries the greatest risk. The danger from light drinking (e.g., less than 1 ounce of absolute alcohol per day) has not been determined, and caution should be exercised to avoid unnecessary guilt in parents who drink and who have abnormal children. There are many other possible etiologies for fetal abnormalities.

CHAPTER 3

Barriers to Treatment

Despite the well-documented and well-publicized costs of alcoholism to our society, the response of the medical profession has been limited and hesitant. This has been as true for psychiatry as for other clinical specialties. How can we explain our diminutive response? Several specific factors bear on our inadequate reaction: training, attitudes, and ignorance of treatability. These areas are seen as barriers which hinder our initial attempts to understand and treat alcoholic patients. Consistent with the theme of this text, the importance of the clinician's gaining motivation, conviction, and confidence as preparation for working with alcoholic patients is emphasized. The reason such exhortation seems necessary lies in deficient training, pessimism, and lack of knowledge of treatment effectiveness.

DEFICIENT MEDICAL TRAINING

The first issue, training in the diagnosis and treatment of any illness, involves a complex process, begun in medical school, refined during residency training, and continued through professional life. Ironically, these experiences ill prepare one for the responsibilities of professional life in regard to alcoholism. This lack of training leads to a combination of pessimism, avoidance, anger, and indifference.

Perhaps this attitude merely reflects our larger society's view of the alcoholic, a view which the novice physician could be expected to share.

Yet a physician's approach to illness is not governed by the ignorance and misunderstanding of the lay public. For example, at first any medical student may share the average man's repulsion for the procedure of an autopsy. But in medical training one learns the value of such procedures in the interest of science and better clinical care.

Some might argue that training is unnecessary since no effective treatment is available for alcoholism. Even if this were true, medicine has always prepared physicians to understand any patient's condition and to do all possible to alleviate suffering. As will be discussed, there is effective treatment and positive results can be expected.

Effective treatment, of course, depends on the potency or intrinsic efficacy of a treatment method and the susceptibility of the illness to current treatment. Training and skill on the part of the physician, however, are needed to render any treatment effective.

Optimal training integrates the physician's cognitive, affective, and behavioral capacities. Several examples may illustrate the importance of these components: At Johns Hopkins Hospital (Inui, Yourtee, & Williamson, 1975) patient compliance with hypertension treatment regimens was noted to be low. The physicians treating these patients were assigned either to a control group or were provided a 1-to-2-hour tutorial on recognition of noncompliance and strategies of intervention. A follow-up study 2 and 6 months later documented that patients of tutored physicians were more compliant with drug regimens and had better control of blood pressure than did the patients of the physicians in the control group. Physician effectiveness can be enhanced by such a straightforward cognitive approach to improved patient care.

At the University of Connecticut (Pinkerton, Tinanoff, Willms, & Tapp, 1980) the intensive education in the techniques of fluoride therapy to family practice residents resulted in no gain in proper clinical management. Subsequently, faculty supervision on a one-to-one basis led to appropriate changes in attitude and in prescribing behavior. This result documents a situation where modeling behavior on the part of faculty was a necessary addition to the cognitive component of training before effective use of fluoride was accomplished.

What should medical training in alcoholism hope to accomplish? Table 3-1 lists goals for the training of psychiatrists.

Few psychiatrists acquire these skills. Why? In part, the cognitive component of training is deficient. In 1970, a survey (Brown, 1979) of 60 medical and 2 osteopathic schools revealed that only 10% offered a formal course or clerkship in alcoholism. A report of the Macy Conference (Macy Foundation, 1973) in 1972 stated that only 45 of 120 medical schools in the United States and Canada had material in the curriculum on alcoholism. By 1977 the situation had improved somewhat. A survey

TABLE 3-1
Goals of Training for the Psychiatrist

1. Readiness to consider the possibility of alcohol abuse or dependence or other forms of substance abuse in any patient or patient's family member.
2. Ability to diagnose alcoholism or other forms of substance abuse.
3. Understanding of the disease concept of alcoholism.
4. Understanding of the possible reciprocal relationship between alcoholism and other psychiatric disorders and establishing treatment priorities.
5. Ability to intervene.
6. Accepting the role of motivating the patient for treatment.
7. Providing detoxification services.
8. Educating, advising, and treating the family of the alcoholic patient.
9. Conducting appropriate psychotherapy.
10. Prescribing disulfiram.
11. Making effective referrals to specific alcoholism or other substance abuse programs.

(Pokorny, Putnam, & Fryer, 1978) of 117 medical schools and 9 osteopathic schools indicated that 102 schools offered at least some teaching about alcohol or substance abuse. Over the four years of medical school an average of 25.7 hours of required training was provided. The proportion of training in alcoholism and substance abuse to the totality of required curriculum ranged from 0.0% to 3.1%, with a total mean of 0.6%. Pokorny and Solomon (1983) randomly re-surveyed 40 of the medical schools in 1981. Of the 35 schools responding, the mean number of required hours over a four-year curriculum was 23.1 hours. The ratio of hours of substance abuse to total required curriculum ranged from 0.05% to 2.3%.

These data document the negligence on the part of American medical schools in providing adequate knowledge about alcoholism and other drug problems. Whether the improvement (however inadequate to the task) which did occur in the decade of the 1970s can be sustained is uncertain. A federally funded Career Teacher Training Program in the Addictions provided considerable stimulation for the gains noted. The program was discontinued in the early 1980s.

As crucial to training as the acquisition of information (cognitive component) is, it is unlikely that improvement in physician effectiveness will occur through attention to information alone (Haynes, Davis, McKibbon, & Tugwell, 1984). Therefore we need to direct our attention to a second component of the training experience: the affective component, a matter of particular concern for the treatment of alcoholism. In the case of alcoholism the affective component consists of a constellation of negative attitudes directed toward the alcoholic patient. In varying degrees we may be conscious of our attitudes, but there is usually a substantial unconscious component. Psychiatrists are trained to examine their own feelings as part of the process of understanding a patient. This process of self-examination will be necessary even before undertaking the treatment of an alcoholic, as attitudes toward alcoholic patients commonly antedate actual clinical experience.

Training in this area is influenced by attitudes of hostility, pessimism, apathy, or indifference. Fisher, Mason, Keeley, and Fisher (1975) show that the process of medical training, from entry into medical school through residency, yields increasingly negative attitudes toward alcoholic patients. In fact, it has been observed that the vigor with which life preservation skills are applied in an emergency room is affected by attitudes—the disheveled alcoholic does not receive the same effort as the apparently well-to-do businessman (Sudnow, 1967). Various studies have indicated that physicians view alcoholics as morally weak, or they do not consider it their role to motivate the alcoholic for treatment (Morse, Mitchell, & Martin, 1977).

The most scholarly effort at understanding attitudes toward alcoholic patients is the work of Chappel, Jordan, Treadway, and Miller (1977), and Chappel, Veach, and Krug (1985) with medical students at the University of Nevada. A reversal of the negative attitudinal trend reported by Fisher et al. (1975) was accomplished by a well-designed substance abuse course emphasizing student participation in small group discussions, clinical problem solving, field experience in substance abuse programs, and Alcoholics Anonymous meetings. In addition to demonstrating the possibility of attitude changes in medical students, Chappel and colleagues documented the fragile and tenuous process of change. The steps necessary for a good outcome are now better explicated and include consideration of when training occurs in the curriculum and the need for sufficient freedom from academic pressure to allow not only knowledge acquisition, but energy for the task of attitude examination.

It is encouraging to note that practicing physicians may be undergoing changes in their attitudes toward alcoholic patients. A survey of 665 Midwest physicians indicated a desire for more knowledge about alcoholism and a more positive feeling toward alcoholic patients than had been previously noted (Morse et al., 1977).

The importance of attitude change deserves emphasis. Attitudes determine our readiness to act or not to act. Negative (or dysfunctional) attitudes set up conditions of withdrawal or potentially harmful action. Positive (or functional) attitudes enable the physician to move toward the patient and act in a helpful way. Chappel (1978) describes functional versus dysfunctional attitudes and these are listed in Table 3-2.

TABLE 3-2
Physician Attitudes*

Dysfunctional	Functional
Insensitive	Sensitive
Indifferent	Curious
Unresponsive	Responsive
Giving Up	Persistent
Impatient	Patient
Hopeless	Hopeful
Inflexible	Flexible
Rigid	Firm
Fearful	Anxious
Helpless	Optimistic
Angry	Concerned
Apathetic	Interested
Resentment (sic)	Challenged

*Reprinted by permission, from the *Journal of Psychoactive Drugs,* Vol. 10(1), p. 30, 1978.

Since what we do is considerably influenced by attitudes, we need to address at this point the third component of training: the behavioral.

The behavioral component involves direct participation in the diagnosis and treatment of alcoholic patients and supervision by experienced health professionals who serve as skilled role models. Clinicians who have greater experience in the treatment of alcoholism are generally more optimistic about treatment and more confident of the validity of the disease concept of alcoholism, a view which trainees can acquire. Rezler (1974) points out that medical students' views of the clinical world are shaped largely by moment-to-moment contact with teachers rather than by changes in curriculum, instructional technique, or grading procedures.

Few role models are available for residents and students but improvement can be expected. The Career Teachers Program involved 60 medical schools. Psychiatric and general hospitals have established increasing numbers of alcoholism treatment units over the past 10 to 15 years (Chappel et al., 1977), and medical schools are affiliating with substance abuse programs for training purposes. In this regard, nearly a doubling of program affiliates occurred in the 5 years between 1976 and 1981 (Pokorny & Solomon, 1983).

Delays in improved training are costly—both in terms of medical expense and human suffering. For example, a large city hospital developed a "treatment catalyst" team consisting of a psychiatrist and social worker. Alcoholic patients admitted to the emergency service were evaluated by this team, who took responsibility for their care and took special effort to demonstrate the desire for help. The patients were then referred to alcoholism treatment clinics. Using the criteria of 5 or more voluntary visits to an alcoholism clinic, the "treatment catalyst" team proved effective in nearly 50% of cases. This compares to a nearly 1% effectiveness rate when the alcoholic was handled routinely by the emergency service (Chafetz, 1968). Another example of improved physician performance is provided by a family practice program. Resident physicians doubled the number of alcoholic diagnoses among clinic patients after they had participated in a weekly course on alcoholism given over a 7 month period (Fisher, Fisher, & Mason, 1976).

Similarly, psychiatry residents given the opportunity to serve as the primary physician/therapist in an alcoholism treatment program rated the experience highly. The best experience for the psychiatry residents occurred when they were able to work as part of a treatment team, when they had participated in group therapy and milieu meetings on the alcohol unit, and when the assignment to the alcoholism program was a regularly scheduled part of the residency. The interest in and competence to work with alcoholic patients was documented to occur in the years following completion of their residency (Nace, 1981).

Some comments from the residents included:

I am more aware of the ubiquity of drug use in psychiatric patients.
Makes you more on the lookout for alcohol and drug problems.
Encourages you to have higher expectations of equally sick psychiatric patients.
Offers an important experience in limit setting and dealing with passivity and hostile dependency. (Nace, 1981)

The director of a psychiatry residency program summarizes his experience with an alcoholism treatment program.

Gradually as I treated patients on the alcoholic unit over the three years that the elective program was in place, I became more aware that a theoretical model did exist and that treatment was successful. Therefore, my education and the positive feedback from the residents were primarily responsible for our accepting a formal (training) program. (Singer, M., unpublished manuscript, 1981)

The receptive attitudes of psychiatry residents to participation in alcoholism treatment should encourage greater emphasis in psychiatry residencies to training in this area. The widespread criticism of psychiatrists for their lack of knowledge in treating alcoholics may be corrected and a major public health problem addressed more adequately.

PESSIMISM

A second barrier is the widespread sense of futility as to whether or not alcoholism is treatable. From the time the student begins clinical work in the third year of medical school through the completion of residency, scores if not hundreds of alcoholics will have been examined, sutured, probed, and prescribed for, but the contact is usually brief, takes place under pressured circumstances, and usually the patient is intoxicated (for example, in the emergency room). Prolonged contact involves only those hospitalized for serious, often end-stage complications such as cirrhosis, esophageal varices, or pancreatitis. The "revolving door" alcoholic patient is the norm during the training years. Alcoholics who recover require acute medical services infrequently, and house officers only witness those who relapse and deteriorate.

A third-year student described his experience on surgery tersely:

A man from Beaumont, my home town, was admitted for treatment of esophageal varices. I worked closely and supportively with this patient and was pleased by the man's genuine appreciation. This satisfactory clinical experience was shattered for me when post-operatively I observed the patient drinking the after-shave lotion at his bedside.

Fortunately, the same student later accepted an assignment in an alcoholism treatment program as part of his third-year clerkship in psychiatry. The student's earlier experience was balanced by the opportunity to work with alcoholic patients undergoing rehabilitation.

We should not underestimate the impact on the student and the physician of attempting to treat alcoholic men and women who, despite the best medical care and well-meaning advice, destructively return to the obvious source of their despair and deterioration. It is asking a great deal of the young physician to persist in his efforts to treat the alcoholic. An alcoholic woman (a nurse) recently told me of her five bouts with pancreatitis within 6 months. This occurred 4 years earlier, and she has now been sober and employed for over a year. I saw her as she struggled to stop drinking, as she endured kidney ailments unrelated to drinking, and as she tolerated the subtle and not so subtle comments of peers upon return to nursing duties. Had my involvement been during her extensive alcoholic binges and bouts of pancreatitis, I don't think I could have avoided feeling hopeless about her.

Pessimism about the treatment of alcoholism has its origins not only in the acute, crisis-centered experiences of the training years, but may develop from intrapsychic conflict and serve a defensive function. The behavioral expressions of this defense include avoidance and rejection. Psychiatrists answering a survey provided reasons for avoidance of alcoholics (Robinson & Podnos, 1966, p. 221):

Alcoholics are too frustrating
Acting out is hard to handle
They are too demanding
Their dependency and passive-aggressivity are hard to tolerate
They are threatening
Alcoholics are not motivated

Lisansky (1975, pp. 1791–1792), utilizing 30 years experience with alcoholic patients, details possible subconscious reasons for physicians' avoiding alcoholics:

1) Anger at the alcoholic who is felt to be willful, uncooperative, and unmodifiable.
2) The presence in one's family of alcoholics. This may serve a positive or negative role in the physician's attitude in his practice.
3) Fears of losing the patient if he is told he is an alcoholic; in general feeling that there is tremendous prejudice against the label of alcoholism; the unwillingness or the feeling of lack of skill in presenting this kind of a diagnosis to the patient in a manner which will be acceptable.
4) Doubts about whether alcoholism is an illness; fears that it has something to do with sin or perversity in the individual.
5) Misgivings about the physician's own drinking pattern; inability to come to a decision about whether he is or is not an alcoholic is being projected onto the patient.
6) Fear of legal reprisal; the diagnosis may not stick.

Alcoholic patients arouse a variety of emotions in the physician. These feelings constitute countertransference reactions, using the term countertransference in its broadest meaning. Consider the physician's usual sense of obligation to conduct himself in a controlled, responsible, predictable manner. In contrast, the alcoholic abandons such restraints, allowing a free-form expression of impulsivity, omnipotence, and regression. This stark contrast may signal an anxious response within the physician as he senses his own vulnerability and wishes to violate cherished values. In addition, physicians may be uncomfortable with an awareness, however fleeting, of anger and disdain toward sick patients.

Avoidance of alcoholic patients is tantamount to avoiding uncomfortable unacceptable feelings within ourselves. Distancing ourselves from prolonged contact with alcoholic patients may indicate an avoidance defense against conflicting feelings of repulsion versus obligation.

Avoidance would seem rational if the physician were able to find continuing reason for pessimism regarding treatment outcome. I am often asked by doctors "What are your results?" Usually the physician has no knowledge of the literature on outcome and therefore finds it difficult to interpret percentages of success or failure. I've learned that the above question is not actually a statistical one, but disguises the query "Is it worthwhile for me to get involved?" If my answer is presented pessimistically, it reinforces a prevailing attitude that you can't do much for an alcoholic. On the other hand, if I explain treatment and its potential to aid in recovery, many physicians show interest in learning more.

An orthopedic surgeon who treated me for tennis elbow asked the "results" question. It provided a chance to explain what we did and why. I was able to do so with confidence that we were doing well with many of the referrals. About one month later, the orthopedist referred a patient to our alcoholism treatment program. The surgeon had refused to operate until the man sought help for a long-standing drinking problem. He wisely saw that this patient's capacity to care for himself properly over a long postoperative course was compromised if alcohol remained in the picture. He also had enough optimism to recommend alcoholism treatment and to make his surgery contingent on the results.

The defensive process of avoidance is bolstered by belief in or acceptance of a pessimistic view of treatment. If this belief prevails, the physician is spared facing a process of intervention that may prove frustrating or disappointing, and is further spared the associated feelings of anger, guilt, or failure. Observing alcoholic patients over the long term is an antidote to this dilemma. It has been observed that psychiatrists report more optimistic attitudes about alcoholism and express a greater willingness to treat alcoholics when adequate programs and facilities become available (Robinson & Podnos, 1966). The psychiatrist who is willing to work with alcoholic patients over a long period of time acquires the perspective that his efforts—medical and psychotherapeutic—are not ordained to fail. He communicates confidence and hope, but not at the expense of denying the reality of the patients' condition. The availability of inpatient and outpatient programs for alcoholics and a willingness to encourage use of Alcoholics Anonymous bolsters the psychiatrist's therapeutic work. The physician can be supported by the spectrum of services available and less threatened by the alcoholic's potential for acting out.

IGNORANCE OF TREATMENT EFFICACY

A third barrier is lack of knowledge about the effectiveness of treatment. Often, reports from the literature reinforce a nihilistic view of treatment. Consider the following examples:

> Two groups of alcoholics received either one counseling session or several months of in- and outpatient treatment. One year later there were no significant differences in outcome between the two groups. (Edwards et al., 1977, p. 1004)

> . . . there is compelling evidence that the results of our treatment were no better than the natural history of the disease. (Vaillant, 1983a, p. 284)

> It is not only that the research literature is poor in reports which suggest that any particular treatment is advantageous; on the contrary, it is rich in reports which demonstrate that a given treatment is no better than another. (Edwards et al., 1977, p. 1026)

Despite the pessimism permeating some of the research literature, the clinician is admonished as follows:

> These findings should not be construed as advocating the elimination of intervention programs for alcoholism. (Stimmel et al., 1983, p. 865)

> The implications of this study must not be seen as nihilistic. (Edwards et al., 1977, p. 1027)

> The fact that we cannot easily alter the long-term course of alcoholism should be no reason for despair. (Vaillant, 1983a, p. 316)

Such reports are discouraging, perhaps demoralizing, for the clinician treating alcoholics. The admonishments to continue ring hollow and, at best, they leave one perplexed.

Do the results of research warrant this degree of pessimism? Are there no data to support the effectiveness of treatment?

Emrick (1974, 1975) reviewed a total of 397 studies of alcoholism treatment reported in the literature between 1952 and 1973. Pooled data on well over 4,000 patients reveal that at follow-up 6 months or longer after termination of all treatment, patients who had been judged to have had minimal or no treatment achieved abstinence in 13.6% of cases. By contrast, the patients who had received more than minimal treatment acquired a 28% abstinence rate. When less stringent criteria than total abstinence were applied 41.5% of the minimal or no treatment group had improved over pretreatment drinking levels. Of those receiving more than minimal treatment 63% improved.

Are these results discouraging? Bear in mind that Emrick's review consists of very varied treatments, samples, and programs. Veterans Administration Programs, state hospitals, and other public facilities may be overrepresented and typically they are not able to provide intensive and sophisticated staffing. They usually treat a more chronic, socially unstable alcoholic population. Also, several studies reviewed by Emrick report on discredited treatments such as the use of hallucinogenic agents.

Costello, Biever, and Baillargeon (1977) reviewed 80 outcome studies. They determined that a 50% success rate 1 year after treatment could be expected in a program that selected its clients and offered multiple treatment components. It is worth remembering that even small statistical differences in improvement may yield substantial savings when medical costs or prevention of lost income are calculated.

Emrick (1974) calculates a range of outcome results which could be used to gauge new reports. The range is based on using one standard deviation above and below the mean. Results outside this range would be atypically poor or atypically good. For abstinence, atypical rates would be below 10.5% and above 53.3%. The rates for deterioration would be atypical if they fell below 0.2% or above 20.6%.

TREATMENT VS. NATURAL HISTORY

A major challenge to alcoholism treatment is the question of whether treatment alters the natural history of the disease. Vaillant (1983a) has argued that treatment does not alter the natural history. Comparing untreated alcoholics as reported in the literature with selected outcome studies, Vaillant concludes that treatment fails to yield results better than those obtained by allowing the disease to run its natural course. This conclusion is premature. For example, Imber, Schultz, Funderburk, Allen, and Flamer (1976) found that an untreated sample of alcoholic men (they had received brief "drying out") had a mortality rate of 12% over a 3-year follow-up. In contrast, Costello et al.'s (1977) review of 80 treated samples report a 2% mortality rate (minimum follow-up period was 1 year). In addition, four separate samples of middle-class alcoholic men and women who received 2 weeks of inpatient treatment plus periodic follow-up visits had an average mortality rate of only .01% during a 1-year follow-up period (Neubuerger et al., 1982).

Further support for the claim that alcoholism treatment reduces mortality can be implied from Pettinati, Sugerman, DiDonato, and Maurer's

(1982) study of 225 treated alcoholics followed yearly for 4 years. In their sample, 16 patients died over the 4-year period, yielding a yearly mortality rate of less than 2%.

The 80 studies reviewed by Costello et al. (1977), the 4 samples followed by Neubuerger et al. (1982) and Pettinati et al.'s (1982) study clearly indicate the advantage of treatment in regard to short-term mortality rates.

Vaillant (1983a) reports on a prospective study of 456 white males chosen from Boston inner city schools. This "Core City" sample was selected in early adolescence with follow-up contacts at ages 25, 31, and 47. The sample was selected partly on the basis of negative history for delinquency at age 14. One hundred twenty of these men were judged to be alcohol abusers during the course of this longitudinal study, and 110 were available for careful study. This is considered an untreated sample although AA was used by many of the men. Of these 110 alcohol abusers, 21 (19%) were found to be securely abstinent, i.e., they remained abstinent for at least 3 years and were abstinent at the last follow-up. The definition of abstinence was at least 12 consecutive months of using alcohol less often than once a month with no more than one episode of intoxication in the abstinent year and that episode less than a week in duration.

Using a more rigorous definition of abstinence, i.e., no alcohol use at all, Pettinati et al. (1982) found that in their sample of 225 treated alcoholics complete abstinence was maintained over 4 years by 29% of the sample. An additional 26% had been abstinent with the exception of occasional slips. If a less rigorous definition of abstinence is applied, similar to that used by Vaillant for the study of the Core City untreated sample, 55% of the treated sample of Pettinati et al. maintained abstinence over a 4-year period.

One of the earliest studies of formal treatment (Voegtlin & Broz, 1949), a follow-up of 2,323 male and female alcoholics treated by the conditioned reflex method, found that 85% of all chronic alcoholics remained abstinent for 6 months or longer, 55% remained abstinent for greater than 3 years, and 25% remained abstinent for more than 10 years. These results are impressive considering that treatment efforts during the period of study (1935–1945) were not assisted by the well-established network of Alcoholics Anonymous meetings available today.

Of particular interest is the outcome of a treatment program at Norristown State Hospital, which selected only chronic recidivist alcoholics (Sheehan, Wieman, & Bechtel, 1981). Inpatient treatment ranged from 6 to 12 months. One and 3 years following hospitalization, 48% to 58% of patients were found to be abstinent, employed, and free of legal problems. Length of treatment was associated with good outcome, a finding that counters previous reports that long-term treatment offers no advantage.

Vaillant's conclusion that treated and untreated alcoholics turn out the same can be challenged on many grounds. First, not all of the untreated sample met the American Psychiatric Association's criteria for alcohol dependence as outlined in the *Diagnostic and Statistical Manual of Mental Disorders, 3rd Edition* (American Psychiatric Association, 1980). Alcohol abusers were lumped with those more clearly dependent.

The selection of the sample avoided including males whose drinking began at a very young age. This may have introduced a bias in the light of Schuckit and Russell's (1983) study of over 1,000 university men, ages 21 to 25. They found that age of first drink (taking a drink on one's own, not a sip from an adult's glass or for religious ceremonies) was significantly related to subsequent alcohol-related problems, drug use, and psychiatric problems. The younger the onset of drinking, the more likely were the latter problems to occur.

The samples studied were not socioeconomically matched. The comparison on outcome was between a blue collar employed sample (untreated) and a socially bereft sample (treated). The latter, the "clinic" sample, were socially unstable with 50% either living in the streets or by themselves. Also, 71% of the clinic sample had a history of being jailed.

The clinic sample was first interviewed at an average age of 45, whereas the Core City sample had been interviewed at ages 25, 31, and 47 years. Fillmore and Midanik (1984) have documented that the stability of alcohol-related problems is low in the age range 20–29 years, but when you find alcohol problems in men ages 40–49 years the problems persist over time. That is, in nonclinical samples, evidence for alcohol-related problems in younger men is much less sustained over follow-up periods than when you begin with a clinical sample of older men. The older males, if they appear alcoholic at one point, are significantly more likely to appear alcoholic at follow-up points as well, but this is not true for younger males. Vaillant's untreated sample had an average age of 35 when they were judged to be securely abstinent. Four of these 21 men who had secure abstinence were under 30, and only 6 were over 40 (Vaillant, 1985). Possibly, the untreated and treated samples represent quite different phenomena as far as alcohol-related problems are concerned.

The treated sample had minimal treatment. Their average length of hospitalization was 5 days, with a range from 1 to 11 days. This was for the purpose of detoxification. Following discharge the patients were encouraged to attend an aftercare group that fostered AA attendance. This treatment effort, although not uncommon in large mental health clinics, can hardly be considered equal to the magnitude of problems which this clinic sample presented.

If the natural course of alcoholism leads to remission at a rate of 2% to 3% a year (Vaillant, 1983a), would not skilled intervention improve these results? Research to answer this question is not complete, but the data indicate that treatment considerably improves the prognosis for the alcoholic, certainly on the short-term and possibly for the long-term. For example:

- Long-term treatment of a chronic recidivist sample produced a 58% good outcome rate (Sheehan, Wieman, & Bechtel, 1981). This result stands in stark contrast to a 5% success rate for a similar sample of alcoholics who had been kept on a waiting list (Kissin, Platz, & Su, 1970).
- Two years after treatment for alcoholism, 83% of Naval personnel are rated effective in duty performance (Skuja, Wood, & Bucky, 1976).
- One year following brief inpatient aversive conditioning, 54% of a large middle-class sample remained abstinent (Neubuerger et al., 1982).
- Patients treated in private psychiatric hospital programs have had good outcome. In one study using conservative criteria, 58% of cases were abstinent an average of 14 months after treatment (Saxon, Nace, & Cammarota, 1983). In another study, 39% were abstinent and/or had good adjustment for 4 consecutive years after hospitalization (Pettinati et al., 1982).

A major difficulty in evaluating the outcome of treatment for alcoholism is the problem of matching the patient to the appropriate treatment approach. Pattison argues that we abandon unitary approaches to treatment and learn to use the varying treatment methodologies currently available (Pattison, 1979). Kissin et al. (1970) provide data to support the wisdom of carefully selected treatment approaches. Nevertheless, a reluctance exists to apply what we have learned about treatment (rudimentary though our knowledge may be). Not only may patients be directed toward a treatment approach not well suited to their needs, but in any given program the staff may fail to adopt the pace of the program to the abilities of certain patients or may overlook cognitive deficits or personality disorders that compromise understanding and acceptance of treatment. When, however, the patient becomes an active and serious participant in a competent treatment program, a good outcome can be expected.

CHAPTER 4

Evaluation and Diagnosis

An evaluation for alcohol abuse or dependence should be routine with any new patient contact. The prevalence rate of alcoholism in our society justifies this consideration alone. There are other reasons as well. The undiagnosed alcoholic patient might be prescribed medications such as sedatives, tranquilizers, or antidepressants which, in combination with alcohol, could be dangerous. The prescribing problem is compounded by the possibility that an alcohol-abusing patient may be using any variety of other drugs as well, and any additions may increase the risk. Furthermore, it is widely recognized that an alcoholic patient is at higher risk for dependence on other substances, including sedatives and the minor tranquilizers. Therefore, prescribing psychoactive medications for an alcoholic poses certain risks, which are not always present with other patients (Chapter 11).

For the patient with whom the psychiatrist is familiar, a reevaluation for possible alcohol or other substance abuse is indicated when a treatment plan is not being followed or there is a failure to benefit from treatment. If alcoholism remains active but unrecognized, psychotherapeutic as well as psychopharmacologic treatment are likely to yield disappointing results. On this point mental health professionals frequently meet criticism from lay circles and Alcoholics Anonymous because alcoholic patients have been undiagnosed or misdiagnosed, and their alcoholism progresses.

Some specific circumstances raise the question of whether alcoholism is part of the clinical picture:

1) *All circumstances where the referral source suspects alcohol or drug abuse*: The adage "where there is smoke there is fire" often applies to alcoholism. The tendency for alcohol problems to be minimized or overlooked by health professionals and others should alert us when recognition has at least reached the level of suspicion.

2) *Any patient with a history of drug abuse or drug dependence*: The poly-drug user often has a history of alcohol abuse as well. Patients who present with a history of abuse of one drug only are exceptional. This applies to patients less than 35 years old particularly since this segment of the population grew up during the drug epidemic beginning in the 1960s. Among users one finds that drugs, including alcohol, are usually interchangeable. Therefore, the teen-ager or college student referred for problems associated with marijuana or other drugs should be evaluated for alcohol abuse and dependence. Because the risk of dependence shifts from one chemical to another, the abuser of street drugs also should have abstinence from alcohol as part of the treatment plan. This is appropriate whether or not alcohol use has reached an abusive pattern.

3) *Referrals from corporations or industry secondary to job-related problems*: Fifty percent of on-the-job problems are alcohol related (Chafetz, 1983). The odds are high, therefore, that a referral from a medical director of a company, an employee assistance program, or a personnel director involves alcohol abuse. Employee assistance programs (EAP) emphasize early detection through monitoring of job performance decrements. Rather than firing the alcoholic employee, the EAP emphasizes referral for treatment and salvaging of the employee. This cost-saving approach has proliferated in the United States, with 4,400 programs in effect in 1980—up from 500 in 1973 (Chafetz, 1983).

4) *Hospital and emergency room consultations*: Not all emergency room patients who have been drinking are alcoholic. But in urban settings alcohol use can be detectable in up to 40% of patients (Keeley, 1982). Because alcohol dependence is underdiagnosed in emergency room settings (Solomon, Vanga, Morgan, & Joseph, 1980), the psychiatrist should have a high index of suspicion regarding alcohol dependence or abuse when seeing emergency room patients. The high rate of alcoholism in general hospital populations also has been documented (Galanter & Sperber, 1982) and warrants the same degree of awareness.

5) *Patients with an arrest for driving while intoxicated (DWI)*: It has been estimated that 2% to 3% of the driving population are legally intoxicated at any given time, and that percentage increases on nights and weekends (*Fifth Special Report*, Department of Health and Human Services, 1983). Findings vary as to how many of the individuals who are arrested for DWI are actually alcohol dependent. DWI cases with a prior history of alcoholism treatment vary from 3% to

9% (Chafetz, 1983). Undoubtedly, more are alcohol abusers or alcoholics without a history of treatment. The percentage of accidents involving legally drunk drivers (blood alcohol level more than 0.10%) is commonly underreported. For example, Texas A & M's Transportation Institute found that autopsy reports document levels of drunkenness in 5% of drivers killed in the 10 Texas counties where such records are kept. The accident reports, however, indicated that only 2% were legally drunk (Paternoster, 1984). At the least, a history of a DWI serves as a signal for careful evaluation for alcohol problems.

6) *A patient with a history of divorce, especially multiple divorces*: Although divorce is common in our society, the rate of divorce for alcoholics is greater than for the general population. One review estimated that separation and divorce occurs 7 times more frequently among alcoholics than in the nonalcoholic population (Paolino & McCrady, 1977).

7) *The patient who expresses even minimal concern or who jokingly expresses concern about alcohol use*: Acknowledgement of a possible problem is counter to expectations in light of the denial usually present in alcoholic patients. But, many alcoholic patients make reference to their alcoholism with physicians, only to be falsely reassured. We should encourage further exploration in any patient who refers, however obliquely, to alcohol-related concerns. The physician should not shy away from the topic for fear of embarrassing the patient. The course of alcoholism always results in pain far more ominous than that incurred by a frank and open discussion.

Before beginning an evaluation, certain points need to be kept in mind:

1) The decision to consider the possibility of an alcoholic diagnosis should not be determined by the patient's status in life, his/her accomplishments, profession, age, physical appearance, charm, or reputation in the community. Probably only 1 of 10 alcoholic persons appears to be alcoholic in the sense of conforming to a stereotyped image; for example, the skid row derelict or the marginally employed, isolated occupant of a single room. A Massachusetts General Hospital study found that physicians were unlikely to make a diagnosis of alcoholism when the patient was employed, married, had a permanent address, was self-referred, or had health insurance (Wolf, Chafetz, Blane, & Hill, 1965).

2) Before the initial interview, obtain as much information as possible. The hospital chart should be reviewed for laboratory findings, results of the physical exam, and information from the history. A referring person should be questioned carefully for details of the patient's condition, and the relationship of apparent problems to

alcohol use. Even if the referral source states, "The problem is alcohol," obtain specific incidents, effects, observations. Further, and most important, obtain permission from the referral source to be quoted (really paraphrased) regarding the information provided. Armed with enough preliminary data, the physician will be able to counter the defensive patient's minimization, denial, and protests. When the alcoholic patient knows the doctor knows, a new level of relationship can be obtained; that is, the patient's confidence in being able to bluff his way through the interview is lessened. Paradoxically, the sense of isolation common to the alcoholic is also lessened, and some hope of being understood is established.

3) The tone of the doctor's voice, which reflects underlying attitudes, will influence whether the alcoholic patient accepts the diagnosis and initiates treatment. The importance of this variable has been documented (Chafetz, 1983). Physicians who approach patients with a hurried, angry, or aloof professional tone have little success with alcoholic patients. Doctors whose voices seem to reflect nervousness or anxiety obtain best results. Patients perceive them to be concerned and caring.

4) Schedule an appointment with a family member or other concerned person prior to the initial interview with the prospective patient. The interview may be held either immediately before or after the interview with the patient. Again, obtain permission to share parts of this interview with the patient. After both interviews, meet jointly with the alcoholic patient and the concerned others. Review the findings, discuss any disparities between the two sources of information, and explain the basis for your diagnosis.

At this juncture, not only does the doctor know, but the concerned person has the support of medical opinion.

DIAGNOSTIC CRITERIA

As mentioned in the Introduction, the heterogeneity of alcoholism lends credence to a biopsychosocial concept of the disease. Let us consider this heterogeneity as it is mirrored in the varied diagnostic criteria formulated over the past several decades.

A social emphasis is clear in the definition provided by the World Health Organization:

> Drug dependence of the alcohol type may be said to exist when the consumption of alcohol by an individual exceeds the limits that are accepted by his culture, if he consumed alcohol at times that are deemed inappropriate within that culture, or his intake of alcohol becomes so great as to injure his health or impair his social relationships. (Kramer & Cameron, 1974)

A biological emphasis is reflected in the criteria established by the National Council on Alcoholism (Criteria Committee, 1972). These criteria are divided into two tracks: The Physiological and Clinical; and the Behavioral, Psychological, and Attitudinal. Twenty-eight major criteria are listed, 25 of which are within the physiological and clinical track. Sixty-four minor criteria are listed, 38 in the Physiological and Clinical track and 26 in the Behavioral, Psychological, and Attitudinal track. A diagnostic level is provided where 1 indicates a definite diagnosis of alcoholism, and 2 a probable diagnosis if two to three such criteria are present. Level 3 suggests a possible diagnosis, but substantially more evidence should be sought.

The *Diagnostic and Statistical Manual of Mental Disorders* (DSM-III) (American Psychiatric Association, 1980) struck a behavioral note and provided temporal orientation. Pathological use of substances was divided into abuse or dependence. The DSM-III diagnostic criteria for alcohol abuse are as follows:

A. *Pattern of pathological alcohol use*: need for daily use of alcohol for adequate functioning; inability to cut down or stop drinking, repeated efforts to control or reduce excess drinking by "going on the wagon" (periods of temporary abstinence) or restricting drinking to certain times of the day; binges (remaining intoxicated throughout the day for at least two days); occasional consumption of a fifth of spirits (or the equivalent in wine or beer); periods of amnesia for events occurring while intoxicated (blackouts); continuation of drinking despite a serious physical disorder that the individual knows is exacerbated by alcohol use; drinking of non-beverage alcohol.

B. *Impairment in social or occupational functioning due to alcohol use*: e.g., violence while intoxicated, absence from work, loss of job, legal difficulties (e.g., arrest for intoxicated behavior, traffic accidents while intoxicated), arguments or difficulties with family or friends because of excessive alcohol use. (pp. 169–170)

The diagnostic criteria for alcohol dependence (alcoholism) are:

A. Either a pattern of pathological alcohol use or impairment in social or occupational functioning due to alcohol use [as described in A and B above].

B. Either tolerance or withdrawal:
Tolerance: need for markedly increased amounts of alcohol to achieve the desired effect, or markedly diminished effect with regular use of the same amount.
Withdrawal: development of alcohol withdrawal (e.g., morn-

ing "shakes" and malaise relieved by drinking) after cessation of or reduction in drinking. (p. 170)

Finally, the CAGE questionnaire (Ewing, 1984; Mayfield, McLeod, &
Hall, 1974), a useful interview technique, should be mentioned. CAGE
provides a mnemonic device for the exploration of the following areas:
Cut down: "Has a doctor ever recommended that you Cut back or stop
the use of alcohol?" Annoyed: "Have you ever felt Annoyed or angry if
someone comments on your drinking?" Guilt: "Have there been times
when you've felt Guilty about or regretted things that occurred because
of drinking?" Eye-opener: "Have you ever used alcohol to help you get
started in the morning; to steady your nerves?"

Positive answers to three of these four questions strongly suggest a
diagnosis of alcoholism.

This detailed description of diagnostic criteria is presented in the interest of clinical accuracy. Of equal importance, however, is the physician's understanding that diagnosing a patient as alcohol dependent is
not simply a label or an arbitrary term applied to distasteful drinking
habits. Rather, it represents the recognition of a distinct syndrome which
may be expressed across a variety of symptoms—biological, psychological, and social.

In addition to the criteria described, various checklists are available for
verification of the diagnosis. These may be helpful for two reasons: 1)
They provide a wide repertoire of questions that can be incorporated into
an interview situation; guidelines for areas to explore and possible
phrasing are provided; 2) They may be given to the patient and family
member for self-administration. Although the answers are easily falsi-
fied, it is more typical for the subject to register surprise at the score and
the fact that some of his own behaviors are included in the rating scale.
The Michigan Alcoholism Screening Test (MAST) (Selzer, 1971) and the
Adolescent Alcohol Involvement Scale (Mayer & Filstead, 1979) are reproduced on the following pages (Table 4-1 and 4-2).

PITFALLS

There are some pitfalls to be avoided. When a patient requests a
definition of alcoholism or of an "alcoholic," it is best to avoid precise,
technical criteria. Too often, the patient can find a loophole which helps
him avoid the diagnosis, for example, "I've never missed any work";
"I've never had the shakes." It is useful to state simply that "an alcoholic
is someone whose use of alcohol has led to medical problems or conflicts
with the family, on the job, or with legal authorities. In other words,
alcohol is beginning to control you instead of the other way around."

TABLE 4-1
The Michigan Alcoholism Screening Test*

1. Do you feel you are a normal drinker?	Yes	No
2. Have you ever awakened in the morning after some drinking the night before and found that you could not remember part of the evening?	Yes	No
3. Does your wife/husband or parents ever worry or complain about your drinking?	Yes	No
4. Can you stop drinking without a struggle after one or two drinks?	Yes	No
5. Do you ever feel badly about your drinking?	Yes	No
6. Do you ever try to limit your drinking to certain times of the day or to certain places?	Yes	No
7. Do your friends or relatives think that you are a normal drinker?	Yes	No
8. Are you always able to stop when you want to?	Yes	No
9. Have you ever attended a meeting of Alcoholics Anonymous?	Yes	No
10. Have you gotten into fights when drinking?	Yes	No
11. Has drinking ever created problems with you and your wife (husband)?	Yes	No
12. Has your wife (husband, or other family members) ever gone to anyone for help about your drinking?	Yes	No
13. Have you ever lost friends or girlfriends/boyfriends because of your drinking?	Yes	No
14. Have you ever gotten into trouble at work because of drinking?	Yes	No
15. Have you ever lost a job because of drinking?	Yes	No
16. Have you ever neglected your obligations, your family or work for two days or more in a row because of drinking?	Yes	No
17. Do you ever drink before noon?	Yes	No
18. Have you ever been told you have liver trouble?	Yes	No
19. Have you ever had DTs (delirium tremens), severe shaking, heard voices or seen things that weren't there after heavy drinking?	Yes	No
20. Have you ever gone to anyone for help about your drinking?	Yes	No
21. Have you ever been in a hospital because of drinking?	Yes	No
22. Have you ever been a patient in a psychiatric hospital on a psychiatric ward of a general hospital where drinking was part of the problem?	Yes	No
23. Have you ever been seen at a psychiatric or mental health clinic, or gone to a doctor or clergyman for help with an emotional problem in which drinking has played a part?	Yes	No
24. Have you ever been arrested, even for a few hours, because of drunken behavior?	Yes	No
25. Have you ever been arrested for drunken driving or driving after drinking?	Yes	No

Scoring
0–2—Social Drinking
3–4—Heavy Drinking
5 or above—Alcoholism

*Reprinted by permission, from the *American Journal of Psychiatry*, Vol. 127, pp. 89–94, 1971. Copyright 1971 by the American Psychiatric Association.

TABLE 4-2
Adolescent Alcohol Involvement Scale*

Adolescent Alcohol Involvement Scale, and Scoring Instructions

1. How often do you drink?
   a. never
   b. once or twice a year
   c. once or twice a month
   d. every weekend
   e. several times a week
   f. every day

2. When did you have your last drink?
   a. never drank
   b. not for over a year
   c. between 6 months and 1 year ago
   d. several weeks ago
   e. last week
   f. yesterday
   g. today

3. I usually start to drink because:
   a. I like the taste
   b. to be like my friends
   c. to feel like an adult
   d. I feel nervous, tense, full of worries or problems
   e. I feel sad, lonely, sorry for myself

4. What do you drink?
   a. wine
   b. beer
   c. mixed drinks
   d. hard liquor
   e. a substitute for alcohol—paint thinner, sterno, cough medicine, mouthwash, hair tonic, etc.

5. How do you get your drinks?
   a. supervised by parents or relatives
   b. from brothers or sisters
   c. from home without parents' knowledge
   d. from friends
   e. buy it with false identification

6. When did you take your first drink?
   a. never
   b. recently
   c. after age 15
   d. at ages 14 or 15
   e. between ages 10–13
   f. before age 10

7. What time of day do you usually drink?
   a. with meals
   b. at night
   c. afternoons
   d. mostly in the morning or when I first awake
   e. I often get up during my sleep and drink

8. Why did you take your first drink?
   a. curiosity
   b. parents or relatives offered
   c. friends encouraged me
   d. to feel more like an adult
   e. to get drunk or high

9. How much do you drink, when you do drink?
   a. 1 drink
   b. 2 drinks
   c. 3–6 drinks
   d. 6 or more drinks
   e. until "high" or drunk

10. Whom do you drink with?
    a. parents or relatives only
    b. with brothers or sisters only
    c. with friends own age
    d. with older friends
    e. alone

TABLE 4-2 (*continued*)

Adolescent Alcohol Involvement Scale, and Scoring Instructions

11. What is the greatest effect you have had from alcohol?
    a. loose, easy feeling
    b. moderately "high"
    c. drunk
    d. became ill
    e. passed out
    f. was drinking heavily and the next day didn't remember what happened

12. What is the greatest effect drinking has had on your life?
    a. none—no effect
    b. has interfered with talking to someone
    c. has prevented me from having a good time
    d. has interfered with my school work
    e. have lost friends because of drinking
    f. has gotten me into trouble at home
    g. was in a fight or destroyed property
    h. has resulted in an accident, an injury, arrest, or being punished at school for drinking

13. How do you feel about your drinking?
    a. no problem at all
    b. I can control it and set limits on myself
    c. I can control myself, but my friends easily influence me
    d. I often feel bad about my drinking
    e. I need help to control myself
    f. I have had professional help to control my drinking

14. How do others see you?
    a. can't say, or a normal drinker for my age
    b. when I drink I tend to neglect my family or friends
    c. my family or friends advise me to control or cut down on my drinking
    d. my family or friends tell me to get help for my drinking
    e. my family or friends have already gone for help for my drinking

Scoring Instructions

The highest total score is 79. An *a* response is scored 1 (except on questions 1, 2, 6, 12, 13, and 14, on which $a=0$; $b=2$; $c=3$; and so on to $h=8$. When more than one response is made, the one with the higher or highest score is used. An unanswered question is scored 0.

Score	Involvement
42–57	— "Alcohol Misuse"
58–79	— "Alcoholic-like drinkers"

*Reprinted by permission, from the *Journal of Studies on Alcohol*, Vol. 40, pp. 291–300, 1979. Copyright by Journal Studies on Alcohol, Inc., Rutgers Center of Alcohol Studies, New Brunswick, NJ 08903

Second, it is well to remember that many patients suffering from the consequences of alcoholism complain that they don't drink any more than their friends and neighbors who apparently are symptom free. This may be true. It is useful at that time to remind the patient that the cause of alcoholism is not known, but that the amount drunk is not as important as the effect of alcohol on his or her life.

It is appropriate that the quantity drunk receives little emphasis. The context and consequences of alcohol use determine the major diagnostic features. Nevertheless, the usual daily, weekly, or monthly quantity should be sought during the diagnostic process. Although defensiveness is high in regard to such queries, the patient may be asked what he or she buys and then how long it lasts. For example, the person who drinks vodka may purchase it by the quart. It may last a week, suggesting about 4.5 ounces of vodka are consumed per day; or if drinking is done primarily on Friday through Sunday, over 10.5 ounces would be consumed per drinking day. Also, inquire about beer and wine use. It is useful to recall that a 12-ounce bottle of beer, a 4-ounce glass of wine, and 1-ounce of 100 proof whiskey are equivalent drinks in terms of alcohol content.

The equivalent drinks contain 15 ml. of absolute alcohol each. Actuarial research (Noble, 1978) has found that drinkers who consumed greater than 1.5 ounces of absolute alcohol a day had a significantly increased mortality rate. Similarly, use of more than 120 drinks per month is associated with syndromes of alcohol dependence and loss of control over alcohol in nearly 40% of cases (Nace, 1984).

A third pitfall is the problem of abuse versus dependence. Patients who meet only the criteria for abuse should not be reassured by that fact. The tendency to minimize may be the only reason the abuse category applies, or they may be close to becoming dependent. A recent study determined that two thirds of alcohol abusers, as measured by a scale of problem drinking, met DSM-III alcohol dependence criteria (Vaillant, 1983a).

DSM-III has recently been revised (American Psychiatric Association, 1987) and the distinction between abuse and dependence modified. Alcohol dependence and alcohol abuse are now subsumed under the general categories of Psychoactive Substance Dependence and Psychoactive Substance Abuse, respectively. The concept of dependence is linked less to tolerance and withdrawal syndromes and broadened to indicate extensive involvement with psychoactive drugs (including alcohol).

The revised criteria are as follows with three or more necessary for the diagnosis of dependence:

1. At least three of the following:
   1) substance often taken in larger amounts or over a longer period than the person intended

2) persistent desire or one or more unsuccessful efforts to cut down or control substance use
3) a great deal of time spent in activities necessary to get the substance (e.g., theft), taking the substance (e.g., chain smoking), or recovering from its effects
4) frequent intoxication or withdrawal symptoms when expected to fulfill major role obligations at work, school, or home (e.g., does not go to work because hung over, goes to school or work "high," intoxicated while taking care of his or her children), or when substance use is physically hazardous (e.g., drives when intoxicated)
5) important social, occupational, or recreational activities given up or reduced because of substance use
6) continued substance use despite knowledge of having a persistent or recurrent social, psychological, or physical problem that is caused or exacerbated by the use of the substance (e.g., keeps using heroin despite family arguments about it, cocaine-induced depression, or having an ulcer made worse by drinking)
7) marked tolerance: need for markedly increased amounts of the substance (i.e., at least a 50% increase) in order to achieve intoxication or desired effect, or markedly diminished effect with continued use of the same amount

Note: The following items may not apply to cannabis, hallucinogens, or phencyclidine (PCP):

8) characteristic withdrawal symptoms (see specific withdrawal syndromes under Psychoactive Substance-induced Organic Mental Disorders)
9) substance often taken to relieve or avoid withdrawal symptoms
2. Some symptoms of the disturbance have persisted for at least one month, or have occurred repeatedly over a longer period of time. (pp. 167–168)

Abuse is defined as:

1. A maladaptive pattern of psychoactive substance use indicated by at least one of the following:
   1) continued use despite knowledge of having a persistent or recurrent social, occupational, psychological, or physical problem that is caused or exacerbated by use of the psychoactive substance
   2) recurrent use in situations in which use is physically hazardous (e.g., driving while intoxicated)
2. Some symptoms of the disturbance have persisted for at least one month, or have occurred repeatedly over a longer period of time.
3. Never met the criteria for Psychoactive Substance Dependence for this substance. (p.169)

Alcohol abusers (i.e., those not clearly dependent) may be followed regularly over a period of 3 to 6 months in order to determine whether alcohol use can be controlled in a nonabusive pattern, or whether the abuse pattern revolves into a clear picture of dependence.

A few clinical vignettes are illustrative:

A purchasing agent, self-referred, expressed fear of becoming an alcoholic. He didn't think he was yet alcoholic and definitely did not want to give up alcohol altogether. His score on the MAST was 12, well within the alcoholic range. We agreed to try, over a 3-month period, to alter his daily use of alcohol and the increasing concern it raised among his friends. The plan was for him to limit drinking to no more than three drinks a day and go for at least 3 days of the week without any alcohol. In addition, he was to make specific plans for evenings (the time of excessive drinking); for example, purchase tickets to a concert series and attend evening classes at a local college. He was able to follow this plan for about 2 to 3 weeks. Then attempts to regulate ethanol intake faltered, and evening activities were ignored. The patient's alcohol dependence became apparent, and his recognition of his predicament sharpened.

I used the term *alcohol dependence*, even though I could not document symptoms of alcohol withdrawal. His tolerance was clearly developing. More importantly for the diagnosis, psychological dependence, as reflected by the priority given to drinking over other activities and his inability to cut down in the face of social consequences (difficulties with friends), was well-established.

Following an automobile accident and a DWI charge, a young attorney sought consultation in regard to the possibility of alcoholism. Although a moderate to heavy drinker, any abuse of alcohol was of brief duration (an evening occasionally), and typically it followed a prolonged period of excessive work. The patient was able to cut back his use of alcohol drastically, modify his patterns of use (e.g., not drink on an empty stomach), and he learned to alter his work schedule so that exercise, leisure time on weekends, and anticipated vacations could be realized. This pattern was sustained over the 18 months of my periodic contact. Neither abuse nor dependence were appropriate diagnoses. The disorder which led to consultation was alcohol intoxication.

A difficult situation was presented by a 54-year-old dentist who had been undergoing treatment for prostatic cancer over the previous 10 months. Since the time of initial treatment any physical symptoms or laboratory findings that could suggest a progression of the malignancy provoked excessive drinking for days or weeks. He met the DSM-III criteria for alcohol abuse. Tolerance or physiological dependence did not develop largely because threats from his wife curbed the pattern of abuse. Of particular significance was the history that for the prior 10 years the dentist had been completely abstinent. In the past, his wife had started divorce proceedings because of a pattern of severe alcoholism which had been present at that time. Although the present pattern was that of abuse, the past history of dependence necessitated an approach of total abstinence, which was accepted and accomplished by this patient. The 10-year period of abstinence would be conceptualized as alcohol dependence in remission.

PRESENTATION OF THE DIAGNOSIS

The word *alcoholic* is a red flag to many people. It connotes skid row or perhaps someone known to the patient who has a notorious reputation or who has been stigmatized by alcoholism. Phrases such as "a person with alcoholism" or "a case of alcohol dependence" are often more acceptable. With time, the alcoholic person may accept the rubric "alcoholic" and utilize its bluntness as an antidote against denial.

Before getting to the issue of diagnosis with the patient, I anticipate common responses to a discussion of drinking practices. For example, I mention that most people feel uneasy when asked *how much* they drink, or *when* they drink, or *what happens* when they drink. Many times they feel very reluctant to be completely open. They sometimes feel that they may be judged unfavorably or criticized. I emphasize that we are dealing only with an issue of health and that the more information they can give me, the better able we will be to figure out what the problem is and how to help with it. My job is not to be critical, but to try to understand.

To proceed with explaining the diagnosis requires that the physician have firmly fixed in mind all facts that document alcohol dependence. These could include laboratory data, physical findings, history from family members, or any of the phenomena included in the diagnostic criteria described earlier.

It is essential that patients understand clearly that your diagnosis is *alcohol dependence* or *alcoholism*. If they ask, "Does this mean you think I'm alcoholic?" you must indicate that, yes, that is the case. Add quickly that the word alcoholic is misunderstood, what you are actually describing is a situation where alcohol is causing harm to health and well-being.

Then explain that, fortunately, this type of problem can be dealt with and many effective ways of helping are available.

"Do you mean that I'm supposed to go to AA?" The answer here is: "I want to talk more with you and then explain different treatment approaches that have helped people. AA is one approach that has been very helpful for many people."

"No one can do this for me. I have to do it myself." Answer: "It's true that nothing can help without your willingness to work hard on this. But experience with alcohol problems has shown that a person who is willing to work with a treatment plan does extremely well. The individual who tries to manage it by himself often has further trouble and usually fails."

To summarize, in presenting the diagnosis, all one's psychotherapeutic skills are utilized in order to accomplish the following:

1) Confronting the denial and using the words "alcoholism," "alcohol dependence," and "alcoholic" clearly and confidently.
2) Providing an explanation of why the diagnosis applies, i.e., the facts that document the diagnosis.
3) Breaking through the prejudice resulting from stereotypes or stigma; recalling that well-known and successful people now share their experience in recovering from alcoholism. There is no stigma to recovery.
4) Communicating concern which is shown by the interest demonstrated and the action taken. Concern should be the background music for all explanations and discussions.
5) Relieving guilt and shame. Alcoholism is a disease, a health problem; it is not a moral issue or weakness. Becoming an alcoholic usually happens without the person's being aware of it.
6) Instilling hope. Successful outcome should be expected; treatment results are very good for those willing to try.
7) Planning ahead. Inpatient facilities should be contacted prior to your interview in order to facilitate admission without delay. It is best if the patient can go directly from an evaluation to an inpatient program. A family member can bring clothes at a later time. If outpatient treatment is decided, however, it is crucial to know the range of services available and to refer to a suitable counselor, social worker, or physician. A contact person in an outpatient program should be lined up to meet with the patient the same day if possible.
8) Initiating a commitment to treatment. Keep the momentum going; avoid cooperating with counterdependent maneuvers such as, "I have to handle this myself." Schedule the next appointment; arrange to meet further with the family; initiate hospitalization or outpatient treatment with a program specifically designed for the treatment of alcoholism; have a person and place prearranged for

the patient to contact; have a local AA meeting schedule available in your office to give to the patient and a schedule of Al-Anon meetings for the family; know several AA members (men and women) who are willing to meet with your patients, discuss AA with them, and accompany them to a meeting.

In conclusion, this chapter outlines the importance of being alert to the possibility of an alcoholic diagnosis and emphasizes the need to be well-versed in criteria that establish the diagnosis. Certain traps or pitfalls in presenting the diagnosis are reviewed, and an outline of objectives that accompany the diagnostic process is presented.

CHAPTER 5

The Disease of Alcoholism

Viewing alcoholism as a disease has distinct advantages. It allows the focus on alcoholism to shift from a moral or legal perspective to one of medical concern. The alcoholic person now has available the resources of the health care system. Scorn and neglect no longer have a place as we encounter the alcoholic individual and his or her family. A second advantage is that alcoholism, as well as other addictive diseases, is now the recipient of scientific investigation. Research monies for the study of alcoholism are small relative to the magnitude of alcoholism's cost, yet the amount and sophistication of research today dwarf the efforts of only 15 to 20 years ago.

Related to the above advantages of the disease concept is the political interest in viewing alcoholism as a disease. Many groups now have a vested interest in viewing alcoholism as a disease. Such groups include health care providers, hospitals, insurance providers, alcoholism rehabilitation personnel, recovered alcoholics, and Alcoholics Anonymous. It would be difficult for organized medicine, the scientific community, or the Department of Health and Human Services to retract their declaration that alcoholism is a disease.

Of course, the fact that there are certain social, ethical, or political advantages to calling alcoholism a disease does not convey scientific validity, without which the positive effects of the disease concept will probably be short-lived. Therefore, can there be found, within the phenomenon of alcoholism, justification from a medical-scientific point of view for the disease concept? This text argues affirmatively in this regard while acknowledging that disease typically refers to malfunctioning or maladaptation of biologic or psychophysiological processes (Kleinman, Eisenberg, & Good, 1978).

As yet, there are no known specific alterations in biologic or psychophysiologic processes that are unique to the state of alcoholism (and which are not a medical complication of excessive alcohol use). In the absence of known specific physiological changes that cause alcohol dependence, some would consider alcoholism best described as an illness. Illness is the personal experience of a disruption in state of being and in social functioning (Kleinman, Eisenberg, & Good, 1978). It is the subjective feeling of being sick. The patient goes to the doctor with an illness and leaves with a disease (Cassell, 1976).

Illness may occur in the absence of disease. For example, nearly half of visits to doctors' offices are for complaints without any discernible underlying alternation in the structure or function of body organs (Kleinman, Eisenberg, & Good, 1978). Disease can also exist without illness. Preventive medicine's thrust is to detect disease states early, that is, before the subjective experience of illness emerges. Routine physical examinations may detect hypertension or cancer before the individual becomes symptomatic.

The terms "disease" and "illness" are commonly used interchangeably. This applies particularly in the field of alcoholism where the terms are used to refer to alcohol dependence and no apparent distinction is intended. The disease underlying the various expressions of alcoholism have no known demonstrable tissue pathology. There are no proven distinctions in brain or other organ functioning between the alcoholic and nonalcoholic. Of course, various patterns of brain and other organ system damage are seen in alcoholic patients but these are secondary to the alcoholism and not responsible for the phenomenon of alcoholism itself.

How does the alcoholic patient fit into this distinction between illness and disease? It would be simple to settle for the term "illness," yet an argument can be developed for the disease concept in the absence of demonstrable biochemical or physiological changes. The changes in structure and functioning, characteristic of disease states, are manifest in alcoholism by alterations in the structure and functioning of the mind (this does not imply that alterations in biological variables do not occur, only that they have not yet been demonstrated conclusively).

Mind refers to all of the individual's conscious and unconscious experiences together as a unit. Mind depends on brain functioning but, as indicated, distinctions in brain functioning between the alcoholic and nonalcoholic at the organic level remain to be discovered. Alterations in structure and functioning in the alcoholic occur at the level of subjective experience and consist of phenomena such as denial and psychological dependence. Such changes from normal functioning are so consistently present as to warrant considering alcoholism as a disease on the basis of changes in the structure of cognitive functioning as well as alterations in affective and conative experiences.

Conceptualization of disease in these terms may be considered "soft" and measurement very difficult. Difficulty in measurement does not imply a lack of validity, however. Psychiatry throughout most of this century advanced the understanding of human behavior and illness by development and refinement of concepts not amenable to precise quantification such as more commonly exists in internal medicine (Pattison & Kaufman, 1982). Obviously there remains a need for concepts which allow greater precision and quantification and which can be linked to brain functioning. This current lack in our biological understanding of alcoholism need not deter us from recognizing alcoholism as a disease. The concepts that justify considering alcoholism as a disease, even in the light of our limited understanding of pathology, are derived from the altered psychological and behavioral experience of the alcoholic patient and are described further in this chapter.

On the other hand, would the term syndrome be preferable to disease? A syndrome is generally defined as a group or set of symptoms which occur together and can be considered a disease. Pattison and Kaufman (1982) have argued that alcoholism be considered a "multivariate syndrome." This concept recognizes the diversity inherent in the phenomenon of alcoholism, including multiple patterns of use and abuse of alcohol, multiple interacting etiological variables, variation in the development of alcohol-related problems over time, and variation in the population of individuals with alcohol problems. The advantage of viewing alcoholism as a syndrome is the recognition that there are many pathways to alcoholism. This conceptualization contrasts with efforts to delineate alcoholism as a strictly biological process, genetically determined and unfolding over the course of a lifetime with a characteristic sequence and predictable outcome. It also contrasts with efforts that attempt to explain alcoholism as the outgrowth of a specific personality type.

No inherent contradiction need exist between considering alcoholism as a disease or syndrome. "Disease" is an applicable term because of the commonality of psychological dependence and related phenomena described in this chapter which exist across the multivariate patterns, progressions, and etiologies. In other words, regardless of how one acquires alcohol dependence or which symptoms predominate, at the subjective level of the patient the disorder manifests a characteristic influence on thinking and behavior.

Until the 1950s the fate of the alcoholic was determined less by physicians than by public policymakers, moralists, and, in particular, an international temperance movement (Chafetz, 1983). Public concern about heavy alcohol use among Civil War troops enabled the temperance movement to gain strength during the decade following the war (Howland & Howland, 1978). The temperance movement reached its pinnacle in 1919 with the passage of the 18th Amendment. Fourteen years later, the 18th Amendment was repealed. Seven years after repeal, the study of alcohol and alcoholism gained scientific respectability by the founding of the Center of Alcohol Studies at Yale University. By 1956, the American Medical Association recognized alcoholism as a disease. Similar recognition by the American College of Physicians followed in 1969.

Official recognition translates slowly into practitioner acceptance. A high incidence of alcoholism among general hospital patients has been documented consistently since the 1960s. Galanter, Karasu, and Wilder (1977) reported in 1977 that 21% of adults admitted to a large city hospital were alcoholic. Identical results were obtained from another hospital, with the additional finding that 13% of admissions were alcoholics in remission (Barcha, Stewart, & Guze, 1968). In a community hospital (Moore, 1971), 10% of admissions (18% of the males and 5.5% of the females) were determined to be alcoholic.

These findings are probably conservative estimates. Yet, with that known probability of a hospitalized patient's being alcoholic, the diagnosis is often missed or ignored. Moore (1971) found that doctors made the diagnosis in only 50% of alcoholic patients. In another study (Abbott, Goldberg, & Becker, 1974), 14 of 16 patients admitted for acute pancreatitis were alcoholic. None was referred for alcoholism treatment because the physicians didn't know how to, felt pessimistic about treatment, or believed the patient was responsible for obtaining treatment for alcoholism.

Although organized medicine recognizes alcoholism as a disease, hospitals continue to oppose providing inpatient treatment, fail to refer for treatment of alcoholism, or fail to diagnose alcoholism (Galanter & Sperber, 1982).

In 1970, and again in 1980, Moore (1982) surveyed alcoholism treatment in private psychiatric hospitals. The percentage of patients admitted for alcoholism treatment increased from 11% to 15% during that decade. Staff attitudes toward alcoholic patients, however, showed a decline in an "accepting" attitude from 88% to 61% and an increase in "reluctant" attitude from 3% to 39%. Explanation for these changes in attitude is not available, but the shibboleth of poor patient motivation would not seem to apply. The same study found that staff members who reported "lack of patient motivation" as a reason for treatment failures had declined from 71% in 1970 to 45% in 1980.

The ambivalence and confusion over acceptance of alcoholism as a disease may lie partly in an uncertainty as to what the disease of alcoholism actually is. If we had a metabolic explanation for the etiology of alcoholism, a greater acceptance of the disease concept and improved service might occur. But we have no such explanation, and most physicians give a vague "lip service" without a sense of conviction to the disease concept. The fragility of our acceptance of the disease concept renders us vulnerable to the idea that the alcoholic is engaging in unacceptable behavior willingly.

Increased acetaldehyde levels (Schuckit & Rayses, 1979), formation of "false" neurotransmitters (Kissin, 1979), and changes in cell membrane structure (McCreery & Hunt, 1978) are tantalizing areas of research, but we lack the explanatory models such as exist for diabetes, gout, and other chronic diseases.

What is the disease of alcoholism? Is it possible to grasp the validity of the disease concept in the absence of a well-defined pathophysiological process? An illness such as schizophrenia is better accepted as a disease in the absence of etiological explanations. Schizophrenic symptoms are alien, bizarre, and unlike our own experiences. By contrast, the person with alcoholism is very similar to us. He or she usually drinks the same beverages at the same time or the same place as we do. Why does the alcoholic overdo it? The overt symptoms of drinking—loquaciousness, slurred speech, uncoordination, intoxication, and hangover—are familiar and similar in any who have overindulged. Most, however, learn to titrate the use of ethyl alcohol more carefully. Why doesn't the alcoholic?

Comparing the alcoholic person's behavior to our own experience with alcohol leads easily to the conclusion that the alcoholic person chooses his or her pattern of alcohol use. In other words, it is a matter of defective will, character, and values. That one should choose such loathsome, obnoxious, and pathetic behavior is perplexing as well as disgusting. (At this point, we have recapitulated the relationship of the alcoholic with his or her larger society across the centuries—a relationship based on a shared experience with the pleasure and pain of alcohol use, but ruptured by an apparent willful indifference on the part of those we consider alcoholic.) Thus the alcoholic has been readily considered a social misfit, a moral degenerate, a source for pity. The disease process has been obscured by the unrealistic expectation that the alcoholic man and woman can simply choose to regulate their use of alcoholic beverages more appropriately.

Understanding the disease of alcoholism will not come from the observation of the external manifestations of alcohol use. Nor does the physician need to wait for a biochemical explanation in order to accept the concept of disease. Acceptance can emerge as one comprehends the subjective experience of the alcoholic patient and the impact of alcohol on the thinking, motivation, and personality functioning of the alcohol-dependent individual. Six constructs make up the essential phenomena of alcoholism: psychological dependence on a chemical, craving, loss of control, personality regression, denial, and conflicted behavior.

PSYCHOLOGICAL DEPENDENCE

To understand the alcoholic we must try to imagine a condition few of us have experienced: psychological dependence on a chemical. This form of dependence is not the state of physical dependence character-ized by tolerance to alcohol and emergence of withdrawal symptoms when alcohol use is discontinued. Psychological dependence precedes physical dependence by at least 5 years, on the average (Mandell, 1983), and remains long after the patient is successfully detoxified. It continues to exert a profound influence on thinking and behavior during the early years of recovery.

Dependence means being influenced, controlled, or determined by something; to rely or trust something other than one's self. This is the effect alcohol has on those who develop alcoholism.

A World Health Organization Panel on Drug Dependence stated:

All of these drugs have one effect in common: they are capable of creating, in certain individuals, a particular state of mind that is termed "psychic dependence." Indeed, this mental state is the most powerful of all the factors involved in chronic intoxication . . . (Eddy, Halbach, Isbell, & Seevers, 1965, p. 723).

Why this state of dependence becomes established in a minority (about 1 in 12) of people who drink is not known, but a combination of genetic, psychological, and social factors is likely involved.

Psychological dependence is the essence of the disease and is the central organizing experience of the alcoholic. This condition of depen-dence is illustrated by profound changes in one's thinking. These changes can be described briefly.

Psychological Primacy

This aspect of psychological dependence describes the evolving *priori-ty* of alcohol in the dependent person's life. For example, in the early stages of alcoholism the person is concerned with the possibility that his drinking will interfere with his work. Later, when psychological primacy is established, the concern is that work may interfere with drinking. The dependent individual finds that his thinking and behavior become increasingly oriented to getting and using alcohol. He may even bring his own bottle to a party, lest the host not have that particular brand or not have an adequate supply.

A judge, admitted to an alcoholism program, showed considerable interest in the medical aspects of alcohol abuse. He was curious about hepatic effects and specifically wanted to know how much alcohol it took to produce liver enlargement or jaundice. The judge's interest in the serious consequences of alcoholism unfortunately was not determined by the decision to stop drinking. He acknowledged, after further severe drinking bouts, that he had been trying to figure out how to titrate his drinking so that liver enlargement either could be avoided or rendered undetectable.

The alcoholic becomes aware that "nothing is more important than alcohol." Family and friends reach a similar conclusion. Gradually the alcoholic man or woman becomes increasingly isolated. As disregard for health, family, and career continues, the emergence of self-loathing, guilt, and shame parallels the developing preoccupation with alcohol. Respect for the strength and tenacity of this process is necessary if one is to understand alcoholism. The alcoholic drinks through the harshness of social disdain, the pain of physical impairment, and the guilt of emotional despair in order to find, again, the effect sought from alcohol.

Self-doubt

A second thought pattern that reflects psychological dependence is self-doubt. The doubt is expressed by a sense that one is unable to cope without alcohol. A conviction that one is inadequate in the face of daily work or family demands reflects the destructive erosion of alcoholism on the patient's thinking. Only the uplifting and sedative effect of alcohol restores confidence.

A young married male found it difficult to remain sober more than a few weeks at a time. When his wife became pregnant his doubts about being an adequate father led to another "slip." Subsequently, doubts about his adequacy as a son were revealed. His mother's life revolved around his father, and he felt that he should have encouraged his mother to do more for herself. The anticipated emptiness of her life should his father die raised doubts about his ability to cope with a widowed mother. Again, he resumed alcohol use. The drinking bouts compounded his doubts about carrying out his family obligations.

This patient's negative thinking (self-doubt) was reinforced by the subsequent euphoria of alcohol use. His alcohol dependence was, in part, manifested by self-doubt, which "drove" him to drink, i.e., legitimized his use of alcohol. In the treatment of his alcoholism it was necessary to reinterpret his doubts or worries as expressions of the addiction rather than realistic assessments of his ability to cope. Such an interpretation enabled him to focus on a target behavior—alcohol use—rather than a set of uncertain future experiences.

Another form self-doubt takes is illustrated by a woman who was severely alcoholic from age 18 to 24. For the two years prior to treatment she drank about a fifth of whiskey a day. During the early months of treatment in an inpatient program it was inconceivable to her that she could live the rest of her life without alcohol. Although her social skills were well established, she was certain she would be a bore socially. Even though her fiancé was instrumental in seeing that she received treatment, she doubted that he would remain interested in her as a sober person. Her sexual experiences had always been associated with alcohol use, and she was fearful and uncertain as to whether she could respond without it.

The antidotes to her self-doubt were first, her gradual and successful reexperiencing of threatening situations in an alcohol-free state; and second, an opportunity to identify with confidence-building role models found among Alcoholics Anonymous members. The emphasis of Alcoholics Anonymous on living "one day at a time" was essential in order for her to avoid feeling overwhelmed by a future without alcohol.

Fear of being unable to cope without alcohol is a very real one for the alcoholic. It seriously erodes self-esteem, and it is vital that the therapist not take such doubt at face value. It is essential to explain to the patient that these concerns are in fact an effect of the alcohol and reflect the destructive impact of alcohol on self-confidence. Such reinterpretation establishes therapeutic priorities—first to avoid alcohol use, then to deal with other problems—and it avoids the uncertainty of addressing character pathology.

Sense of Loss

The possibility of living without alcohol fills the alcoholic with a pervasive dread. Life would not be worthwhile (even if one could cope). Boredom, loneliness, and a void are expected to follow abstinence from alcohol. ("It's all I have left. Don't take this from me.")

Such thoughts were recalled by a young patient as she described her anger at films portraying alcoholism. Recognition that drinking may be incompatible with a manageable life made her angry and threatened what seemed to her a life-sustaining relationship.

The "loss of my best friend" expresses the grief reaction that sometimes accompanies the discontinuance of alcohol. Such a reaction was portrayed by a man in his 50s the day after he began use of disulfiram. He recognized that a commitment to disulfiram use precluded his turning to alcohol in time of "need." He was surprised at how let down and depressed he felt. In a more positive sense he also gained a deeper appreciation of how fully dependent he had become on alcohol.

The sense of loss may be experienced as the removal of all joy or zest from one's existence. A physician recalled, after noticing a travel poster of the Rhine River, that he had vacationed in Germany a year earlier. He had sampled wines and taken a trip down the Rhine, and such pleasures now seemed lost for him. Without alcohol the pleasures of foreign travel, experiencing different cultures, and partaking of varied cuisines seemed pallid for this newly sober alcoholic patient. As with any grief reaction, he needed to be encouraged to express his feelings and helped to a healthier lifestyle.

Inability to Abstain

Less apparent than the above manifestations of psychological dependence is the conviction of the alcoholic that he cannot stop drinking. This thought is usually repressed and rarely verbalized. The conviction that "I can't quit" is partially understandable from the repeated efforts and failures at reducing or refraining from alcohol use, which most alcoholics attempt periodically. The fear of not being able to quit drinking is particularly ominous to the alcoholic patient. For example, if a doctor makes a diagnosis of alcoholism, the patient promptly draws the logical conclusion that the next recommendation will be "you must stop." The patient is aware that this is not easy. The patient feels misunderstood—that if the doctor understood he would know the prescription to stop is impossible or, at best, very unlikely.

Consider the dilemma of the patient at this point: The doctor's perfunctory prescription to stop drinking increases the isolation of the patient and he feels misunderstood and, therefore, even more anxious, but he is too ashamed to acknowledge his inability to quit. This is one reason the alcoholic often lies about his drinking. If the doctor knew how much the patient really drank, the patient would be expected to quit. He can't, he thinks.

The patient's dilemma, however, is not contained at this level. The diagnosis of alcoholism is proffered with a cure—"quit drinking." For the alcoholic to be offered a cure which he knows is impossible is to create a psychological bind. "If I'm an alcoholic and my cure is to quit drinking (but I can't), then I'm incurable (hopeless)."

Such a conclusion is not well-tolerated under any circumstance, and the alcoholic quickly finds an escape from this dilemma: denial—"I'm not alcoholic (therefore, I don't have to face the possibility of not being able to quit)."

Some patients display another version of this dilemma: "I wish I wanted to quit." The implication that one could quit if he or she only wanted to protects the alcoholic from the anxiety associated with the uncertainty of being able to abstain.

This facet of psychological dependence (inability to abstain) will be influenced by experience, that is the daily "one day at a time" experience of sober living. The recovering alcoholic is taught to value each 24-hour period that is free of alcohol. Each challenge, disappointment, or accomplishment endured without alcohol must be seen as evidence that the impossible—not drinking—is increasingly within one's grasp.

Psychological dependence not only affects cognition, but also undergirds the craving, loss of control, personality regression, denial, and conflicted behavior, which could not develop or flourish without the underlying "need" created by psychological dependence.

These additional five constructs of the disease concept are now discussed with the understanding that they revolve around the primary construct of psychological dependence.

CRAVING

Within the context of alcohol abuse, craving may be defined as a subjective experience of desiring, needing, or longing for the euphoric and tension-relieving properties of ethyl alcohol. Craving has not been defined as a compulsion because the quality of feeling compelled to drink is but one of a variety of possible manifestations of craving. Isbell (1955) describes two origins of craving:

1) Physiological ("nonsymbolic") craving occurs in conjunction with decreasing blood alcohol levels and the concomitant appearance of withdrawal symptoms; it is a physical dependence and reflects a physical need for relief from withdrawal symptoms.
2) Psychological ("symbolic") craving represents a conditioned response that originates in the reexposure to stimuli that the patient associates with alcohol use. Psychological craving does not depend on physical dependence, but reflects a "need" for the euphoric tension-relieving properties of ethyl alcohol.

Ludwig and Wikler (1974) hypothesize that craving is "a psychological or cognitive correlate of a subclinical conditioned withdrawal syndrome which may be evoked by any state of psychological arousal resembling the syndrome" (p. 108). In other words, the alcoholic desires a drink (craving) when he walks by a bar or is in the presence of other people drinking because he is then reexposed to cues associated with prior alcohol use and the subsequent withdrawal symptoms. Thus a conditioned withdrawal syndrome is believed to be established, which is *subclinical*, not detectable except for its cognitive component, craving. The elaboration of a conditioned withdrawal syndrome under these stimuli (bar, drinking companions, etc.) is considered exteroceptive conditioning. Interoceptive conditioning may also result in a subclinical conditioned withdrawal syndrome and craving. This is believed to occur when the alcoholic drinks alcohol. Because of prior withdrawal experiences, the effect of the alcohol on the neurons or viscera triggers a conditioned response of withdrawal, which is detected as a "need" for more alcohol (craving).

A third way in which craving can be elicited is by the experience of emotional states (e.g., anxiety, anger, apprehension, depression) or states of physical discomfort that impart a degree of physiological arousal similar to that occurring during withdrawal. Increased heart rate, tremors, and insomnia characterize alcohol withdrawal and may trigger craving when reexperienced, for whatever reason.

Neither the concept of craving nor this theoretical explanation is accepted universally: Mello (1972) and Nathan and Lisman (1976) reviewed behavioral approaches to alcoholism as studied under laboratory conditions. Behavioral studies challenge the concept of craving and its role in triggering relapse (Caddy & Gottheil, 1983). Some researchers consider the concept tautological, superfluous, and useless (Mello, 1972).

The behavioral studies, which trivialize the concepts of craving and loss of control, are limited in generalizability because they are conducted under very artificial laboratory conditions, and the conclusions usually fail to take into consideration the demand characteristics of the laboratory (Orne, 1962). Behavioral studies set up as a "straw man" the notion that once alcoholics take a drink a physiological mechanism drives them to drunkenness—invariably. These studies fail to appreciate what clinicians working with alcoholics always observe: alcoholics' consumption of alcohol and their behavior while drinking are influenced by many factors including access to alcohol, expectations from others, environmental setting, and competing demands, as well as emotional and physiological factors.

Several studies that minimize the phenomena of craving and loss of control report that the alcoholic subjects still consumed significantly greater quantities of alcohol than nonalcoholic controls and often maintained blood alcohol levels between 150 mg. to 200 mg. per 100 ml.* (Cutter, Schwaab, & Nathan, 1970; Marlatt et al., 1973).

Further, a study conducted in England (Merry, 1966) claims that nine alcoholics reported the same amount of craving after being given either a placebo or 1 ounce of 65 proof vodka in a disguised mixture. On the last day (day 18) of this experiment, however, the amount of disguised vodka was doubled, and on that day, all nine subjects reported craving. Yet, this study is touted widely as debunking the concept of craving.

An amelioration of the earlier behavioral view seems to be emerging, as Nathan and Lisman (1976) state ". . . it is clearly possible that craving is a factor in the decision of some alcoholics, enmeshed in certain specific environmental situations, to resume drinking" (p. 502).

Reports of craving are readily elicited from alcoholic patients. In a study (Isbell, 1955) of 60 alcoholics, 78% reported craving. When the concept was more carefully explained to them, 95% reported craving. Nearly two-thirds of the patients stated that craving increased after one or two drinks, and about one-half of the patients reported an increase in craving when around people who were drinking or in places where alcohol was available. Mathew, Claghorn, and Largen (1979) found 88% of alcoholics reported craving. Duration of alcoholism was not related to the intensity of craving, but length of sobriety was. The longer the period of abstinence, the less frequent and less severe the craving. Alcoholics who reported no craving had been abstinent a mean time of 19 weeks compared to 3 weeks for those who reported severe craving.

It is important that each patient learn to recognize his personal vulnerabilities to craving (Nace, 1982). Excursions from a treatment program to home can be encouraged so the individual can learn to appreciate the circumstances likely to precipitate a feeling of need for alcohol. This experience helps the patient get past the overconfidence that develops in residential treatment when no desire for alcohol is experienced. The rules of the hospital, for example, prohibit alcoholic beverages; no alcohol is visible, no drinking opportunities provided, and the staff reinforces these rules with a negative attitude toward alcohol use. All contribute to an absence of desire for alcohol that surprises many patients and leads them to believe they "have it made."

The various precipitants of craving that patients should be aware of are:

---

*The legal definition of drunkenness in most states is 100 mg. per 100 ml.

- *General Environmental*
  Visual and auditory stimuli. Advertisements for alcoholic beverages, scenes, depicting alcohol use in films or novels, discussions of alcoholism in therapy sessions or AA meetings.
  Merchandise exposure. Confronting shelves of wine in the supermarket, proximity to the bar or cocktail lounge in a restaurant, any instance in which one may encounter the availability of alcohol in a situation not typically or necessarily associated with drinking.
- *Specific Environmental* (refers to idiosyncratic associations to alcohol use)
  A particular chair or room in the home.
  A particular tavern or bar.
  Specific drinking companions.
- *Temporal*
  Seasonal or cyclical. Holidays, anniversaries, celebrations
  Daily. Periods associated with drinking such as the end of the work day, prior to an evening meal, lunch, etc.
- *Affective* (refers to the use of alcohol in association with various emotional states)
  Egodystonic. In times of anger, boredom, or anxiety
  Egosyntonic. To express satisfaction, joy, or relief
- *Physical* (refers to the prior use of alcohol for relief of physical discomfort, such as withdrawal symptoms, fatigue, insomnia, thirst, hunger, or pain)

In one study (Mathew et al., 1979), external factors associated with alcohol (e.g., an empty beer can) precipitated craving in 48% of alcoholics, while 25% reported craving when they experienced mood changes.

An understanding of craving is useless for alcoholics if they cannot identify it within themselves. Alcoholics frequently are not aware of the subtle expressions of urges to drink. Learning the variety of possible manifestations of craving widens their spectrum of awareness.

For example, an alcoholic woman wanted to bring wine into the home during a particular religious holiday "so that the children could see that wine can be around without causing harm." She disavowed any interest in drinking; no guests were anticipated, and no one else in the family drank. Her husband and children were alarmed at the implications of her proposal, and the woman was equally dismayed at their alarm. Through group therapy sessions she became aware of her subtle fantasies and yearnings for a return to social drinking.

The different manifestations of craving are listed below:

- *Physical.* The patient feels as though he or she can taste the beverage and has sensations of dry mouth, thirst, and a gnawing feeling in the gut.
- *Compulsive.* The patient cannot think of anything else.

- *Cognitive.* The patient's thoughts of alcohol use are unaccompanied by physical sensation or compulsive urge. Typical expressions include rationalizations such as "I have to have alcohol in the house in case friends drop by" and euphoric recall of drinking experiences. The individual may or may not be aware that his or her thinking reflects impulses to drink.
- *Affective.* The patient experiences dysphoric mood states characterized by irritability, depression, anxiety, and resentment. The individual is usually unaware of the relationship between the current affective state and the frustrated need for alcohol.

Typically the experience of craving is considered by the alcoholic to be a negative reflection on himself. Impulses to drink are assumed by the alcoholic patient to represent character flaws or weaknesses. The following negative interpretations of craving are reported repeatedly:

- *Bad.* Impulses to drink are wrong or immoral.
- *Greedy.* Craving is self-centered and lacks consideration for others.
- *Empty.* The desire for alcohol reflects an inner void and lack of substance.
- *Stupid.* Continuing urges to drink reflect an inability to learn from experience.
- *Hypocritical.* Craving indicates that the patient's efforts to curb drinking are false or deceptive.
- *Weak.* The patient lacks will power.

The discouragement, guilt, and shame that accompany such interpretations necessitate that the therapist reinterpret the experience of craving for what it is: a manifestation of the disease process of alcoholism, not a character flaw.

It is particularly important that the alcoholic appreciate that his craving is either biologically determined, as during the withdrawal phase, or, as occurs later, within the realm of basic conditioning psychology. This realization helps to demystify the experience, placing it within familiar human experience. It is useful to point out that we do not condemn the person who is dieting when he experiences a longing for sweets. Similarly, there is no need for a person to castigate himself or herself for desiring alcohol.

The therapist is cautioned not to arrive mistakenly at a poor prognosis or conclude that a patient lacks motivation because he demonstrates, verbally or otherwise, a strong subjective preoccupation with alcohol use. The patient's preoccupation with alcohol does not occur in a vacuum, but is integral to the defensive coping capacities of the individual. Using the concept of ego mechanisms of defense, the clinician can assess the alcoholic's current level of psychological functioning and observe shifts in functioning—adaptive or maturational versus nonadaptive or regressive—as the patient experiences craving, which is processed by the ego according to the individual's characteristic defensive style. The experience presents, for the alcoholic, a conflict between a perceived inner need (biological and/or psychological) and external reality. The external reality is represented by the destructive effects of drinking (e.g., loss of job, impaired health, family disruption). Eventually, internal prohibitions also are brought into conflict with impulses to drink.

Clinical vignettes illustrating the emergence of defensive style against the conflict over drinking impulses are presented below. The clinical examples illustrate the hierarchy of defenses, as described below, proceeding from the most regressed to the mature (Vaillant, 1971).

Ego-functioning at the psychotic level is illustrated by a middle-aged male who, after a recent recovery from an episode of mania, entered an alcoholism treatment program. Concomitantly, he increased his contact with his wife and children and confronted his wife about several long-standing marital conflicts.

The resulting stress stimulated impulses to drink which, in turn, produced further conflict. The patient became delusional in reference to his family, accused them of ruining him financially by their "meddling," and wished to leave the treatment program because his "cure" had been effected by God. He left the program, drank for a brief period of time, and was then persuaded to return for treatment. The drinking impulse and the subsequent conflict certainly were not the only stresses compromising this patient's emotional equilibrium, but they added to the state of ego regression as was characterized by use of the defenses of delusional projection and distortion ("cured by God").

Ego-functioning reflecting a severe characterological impairment (immature defenses) is illustrated by a divorced, chronically unemployed male. While on a brief excursion, he telephoned the hospital and angrily accused the staff of not allowing him sufficient time for his errands. (In fact, he had been granted the amount of time he had requested.) He felt that he was being "tested" in order to see if he could "take the frustration." As the staff learned later, he had experienced strong cravings for alcohol when exposed to his neighborhood environment and had felt conflicted, guilty, and frustrated. He projected his self-loathing and lack of self-image onto the staff, whom he saw as harsh and inadequate.

A second example of ego-functioning at the level of immature defenses is provided by a 35-year-old married woman who periodically expressed strong wishes to drink. She felt that it was unfair that she continued to experience such urges after not drinking for over a year. Her characteristic response was passive-aggressive: she cancelled therapy sessions or refused to talk during sessions. At home, she typically went to bed for 12–24 hours. This behavior reflected the defense of schizoid fantasy, as it represented an autistic retreat to gratify unmet regressive needs (formerly provided by alcohol). In addition, it served to avoid hostile feelings toward those who put demands on her, namely her husband and family.

A healthier state of ego-functioning is observed when craving for alcohol and the resulting conflicts are processed at the level of "neurotic defenses." A 19-year-old male observed several people drinking beer at a basketball game. Strong desires for alcohol developed, but simultaneously he thought of his brother and the disappointment of his family. The feeling of craving was then replaced with a sense of disgust for those drinking, thus illustrating the manifestation of reaction formation to curb an unacceptable desire.

A female patient was unable to recall any thoughts or circumstances that precipitated her periodic impulses to drink. She acknowledged that this was characteristic of her handling of emotionally conflicted material. As treatment progressed, her defense of repression was lessened, and the environmental and affective concomitants of the impulse to drink became available to memory.

The defense of isolation is noted in a middle-aged woman whose sense of craving was limited to the thought "I want to drink." No affect was experienced in relation to this thought or the possible consequences of such an action. In fact, the thought "I want to drink" usually developed during group therapy sessions. The patient was distressed that the thought did not disturb her more, for she knew that further alcohol use would be harmful to her. The use of defenses such as isolation, repression, and reaction formation is characteristic of the alcoholic who is well enough to function at a neurotic level.

At the mature level of ego-functioning, the patient responds to craving in a manner largely free of strong negative affect and the gross distortions that accompany ego-functioning at lower levels. Defenses or coping mechanisms such as humor, sublimation, suppression, and anticipation are observed. For example, a professional woman experienced considerable anxiety and the urge to drink on excursions from the hospital. She coped effectively by anticipating her return to the hospital and the opportunity to discuss her feelings.

A businessman realized how strongly he felt a desire to drink the first time he visited his family. At first he was anguished by this, but was able to joke about it with his wife. In doing so, he did not deny or minimize the strength of the craving but, rather, through humor minimized his disappointment in not being able to drink.

The observing capacity of the ego will be strengthened as the patient understands the phenomenon of craving. For such comprehension to be complete, each patient must gain an appreciation not only of the origins, precipitants, and manifestations of drinking impulses, but also of the emotional impact or meaning the experience has for him or her.

Information helps to demystify craving and counters the common feeling that one is a victim of fate. It provides guidelines for recognizing subtle forms of craving and stimulates thinking as to how to avoid or minimize situations that are likely to stimulate a desire to drink.

An understanding of the material increases the patient's awareness of an important determinant of his behavior, facilitating the shift from passive acquiescence to active resistance when confronted with an urge to drink. When the alcoholic patient demonstrates mature coping mechanisms, the ego's observing capacity is sufficiently strong to ward off impulses to drink.

In the early months of recovery, treatment must attend the experience of craving. A majority of alcoholics (68%) report that craving is dealt with best by their associating with nondrinking alcoholics (Mathew et al., 1979). Jogging, sex, and exercise as well are reported as very helpful in combating craving. The patient requires support while struggling to avoid drinking. The patient may learn to function at a higher level than he or she had functioned before attempting to stop drinking. Commonly, the ability to endure frustration and dysphoric affect is strengthened during this period. In addition, as the patient gains experience in recognizing and coping with craving without the use of alcohol, a sense of mastery and hope become established.

LOSS OF CONTROL

Closely related to craving is loss of control. Craving usually precedes loss of control. That is, the alcoholic experiences a need to drink, drinks, craves more, and a vicious cycle leading to intoxication begins.

Before proceeding further the following points need to be kept in mind:

1) Why one loses control is not known, but it is the pathognomic sign of alcoholism (Keller, 1972). If we understood the cause of loss of control, the etiology of alcoholism might be explained.
2) Loss of control is relative. It is not always operating in the alcoholic person. That is, sometimes the alcoholic can drink normally and not experience any harmful consequences. But for how long and how much is highly variable from person to person. Glatt (1967)

postulates that it may take a certain blood level of alcohol over a period of time before the alcoholic loses control.

3) Loss of control is believed to be initiated by cues, often subtle or unconscious (Mathew et al., 1979). These cues may be environmental or internal. In this sense, loss of control may be initiated by the same process as craving, and one major theory (Ludwig, Wikler, & Stark, 1974) of loss of control assumes craving to initiate the drinking, which results in loss of control. Craving does not necessarily lead to drinking, however, and therefore does not invariably lead to loss of control.

4) Loss of control begins before the first drink. The alcoholic seems to be that person who has consistently found alcohol to be useful, desirable, or necessary for increasingly varied purposes. When exposed to stimuli associated with the euphoric or relief-producing properties of alcohol, one's ability to say "no" may be lost. The same cues that initiate loss of control may also produce craving. Craving and the pre-drinking phase of loss of control are not necessarily identical. A common experience probably initiates both, and craving is "useful" as it labels the need for alcohol. Can the alcoholic proceed to the loss of control drinking without craving? This is not known for certain, but in studies of craving there are alcoholics who experience loss of control, but do not report craving (Mathew et al., 1979).

5) Keller (1972) provides a most useful conceptualization of loss of control as a "double disablement—disablement from consistently choosing whether to drink, disablement from consistently choosing to stop if drinking is attempted" (p. 165).

Loss of control does not mean that the alcoholic who ingests an initial amount of alcohol invariably proceeds to drunkenness. The idea that a physiological chain reaction triggered by a small amount of alcohol constitutes loss of control is rooted in the history of this concept. Keller (1972) clarifies the historical errors that led to a reification of this narrow view.

There are two sources for this error: The first is a well known AA slogan "One drink, one drunk." This slogan does not fully describe the alcoholic's drinking history. It would be very rare to find an alcoholic who had not from time to time and for varying lengths of time taken a drink or two and had not gotten drunk nor drunk in any way that could be considered pathological. However, AA, in its wisdom, knew that the alcoholic man or woman could never be sure that one drink in fact might not lead to "one drunk." Therefore, the slogan indicating that the alcoholic is "one drink away from a drunk" is a practical reminder, a useful policy to prevent relapse.

Keller also documents the second source of misunderstanding of loss of control. This misunderstanding arose from a scientific report published by the World Health Organization in August, 1952. The report, written by E. M. Jellinek, states that "as soon as any small quantity of alcohol enters the organism a demand for more alcohol is set up, which is felt as a physical demand by the drinker . . ." and that "this demand lasts until the drinker is too intoxicated or too sick to ingest more alcohol" (Jellinek, 1952, as reported in Keller, 1972, pp. 154–155, 157).

Then, in a fascinating piece of behind-the-scenes science, Keller (1972) reports as follows:

> I saw this version soon after, and immediately questioned him (Jellinek) about it, pointing out how unlike it was to the reality that we both knew. He agreed at once, explained that it was a slip that had passed his notice in the haste of going to press in Geneva, and wished it could be unsaid. (p. 157)

A correction was provided four months later in the December, 1952 issue of the *Quarterly Journal of Studies on Alcohol* (Vol. 13, p. 673). In the latter volume, Jellinek stated that it may take an alcoholic weeks of drinking before loss of control develops. Thus, it is not inevitable that one or two drinks will lead to drunkenness.

The concept of loss of control was further refined by Marconi (1959). He adds the concept of inability to abstain to the more widely understood view of inability to stop. Keller points out that inability to stop and inability to abstain express the fact that the alcoholic has lost control not only over how much he may drink once drinking has begun, but has also lost control over whether or not he will refrain from alcohol use.

By now a better understanding of loss-of-control has been derived: *Loss of control refers to the inability of the alcoholic to choose invariably whether or not he or she will drink and to the inability to regulate predictably how much will be drunk.*

What accounts for loss of control? The earliest theories were physiological in nature. Activation of hypothalamic centers (Marconi, Poblete, Palestine, Moga, & Bahomondes, 1970) and paralysis of control centers in the brain (MacLeod, 1955) are two such examples. In addition, Jellinek postulates altered cellular metabolism conditioned by the signal of the first drink (Jellinek, 1980).

The strong emphasis on physiological factors has necessarily been modified by recent studies investigating cognitive and behavioral variables. Laboratory studies have consistently demonstrated that alcoholics do not necessarily drink to the point of intoxication when given free access to ethanol (Griffiths, Bigelow, & Liebson, 1974; Nathan & Lisman, 1976). Chronic alcoholics have been shown to drink moderately in order to maintain social relationships on a ward (Cohen, Liebson, Faillace, & Allen, 1971) or to gain access to a more favorable ward setting (Gottheil, Crawford, & Cornelison, 1973). Even without tangible "rewards" for moderate drinking, Gottheil et al. have demonstrated that chronic alcoholics can modify their use of alcohol in a hospital-based program, where alcohol is in ample supply 12 hours of the day. Of 98 patients, 55 drank at some time during a 6-week program. Only 23 of the 98 failed to modify the amount drunk, compared to their prehospitalization levels, while participating in the program (Gottheil et al., 1973).

Marlatt et al. (1973) demonstrated that the amount of beverage consumed is influenced, in part, by the subjects' expectancy of what a beverage contained rather than its actual alcohol content. For both alcoholics and social drinkers the amount of beverage consumed was greater if the subjects were led to expect that alcohol was present and was substantially less if told only tonic was present (even if alcohol was actually present in the tonic). The study is further evidence that physiological factors alone do not account for the quantity drunk by alcoholics (Marlatt, Demming, & Reid, 1973).

Marlatt, impressed by the role of expectation in shaping drinking behavior, put forth a cognitive-behavioral explanation of loss of control (Marlatt, 1978). Loss of control results from the alcoholic's expectation and conceptualization of drinking rather than any actual physiological effect of alcohol. According to this theory, if the alcoholic slips, it becomes necessary to modify his or her self-image in order to justify the drinking behavior. Marlatt coined a term "Abstinence Violation Effect," which blends cognitive dissonance theory and attribution theory (Litman, 1980). To put it simply, the alcoholic may attribute a return to drinking as due to personal weakness and, as a result, expect to continue to fail (hence more drinking). Or the cognitive dissonance (e.g., guilt) caused by a slip may be responded to by the view that the disease has come back (a justification for further use of alcohol).

The cognitive-behavioral theory of relapse and loss of control can be diagrammed as shown in Figure 5-1. Marlatt's theory emphasizes environmental factors as the important precipitants of relapse (high-risk situations) and cognitive-behavioral responses (coping responses) as determinants of whether drinking resumes. In accord with this theory, a study of the effect of training alcoholics in social skills to cope with high-risk situations was conducted. Significant decreases in the duration and severity of relapse were demonstrated initially, but failed to be sustained beyond a 3-month period (Chaney, O'Leary, & Marlatt, 1979).

In contrast, Ludwig, Bendfeldt, Wikler, and Cain (1978) postulate a neurophysiological feedback dysfunction in alcoholics, whereby the intake of alcohol fails to be governed by the usual exteroceptive cues (e.g.,

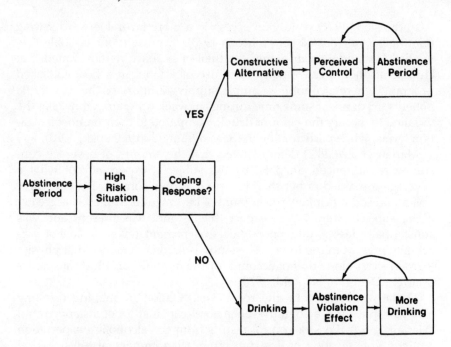

Figure 5-1. Cognitive-behavioral theory of relapse
(reproduced from Marlatt, 1978, by permission).

number of drinks) or interoceptive cues (e.g., perceived intoxication, ataxia).

A test of this hypothesis was conducted (Ludwig, Wikler, & Stark, 1974) by comparing drinking decisions in alcoholics and controls. Both groups were instructed to try to maintain a previously experienced blood alcohol level. The alcoholic subjects obtained significantly higher blood alcohol levels and displayed a poorer capacity to regulate blood alcohol levels over time, regardless of the feedback provided. This apparent inability to attend to interoceptive and exteroceptive cues was defined as loss of control.

The data from the study are compatible with the theory of a defect in feedback regulation, but fall short of demonstrating that that is the mechanism involved. A verbal report from the alcoholics as to how they were subjectively responding would have been helpful. As it is, we do not know whether they were aware of the same cues as the controls. Perhaps, the alcoholic group experienced the feedback identically to the controls but were affected by other factors (e.g., a compulsion) which overrode the usual regulatory cues.

A summary of the Ludwig-Wikler theory of loss of control is diagrammed in Figure 5-2.

A neurophysiological explanation for loss of control has not been established. Nor should data from the cognitive-behavioral studies be taken as a refutation of a neurophysiological process. It is interesting that in behavioral studies (Cutter et al., 1970; Marlatt et al., 1973) in which loss of control was considered a shibboleth, the alcoholic subjects still consumed significantly greater quantities of alcohol than control subjects and often maintained blood alcohol levels between 150 mg. to 250 mg. per 100 ml. These subjects were not "stressed" nor forced to drink. What drove these subjects to drink to levels beyond the usual social levels (55 mg. per 100 ml. or less) remains undetermined.

Clinically, a synthesis of the neurophysiological and cognitive-behavioral views seems appropriate. Figure 5-3 provides a synthesis illustrating various paths both to drinking and loss of control and also to the alternative, maintenance of abstinence. This synthesis differs from the purely neurophysiological view in that craving is not believed necessary to initiate drinking, although it often does. By the time loss of control has occurred, however, craving would be expected to be antecedent to and provide further impetus for the drinking. This does not mean that craving causes loss of control, but that these two are closely associated. The abstinence violation effect is assumed to operate when the alcoholic has

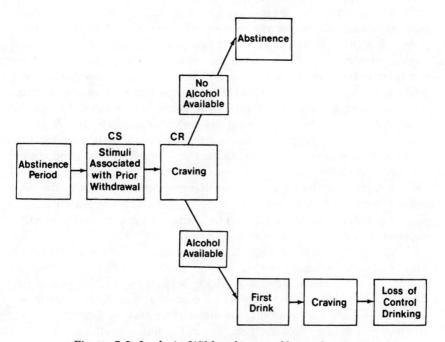

Figure 5-2. Ludwig-Wikler theory of loss of control
(reproduced from Marlatt, 1978, by permission).

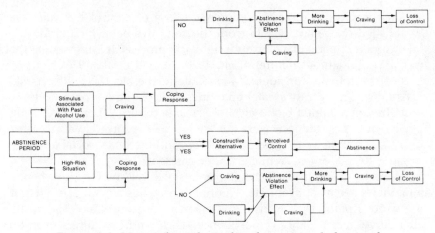

Figure 5-3. Neurophysiological and cognitive-behavioral
synthesis of loss of control.

a relapse and, along with craving, drives the drinking. In the untreated
alcoholic, ignorant of his or her problem and protected by denial, the
abstinence violation effect may be absent.

To review Figure 5-3: First, after a period of abstinence, the alcoholic
may encounter stimuli associated with prior use of alcohol. Such stimuli
may be internal, such as heightened autonomic nervous system activity
associated with anxiety. A desire for alcohol is reexperienced. Or the
stimuli may be external, such as a call from a drinking buddy or driving
past a liquor store. Again, craving may be experienced. If craving occurs,
the alcoholic may or may not cope effectively. A noneffective response
would be to drink. An effective coping response would be to call an AA
sponsor or to leave the place where alcohol was available. Or the individual may simply recognize these cues for what they are and cope appropriately. The latter may include avoiding former acquaintances and lo-
cales or examining the circumstances that provoke anxiety. No subjective
sense of craving may be felt. Exposure to stimuli connected with prior
alcohol use may, as if by habit, lead to taking a drink with no intervening
experience of craving apparent.

Secondly, the alcoholic may encounter a high-risk situation not necessarily associated with previous drinking. The death of a loved one or an
accident may stimulate adequate coping responses, such as turning to
friends or family for support, by which control and abstinence are maintained. The high-risk situation may also induce craving directly, and the
chain of possibilities described above can become operational. Finally, a
high-risk situation may lead to the realization that coping responses are

inadequate, and this may lead to drinking that is unmediated by the experience of craving; or craving may result from the sense of inadequate coping responses and either be dealt with effectively (avoidance of alcohol) or lead to drinking.

Clinical vignettes will further illustrate these alternative experiences:

Reexposure to alcohol-related cues→craving→failure of coping responses.

George, resentful that his wife took a beer some evenings when she returned from her job, finally exploded with anger. Concomitantly, he felt a "gnawing sensation" in his gut and knew he had to get a drink. A binge followed.

Reexposure to alcohol-related cues→craving→effective coping responses.

Dan was beginning to enjoy his newly acquired sobriety and was pleased by his loss of interest in drinking. On a fishing trip, the first since he had stopped drinking, he developed a strong urge for beer. At first he was somewhat discouraged and puzzled, but quickly realized that on all previous fishing trips the bottom of the boat was filled with cold beer. He was able to laugh about this and finish the day without difficulty.

Reexposure to alcohol-related cues→no craving→failure of coping responses.

A man early in his recovery arose from watching TV during the beer commercial. Without apparent awareness he went to the refrigerator, opened a beer, and began to drink. He quickly "caught himself" and was fortunate not to lose control over this incident. The failure in coping in this example was the delayed awareness of his vulnerability to resuming a long-standing habit and his lack of appreciation for the need to keep alcohol out of his house.

Reexposure to alcohol-related cues→no craving→effective coping responses.

A middle-aged male telephone company employee readily acknowledged that he had more fun during his drinking days. He was quick to add that he did not wish to return to or attempt to repeat those stormy days. He was enterprising enough to make the acquaintance of a recovered alcoholic prostitute. The two of them went out for an alcohol-free evening of dinner, motel, and so on, recapturing the nondrinking part of similar evenings from the past.

High-risk situation→craving→failure of coping responses.

John learned that his wife had cancer. Not to return to alcohol seemed inconceivable, and a steady level of drinking was reinitiated.

High risk situation→craving→effective coping response.

A young girl in her early twenties was newly sober and had befriended an older woman. During an excursion from the hospital she visited her friend, was offered a homosexual relationship and a drink. Strong craving for the drink was experienced. By anticipating that the hospital staff expected her to return soon she successfully avoided the drink and the sexual advance.

High risk situation→no craving→failure of coping responses.

An employed woman, recovered from alcoholism, attended a business convention in a distant city. Her business associates, unaware of her alcoholism, quickly provided a variety of drinks. She was taken by surprise, did not wish to drink, but feared that to refuse would identify her as an alcoholic. The potential embarrassment was avoided by going along with the drinkers. She proceeded to lose control over her alcohol use and was readmitted to a rehabilitation program several weeks later.

High risk situation→no craving→effective coping response.

An affluent woman was returning from a Middle-East vacation when her flight was "hijacked." Stranded on a hot runway for hours, the captors allowed drinks to be served freely. Concerned mainly about her safety she experienced no desire for the alcohol. She helped calm the nerves of her fellow passengers by serving drinks and playing the part of hostess.

To conclude, loss of control is believed to be initiated prior to the first drink. It is initiated by cues or stimuli specific for the individual. The cues often are unconscious and usually signal a "need" for the sedative or euphoric-producing properties of alcohol (craving).

Treatment should be directed first toward helping the alcoholic recognize that loss of control is a reality and confront the denial that commonly accompanies this experience. Second, treatment should assist the alcoholic in recognizing and conquering circumstances that render him or her vulnerable to loss of control. For some, this involves gaining mastery over internal drives, developing tolerance of affect, or maturing. For others, environmental or lifestyle changes are necessary.

Since the pharmacologic effect of alcohol, itself, may be a stimulus to trigger loss of control, treatment is not expected to remove all one's vulnerability to loss of control, which would allow one to resume normal use of alcohol. Abstinence, therefore, remains the cornerstone of treatment efforts. It is hoped that treatment will render one less vulnerable to loss of control by increasing one's mastery over environmental and internal triggers.

PERSONALITY REGRESSION

The pathological effect of alcohol on the liver, pancreas, brain, or other organ systems is well known and capable of verification by a variety of techniques ranging from physical examination to electron microscopy. Less well known and less well documented is the erosive effect of alcohol on personality functioning. The effect referred to is not the state of intoxication. Intoxication, with its familiar signs and symptoms, is similar in all who drink to excess. The effect on personality functioning referred to in this section is that of regression and is a toxic effect of chronic alcoholism.

A neuropsychological explanation of this effect of alcohol is being developed (Ryan & Butters, 1983). Alcohol has been demonstrated to impact on the information processing strategies of intoxicated individuals. Less efficient modes of information processing requiring less mental effort are the result. By virtue of experiencing hundreds or thousands of intoxications, the alcoholic may become habituated to cognitive strategies requiring less mental effort, and such strategies may generalize to nonintoxicated states as well. Although this explanation is speculative, these "lesser" strategies may contribute to the clinical phenomenon of regression as described below.

Regression is a return to an earlier mode of psychological functioning. Regression may be conceptualized as a shift in psychological defenses from the more mature to the less mature. For example, immature defenses such as acting-out, passive-aggressiveness, or somatization prevail over mature mechanisms of defense such as suppression, humor, or anticipation (Vaillant, 1971).

This effect of alcoholism may be confused with personality disorders. Personality disorder is a common antecedent of alcoholism, but alcohol itself may lead to personality changes independent of a preexisting character disorder. The symptoms of the regressed ego state are not necessarily part of a personality disorder but can be an effect of chronic alcohol abuse. The alcoholic often seems to be personality-disordered during the active phases of the illness. Not all alcoholics continue to show character pathology when sober (Nace, 1983; Schuckit, 1979). Because of a paucity of studies, how often alcoholism is preceded by a personality disorder has not been accurately determined. Nor is it known whether character pathology that remains after sobriety is achieved is a manifestation of a preexistent personality disorder or an effect of chronic alcoholism.

The changes in character to be described as manifestations of chronic alcohol abuse are grafted on the preexisting personality structure. Sometimes the alcohol nurtures latent or mild pathological features and brings such features into full bloom. In other cases the change in character is in pronounced contrast to the alcoholic's basic character.

Manifestations

The manifestations of personality regression in the alcoholic result from the rapid, predictable, and pleasurable pharmacologic action of ethyl alcohol. Any experience that has such euphoric effects will be highly reinforcing. The personality's capacity to delay gratification and to tolerate frustration is weakened by the experience of immediate gratification, and regression occurs. Specific traits or behaviors are then observed: e.g., grandiosity, impatience, decreased tolerance of frustration, impulsivity, and passivity.

Grandiosity is an exaggerated sense of self-importance; an observer can note an inordinate need for attention and an expectation that one is entitled to such attention from others. The attention may be expected because of one's qualities or strengths (which have never been fully appreciated) or because of one's suffering (which has not been adequately recompensed or acknowledged). A sense of grandiosity also leads to unrealistic expectations of oneself, expectations which, if unfulfilled, yield guilt and a sense of inferiority. Further, grandiosity may promote an air of self-sufficiency, which may impede recognition of the alcoholic's real need for help.

Impatience is manifested by the tendency to want to do everything in a hurry. This can be observed at the beginning of treatment: "How long will it take?" "I can't stay four weeks, I've got to be back to work before that." Conclusions are reached rapidly, and plans are grand. Demands to return to work, to meet with spouse, and to see the counselor more often reflect the fast pace the alcoholic wishes to pursue as he or she continues on a course of "crisis living."

Decreased tolerance of frustration is evident in the anger, anxiety, or despair which results when plans fail or delays result. Temper tantrums are common among alcoholics, and alcoholics are critical of those responsible for the delays. One woman patient signed out of the hospital on her first night because she learned that an appointment with a hair dresser would take a week and that dry cleaning was not available on the premises.

Impulsivity describes behaviors that fail to take into account the consequences of one's actions. An alcoholic allows whims or passing fads to overshadow his or her deeper needs. Such superficial behavior fosters premature relationships, faulty decisions, and poor self-care.

Passivity is characteristic because alcohol provides a high yield for very little behavior. Natural "highs," such as one derives from jogging or the practice of yoga, are obtained through sustained effort and discipline, but the route with a drug is easier and much quicker. Thus, an alcoholic perceives effort as a "hassle" and alternatives to drinking as a "bore."

Today, because of the widespread use of alcohol and drugs among young people, clinicians are recognizing the destructive effects of alcohol and other drugs on the developing ego. A weakening of ego controls and disregard of future consequences are commonly noted (Dupont, 1984).

The destructive impact of alcohol on adult ego functions was recognized early in the history of AA. The "Dry Drunk Syndrome," as it has been referred to, describes a condition of the alcoholic who is not drinking ("dry"), but whose behavior and attitude reflect a pathological condition ("drunk"). The dry drunk is pompous, bored, easily distracted, self-absorbed, and caught up in wishful thinking (Solberg, 1983). Deflating the ego is considered necessary to counter this syndrome, so that the alcoholic may recognize the need for a higher power (Tiebout, 1949).

Tiebout, a psychiatrist who pioneered in studying the dynamics of AA, wrote on the pathological effects of alcohol on ego functioning (Tiebout, 1949). Inflated ego in this sense means the persisting presence in the adult psyche of the original infantile nature. Freud's phrase "His majesty, the baby" summarizes this concept. Drinking nurtures and reinforces the infantile omnipotence. The inflated ego, that is, the immature traits of childhood, must be surrendered, given up, for the alcoholic to remain sober. Surrender does not mean simply submission. Rather, it emphasizes the developing capacity for acceptance of one's limitations and powerlessness over alcohol (Tiebout, 1953).

To summarize, chronic alcohol abuse affects personality structure independent of preexisting character pathology. The resulting state of regression is characterized by traits noted in the earlier literature on alcoholism. Clinically, sufficient time in an alcohol-free state is necessary before the regressive effect of alcohol can be separated from preexisting character pathology.

DENIAL

Denial is the mechanism of defense that gives alcoholism a bad name. It functions partly like armor, repelling the efforts of those who point out reality to the alcoholic, and partly like radar, detecting any movement that threatens the drinking position. Denial operates at the interface of the disease and clinical intervention. It commonly invokes anger, discouragement, disgust, distance, and frustration in those who approach. Indeed, that is its function. The clinician who is provoked to contempt or despair has been incapacitated as an effective intervener. The alcoholic patient thereby continues to avoid recognizing the destructive effect of alcohol, and protects himself or herself from lowered self-esteem.

Psychiatrists who learn to avoid the emotional "bait" which denial provides experience a great leap forward in clinical effectiveness. It is important to remain aware that denial is a process that:

1) Differs from lying and conscious deceit and is largely unconscious
2) Protects the option to continue to drink, which is for the alcohol-dependent individual the sustenance of life itself
3) Prevents the thin and fragile shell of self-esteem from being crushed by the heavy weight of reality
4) Bolts the door that opens into the horrors of personal hopelessness

For the person caught up in the throes of dependence on alcohol, denial is vital to preserve ego integrity. The alcoholic feels as if he or she can't cope without alcohol, doesn't want to live without alcohol, and can't stop drinking anyway. To recognize one's helplessness over alcohol use is tantamount to acknowledging the necessity to quit. Hope lies in giving up alcohol—the one act the alcoholic knows to be beyond his grasp. With this logic in mind, the alcoholic's mind cannot escape the conclusion that he is hopeless, as well as loathsome. Such logic bears too much pain, and the mind mercifully offers an illogical alternative: Denial.

Denial, as an ego mechanism of defense, enables the alcoholic to alter the perception of both internal and external reality (Freud, 1946). It wards off the painful feelings of helplessness over the inability to control alcohol and blocks an accurate appraisal of the consequences drinking has on health, social functioning, and personal relationships.

Denial's work of altering reality is bolstered by other commonly observed ego mechanisms of defense: rationalization, projection, minimization, avoidance, and delaying (Bean, 1981). Bean (1981) has provided lucid descriptions of the role of the latter defenses as the alcoholic attempts to justify, conceal, or preserve drinking. These "adjunctive defenses" (Bean, 1981, p. 78) are listed below:

- Rationalization is redefining drinking so as to make it seem plausible. A woman broke abstinence by drinking wine at a Passover celebration "so the children won't grow up thinking alcohol is evil."
- Projection is attributing one's own motivation to others. A retired naval officer blamed a recent binge on his new employer's "suspi-

cion" that he had been late to work one morning because of a hangover.

- Minimalization is acknowledging only part of the truth. Early in treatment patients may acknowledge a "problem" during the past couple of months when, in reality, the overindulgence has gone on for years.
- Avoidance is removing oneself from situations which raise the question of a drinking problem, e.g., a refusal to read literature on the subject, see a doctor, or brook any discussion of the topic.
- Delaying is a largely conscious tactic that postpones the inevitable moment of discomfort. Patients who are sent to me for an evaluation are sometimes interviewed first by medical students, who are often left feeling perplexed about the referral as the alcoholic delays (or minimizes) the painful revelations of their dependence. The patients know I am the "alcohol specialist" and generally admit a problem with alcohol.

Denial differs from a delusion, which consists of an actively functioning, fixed, false belief that has a sense of reality for the individual. Denial wards off reality rather than finds a substitute for it. Denial also differs from neurologically derived defects in memory seen in Korsakoff's psychosis and from symptoms of anosognosia (denial of disease), which are the result of specific central nervous system lesions and are not dynamically related to the ego's attempt to preserve self-esteem.

Denial, however, is reinforced not only by its dynamic usefulness to ego integrity, but also by several specific effects of alcohol on memory functioning. Blackouts, euphoric recall, repression, and the organic brain syndrome associated with chronic intoxication are memory-related events, which may contribute to the process of denial.

Blackouts are a physiologically induced state of amnesia produced when the blood alcohol level is sufficiently high to impair memory encoding in the neuron. This term does not refer to loss of consciousness. Persons experiencing blackouts have lost segments of their drinking experience. It differs from repression, which is emotionally motivated "forgetting," and is not physiologically induced. Repression is an active defensive process against painful or conflicted associations, but the material repressed, unlike that lost to a blackout, may be retrieved by therapeutic techniques.

Euphoric recall (Johnson, 1973) is the experience of remembering only the positive feeling associated with alcohol use, not the behavioral consequences. For example, when a beer advertisement is played on television the alcoholic may promptly "taste" the beer, long for a can of cold beer, and miss the anticipated pleasure keenly. The alcoholic's experience with beer is much more extensive than the euphoric recall suggests, but the hangovers, quarrels, or sickness is not retrieved. Since the euphoric effect is more closely associated in time with drinking than are the painful consequences, recalling the pleasures of alcohol use gains priority.

The three distortions—blackouts, repression, and euphoric recall—serve to block or distort the reality of the alcoholic's drinking and, thereby, contribute to the process of denial. The fourth effect of alcohol—the repeated insults to consciousness proffered by frequent bouts of intoxication—take a toll on concentration, clarity of thought, as well as the functioning of memory. The alcoholic is at the least temporarily brain-damaged and may become so permanently. Denial is reinforced by the distortions of cognitive processing that occur from the effects of alcohol. In addition, defensive thinking and behavior are stimulated as the alcoholic's sense of integrity and adequacy is threatened by the growing disability (Bean, 1981).

The effective resolution of pathological denial is the *sine qua non* of alcoholism treatment. It is worthwhile to note that denial is not an all or none phenomenon. It is not removed all at once, but seems to fold back in layers, progressively revealing more and more of one's experience. These layers of denial can be observed clinically. The first to be dealt with is the acknowledgement that one is alcoholic. The first step in AA expresses it well: "We admitted we were powerless over alcohol—that our lives had become unmanageable" (Wilson, 1957b). When the alcoholic accepts this first step, the initial layer of denial has been removed. The alcoholic can now see the consequences and admit that alcohol has caused his or her problems.

The second layer of defense is that which denies the need for alcohol. The alcoholic in treatment usually is able to admit that alcohol led to being fired, divorced, or sick. Slower to be recognized is how psychologically important alcohol actually was (and may be still). The alcoholic likes to think that he can take it or leave it. He wants to avoid the knowledge of how vulnerable he is to its seductive powers. This point is illustrated by alcoholics who deliberately go to a bar and order ginger ale. They are trying to convince themselves that alcohol isn't important to them. One man put a bottle of whiskey on his dining room table to prove he wouldn't give in. Until this level of denial is dealt with, the alcoholic hasn't learned that he is powerless over alcohol. It is painful and humbling for the alcoholic person to realize fully that a chemical has been more important than children, career, or health.

The third layer of denial to be unfolded is that which allows the alcoholic to sense the guilt and shame which were repressed or denied during active phases of the illness. The lost years, missed opportunities, broken relationships throb with intensity. Support and assistance are essential for the alcoholic to integrate at this stage and avoid despair or a return to the denial-evoking properties of ethyl alcohol. Steps four, five and six of AA (see Chapter 13) address a process which assists the alcoholic in tolerating the absence of denial at this level.

In Figure 5-4 the function of denial is illustrated. It protects the addiction by shielding from the rational conscious aspects of the mind the consequences of alcoholism. This formidable barrier is the initial focus in the treatment of alcoholism as will be described in Chapter 11.

CONFLICTED BEHAVIOR

The sixth construct of alcoholism is conflicted behavior. As with denial the behavior of the alcoholic is very apparent to those close to the alcoholic. What is less apparent is the conflict this behavior produces.

The variety of behaviors which result from dependence on alcohol include pathological patterns of drinking such as morning drinking, binge drinking, and frequent intoxication. Other common behavioral manifestations are decrements in job performance, child or spouse abuse, reckless driving, accidents, and a progressive deterioration in judgment and sense of responsibility.

The behavioral manifestations of alcoholism have the same initial effect on those concerned about the alcoholic as does denial. Anger, con-

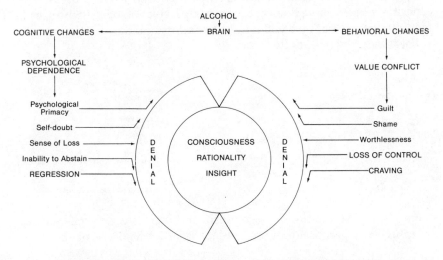

Figure 5-4. Denial shields the conscious mind from the painful consequences of alcoholism. (Reprinted by permission from *Texas Medicine*, 79, 38, December, 1983.)

tempt, frustration, and rejection are normal responses. Less apparent to those close to the alcoholic is the conflict the alcohol-driven behavior produces. An educational film on alcoholism entitled "If You Loved Me"* illustrates the point. The wife in the film protests that her alcoholic husband would not put the family through this—arguments, loss of income, neglect—if he loved them. She assumes his behavior is an expression of his values or priorities rather than a manifestation of his illness. Her response and her perplexity are understandable—she does not understand that his behavior conflicts with his usual (i.e., prealcoholic) sense of values. Prior standards and expectations are overrun repeatedly. Guilt, shame, and a sense of worthlessness accumulate.

To illustrate the effect of the alcoholic's repeated transgressions against self and others, I ask medical students to recall instances when they were chastised, however mildly, for overlooking a physical finding, being late for rounds, or forgetting to order a proper study. The feeling of having let down a teacher or a patient is poignant and agonizing. If those infrequent instances and their painful affects were to occur daily or weekly over a decade or more, the magnitude of conflict for the alcoholic can be sensed.

Such is the dilemma of the alcoholic patient. Each manifestation of the illness influences the sense of self-worth and the integrity of the ego. Figure 5-5 summarizes the contribution which each facet of alcoholism makes to self-esteem. Psychiatrists and other mental health professionals are in a pivotal position to interrupt this destructive process. Our capacity to be effective does not depend upon technological advances in medical science, but on a willingness to understand those suffering from a disease worthy of our effort and skill.

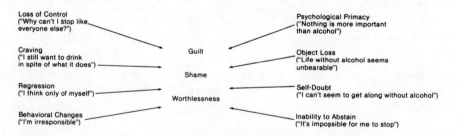

Figure 5-5. Manifestations of alcoholism and their effect on self-esteem. (Reprinted by permission from *Texas Medicine, 79,* 38, December, 1983).

---

*Gerald T. Rogers, producer.

With recognition of the pervasive and primary effect of psychological dependence in the experience of the alcoholic patient, an understanding of the disease concept emerges. The constructs of craving, loss of control, denial, regression, and conflicted behavior round out the disease concept. As clinicians better understand the disease concept and communicate this understanding to patients, the process of recovery becomes substantially strengthened.

CHAPTER 6

Marriage and Family

Before addressing the specific steps and issues in treatment it is necessary to review the family context of alcoholism. Successful treatment often hinges on effective involvement of the spouse or other family members. For this to be accomplished an understanding of the impact of alcoholism on marriage and the family is essential.

Recent statistics indicate that 40% of cases before family courts involve alcoholism (Jacob & Seilhamer, 1982). It is unclear whether family malfunction or alcoholism comes first. Simplistic notions that a nagging spouse causes the mate's alcoholism, as exemplified by W. C. Fields ("A woman drove me to drink. I never even thanked her."), have been replaced by recognition that alcoholism itself can produce marital and family pathology. In addition, the family system may enable or sustain pathological drinking, but can hardly be considered a sufficient cause.

THE ONSET OF ALCOHOLISM

Generalizations become untenable as data on alcoholic marriages accumulate. This is certainly true in the time relationship between onset of alcoholism and marriage. Paolino and McCrady (1976), in an extensive review, discuss the paucity of research in this area and the value that such data would have in understanding the alcoholic marriage.

Rae and Forbes (1966) found that wives with an MMPI Psychopathic Deviation (PD) scale elevation greater than one standard deviation were significantly more likely to have known that their husbands were excessive drinkers prior to marriage. Wives scoring high on the Depression, Psychasthenia, and Hysteria scales were more likely to have witnessed the alcoholism develop after the marriage was established. Further, the wives with high PD were seen as indifferent to their husbands' alcoholism, whereas the depressed/hysterical wives were better motivated to seek help for themselves and to try to understand the dynamics of their marriage.

Jackson (1954) found that in her study of 50 wives none had married an active alcoholic, whereas Clifford (1960), in a study of 50 wives of alcoholics, found that all had known their husbands to be alcoholic at the time of marriage. These discrepancies have been clarified by further data (James & Goldman, 1971; Lemert, 1960). Wives who go to Al-Anon, or who seek therapy for themselves, or who volunteer for clinical research are most likely to have married before their husbands became excessive drinkers. Wives obtained for study from probationary sources or the divorce courts are substantially more likely to have a marriage antedated by alcoholism in the husband.

Sample selection, therefore, accounts for much of the variance in the literature. Although most clinicians encounter the woman who marries several alcoholic men successively, the hypothesis that marriage to an alcoholic is no accident is unproven.

The most commonly encountered alcoholic marriage is that in which the husband is alcoholic, followed by the marriage where the wife is alcoholic, and then marriage where both spouses are alcoholic. In a study by Moos, Bromet, Tsu, and Moos (1979), the husband was alcoholic in 88 couples, the wife alcoholic in 23 couples, and in 2 couples both were alcoholic. Wolin, Bennett, Noonan, and Teitelbaum (1980) reported on 18 families with an alcoholic husband, 5 with an alcoholic wife, and 2 in which both husband and wife were alcoholic. In a study (Wood & Duffy, 1966) of women alcoholics, 4 of 68 had been or were married to an alcoholic husband.

Current data support the contention that men and women who develop alcoholism do not differ from the general population in marital rates (Paolino & McCrady, 1977). When nonpsychotic conditions are considered (Malzberg, 1949) and middle- and upper-class men studied (Paolino & McCrady, 1977; Wellman, Maxwell, & O'Holloren, 1957), the percentage who have ever married is at least as great as that of the general population. These data hold true for women as well, at least among the middle class (Lisansky, 1957; Rosenbaum, 1958). The notable exception is among patients (nearly all male) in public inebriate programs, in which 33% are reported never to have married (Towle, 1974).

Divorce

Marital disruption by divorce or separation is significantly greater when alcoholism is present. Wolf (1958) found disruption more prevalent among alcoholic marriages than among matched nonalcoholic psychiatric controls. In private psychiatric hospital samples, rates of divorce and separation were reported to be 23% (Paolino & McCrady, 1977; Wellman et al., 1957) and 35% (Saxon, Nace, & Cammarota, 1983). In an alcoholism outpatient clinic 30% of those ever married were either separated or divorced (Mayer & Myerson, 1970). The Fourth Special Report to the U.S. Congress on Alcohol and Health (1981) estimates a 40% divorce rate for alcoholics. All of these rates are considerably greater than age-corrected rates for the general population. By the same token, the divorced and separated have significantly higher rates of alcoholism.

Spouse Abuse

A review of spouse abuse (Hamilton & Collins, 1981) determined that alcoholism or alcohol abuse was involved in 45% to 60% of cases. The etiologic role of alcohol is not easily determined as blood alcohol levels are usually not available. The victimized spouse makes the report and may exaggerate the role of alcohol rather than acknowledge other problems. Some theorists dismiss the role of alcohol, arguing that alcohol provides an excuse for being abusive or sets up expectations of violence unrelated to any disinhibitory functions of the drug (Gelles & Straus, 1979; Wilson, 1981).

Given the strong association between alcohol use and violence, it seems unlikely that the "expectation" or "excuse" value of alcohol is solely involved or even a major consideration. The presence of alcohol during or immediately prior to a homicide in either the victim or offender (or both) is found to occur in about 55% of cases. The same is true for aggravated assaults and sexual offenses as alcohol is present in approximately 50% of these incidents (*Fifth Special Report*, U.S. Department of Health and Human Services, 1983).

It seems likely that an interactional effect operates in the case of spouse abuse. Arguments about drinking can easily spread to other areas of conflict within a marriage. Marriage, representing a highly intimate relationship, is expected to have a higher level of conflict than less intimate relationships (Steinmetz & Straus, 1974). The capacity for conflict mixed with alcohol's capacity to alter reasoning and control of behavior yields conditions of rape and abuse.

Spouse abuse is almost invariably described as the husband offending the wife. Obvious factors such as the greater amount of alcohol abuse among males and the male's advantage in physical strength contribute to this skewed relationship. There is also evidence that women who remain in a relationship with a violent alcoholic male have come from a background that suggests the marriage is a carry-over from their family of origin (Hanks & Rosenbaum, 1977). Several patterns are discernible. One, the wives, as had their mothers, married men who needed rescuing, but who were sensitive to criticism and responded violently by beating their wives or daughters. A second pattern involved women from homes where the wives were submissive and abused. These marriages were marked by frequent separations. A third characteristic background is that in which the mother had multiple husbands and left one after the other in order to return to her own mother. In these cases, the daughters were often neglected and subjected to abuse from the abandoned father or relatives. The common factor in the backgrounds of wives who endure abuse is seeing their mothers abused or being abused themselves.

Abuse is not always one-way. Wives inflict violence on their husbands, but little information is available on this pattern. Clinically, one encounters husband abuse from time to time as illustrated by the following example:

A woman in her early fifties had become apparent to her family as an alcohol abuser. Her husband had been chronically ill with scleroderma and been expected to die for years. She tried to care for him in between his long hospitalizations. Bedridden and relatively helpless, he was subjected to alcohol-induced tirades, including being struck by her fists. He shielded her from exposure as long as possible and minimized her drinking and behavior.

Sexual Dysfunction

The most common sexual dysfunction of the alcoholic marriage is in the affective component: intimacy. The capacity or willingness to share, show caring, or take risks is always severely compromised. The familiar question of which came first—alcoholism or impaired relationship—is, of course, appropriate and requires longitudinal studies.

The most common reason for sexual dysfunction in a marriage where alcoholism is present is the drinking itself. The behavior emanating from the dependence on alcohol, the changes in personality, the fear, shame, or guilt experienced by both partners preclude optimal marital functioning. The energy of the family becomes directed increasingly toward coping with the alcoholic member. Jackson (1954) has outlined this process through her studies of the wives of alcoholics. The same general course of events occurs when the wife is alcoholic, but the possibility that divorce will terminate the relationship is much greater.

In therapy with a marriage where alcohol abuse or dependence has not developed, but the use of alcohol facilitates sexual behavior or expressions of intimacy, attention to the relationship would be indicated rather than prescribing treatment for alcoholism per se. In some marriages alcohol use serves as a means of coping when a relationship has declined and the couple is emotionally divorced. Such a marriage is at high risk for the development of alcoholism in either one or both partners. Alcohol becomes a coping mechanism and as such precludes the use of more constructive efforts.

A middle-aged physician resented his family's complaints about his alcohol use. He felt all problems were laid at his feet. Alcohol was a solace. It helped him cope with his wife's depression and his daughter's acting out. Although not an alcoholic or a chronic abuser, the physician's use of alcohol obviously failed to address, aid, or correct his troubled family. Eventually, the daughter's treatment and the counseling for her parents substantially improved their home situation. The physician was carefully evaluated for alcoholism and counseled regarding the risks his symptomatic drinking posed.

In addition to alcohol's impact on one's capacity for intimacy, sexual performance itself may be adversely affected. Erectile dysfunction is a well-known consequence of alcoholism, but until recently was attributed to liver disease. It is now known that abnormal liver function is not necessary for this effect. Alcohol adversely affects the production of testosterone in the testes (Van Thiel, Gavaler, Lester, & Goodman, 1975) and has been demonstrated to interfere with the pituitary hormone, gonadotropin, which stimulates the gonads to make testosterone (Van Thiel, Lester, & Vartukaitis, 1978).

Impotence may occur transiently from acute alcohol ingestion. When the blood alcohol level exceeds 50 mg./100 ml., erectile function may undergo impairment (Karacan & Hanusa, 1982). Plasma testosterone levels have been reported to drop within hours after ingestion of approximately seven drinks (*Fifth Special Report*, U.S. Department of Health and Human Services, 1983). The chronic alcoholic will commonly have decreased libido, impotence, and gonadal atrophy. Other forms of male sexual dysfunction such as premature ejaculation or retarded ejaculation do not seem to be alcohol-related (Whalley, 1978).

A controlled study evaluating alcoholic male sexual dysfunction found that 63% of alcoholics experienced sexual dysfunctions compared to 10% of controls. Erectile dysfunction and reduced libido accounted for the large majority of sexual dysfunctions. Premature ejaculation occurred with the same frequency in the alcoholic males and the controls

(10%). Retarded ejaculation was more common in the alcoholic males, but may have been related to the use of disulfiram (Jensen, 1984).

Sexual behavior of female alcoholics clusters around two extremes: promiscuity or relatively few contacts and little interest (Levine, 1955). Reduced or absent menstruation is also common, as is loss of secondary sex characteristics such as breast tissue and pelvic fat accumulation. Women who have died of cirrhosis show ovarian atrophy even when under 40 years of age (*Fifth Special Report*, U.S. Department of Health and Human Services, 1983). A national survey of drinking and reproductive dysfunction among women found a strong association between dysmenorrhea, heavy menstrual flow, and premenstrual discomfort as drinking levels increased. Lifetime rates of obstetric disorders were significantly elevated for miscarriage, stillbirth, prematurity, infertility, and birth defects. These disorders were associated with drinking levels of six or more drinks a day, three to five times a week. Causality was not determined in this study, and it remains to be determined whether the drinking preceded or was a consequence of the reproductive dysfunction (Wilsnack, Klassen, & Wilsnack, 1984). In a controlled study of 30 alcoholic women (ages 30–45), orgasmic dysfunction and reduced libido occurred at virtually the same frequency (20%) as in controls (23%) (Jensen, 1984).

PSYCHOPATHOLOGY OF OTHER MEMBERS

Wife

The earliest formulations of the alcoholic marriage were derived from psychoanalytically oriented clinical observations. Dominating the literature was the concept that the wife's psychopathology had been present prior to marriage (Bailey, 1961). The wife of the alcoholic was often described as being "dependent." Frustrated oral needs (Lewis, 1954), resentment (Price, 1945), and decompensation of the wife when the alcoholic husband failed to meet her strong dependency needs (Bullock & Mudd, 1959) characterized the initial formulations. These formulations were gradually expanded and led to the classic description of the dominant, hostile-to-men wife who needs a sick, inadequate dependent husband to cover her own inadequacies. The husband's drinking served the wife's masochistic needs (Bergler, 1946); served to cover up the wife's sexual frigidity and fear of sex (as the alcoholic husband was impotent and repulsive); and he served as a foil upon whom she could unconsciously project her own inadequacies (Futterman, 1953).

Whalen (1953) characterized four types of alcoholic wives: the "suffering," the "controlling," the "punitive," and the "wavering." Although her work continues in the tradition of the subjectively derived clinical impression characteristic of studies on the alcoholic marriage in the 1940s and 1950s, it has the merit of recognizing a diversity of personality styles in wives of alcoholics.

Implicit in each of these formulations are the assumptions that (a) women choose alcoholic husbands to meet unconscious needs of their own; and (b) the wife would decompensate if the husband stopped drinking (Futterman, 1953; MacDonald, 1956). These assumptions have been referred to as the "disturbed personality hypothesis" and the "decompensation hypothesis" (Paolino & McCrady, 1977). Neither hypothesis has been supported by objective and better-controlled studies.

The disturbed personality hypothesis. A controlled study by Corder, Hendricks, and Corder (1964) comparing 43 Al-Anon wives with 30 women who were not married to alcoholics found both groups to be within the normal range of each MMPI scale. Similarly, Paige, LaPointe, and Krueger (1971) obtained MMPI data from 25 wives of alcoholics. Scores fell within the normal range (T-scores under 70) on the regular scales. Rae and Forbes (1966) found the group MMPI profile of 26 wives of alcoholics not to be pathologically elevated. Kogan, Fordyce, and Jackson (1963) reported that scales derived from MMPI data distinguished wives of actively drinking alcoholics who sought help from community agencies from a control group of wives without an alcoholic husband. On Welsh's Anxiety Index (1952), on 2 of 3 of Modlin's (1947) measures of personality impairment, and on the Psychotic Triad of Gough (1947) the wives of the alcoholics showed significantly greater impairment. However, 50% of the wives of alcoholics in the Kogan et al. (1963) study had normal scores on the Modlin measures and had normal or questionable scores on the Psychotic Triad. It is important to keep in mind that this study included only wives whose husbands were still drinking.

Paolino et al. (1976) used 3 of the 5 scales of the Psychological Screening Inventory (Lanyon, 1970) as a measure of psychopathology. Forty spouses of alcoholics were contrasted with the normative data established for the Inventory. Both male (N = 15) and female (N = 35) spouses scored significantly higher on a scale of defensiveness, but did not differ from the normative sample on scales of alienation and discomfort. As these data were obtained during the first 3 weeks of the alcoholic's hospitalization, the authors (Paolino et al., 1976) speculated that the results may reflect the commonly observed guilt and defensiveness seen in families of hospitalized patients.

At the very least, these studies demonstrated variable personality functioning among the wives of alcoholics, thus weakening the earlier clinical stereotypes of "domineering" or "dependent" wives. It has become apparent that the wife of an alcoholic is not necessarily the bearer of preexisting psychopathology.

The decompensation hypothesis. The same trend is noted regarding the decompensation of the spouse when the alcoholic ceases drinking. Reports of marked anxiety (Igersheimer, 1959; Mitchell & Mudd, 1957), somatic disorders (Kalashian, 1959), obesity (Paolino & McCrady, 1977), and severe emotional decompensation (Kohl, 1962; MacDonald, 1956) have been reported in spouses after the alcoholic has stopped drinking. Rae (1972), in a carefully done follow-up study, reported that only 4 of 58 wives of alcoholics required hospitalization for serious depressive illness within 6 months after their husbands stopped drinking.

Disturbance in the wife, whether severe or mild, often has been assumed to be the result of cessation of the husband's drinking. However, methodologic flaws such as lack of controls, unavailability of epidemiologic data for comparison, unsystematic means of data collection, and uncertainty of the temporal relationship between onset of the spouse's symptoms and change in the alcoholic's drinking severely weaken the foundation of the decompensation hypothesis.

Other studies, conducted more systematically, provide data that tend to modify or refute the decompensation hypothesis. Bailey, Haberman, and Alksne (1962), in a well-conducted study, found that 65% of wives living with drinking alcoholics reported a high level of psychophysiologic symptoms. The wives of abstinent alcoholics (43%) reported a similar level of symptoms, as compared with 35% of wives in a representative sample of married women. Similarly, Kogan et al. (1963) found that, on three measures of personality disturbance, wives of inactive alcoholics were midway between wives of active alcoholics and wives of nonalcoholics. Haberman (1964), using valid and reliable instruments, reported that 85% of wives showed fewer symptoms when their husbands were abstinent. More recently, Saxon et al. (1983) found a significant relationship between decrease in drinking and both improved sexual functioning and diminishing family conflict in alcoholic marriages evaluated an average of 13 months following hospital treatment of the alcoholic.

A major difficulty with the decompensation hypothesis is the assumption that changes in the wife's mental state coincident with a decrease or cessation of drinking in the alcoholic husband reflect the wife's "need" for a continuous pathological process in her spouse. It is certainly plausible and, in fact, commonly observed that the pathological drinking and behavior of the alcoholic "stresses" the spouse to a point that symptoms develop (Jackson, 1954). The breakthrough of symptoms in the nondrinking spouse may provoke her to seek help for herself or her alcoholic husband. In either case, outside influence is brought to bear.

This influence may lead to creation of the crisis so often necessary before an alcoholic will accept treatment. Thus, the "decompensation" noted in the spouse may be secondary to the stress of living with an alcoholic and may trigger the intervention process that, in turn, can result in a change in the alcoholic's behavior (less drinking). This, of course, has profoundly different implications from the view that a change in drinking (less drinking) leads to spouse decompensation.

The decompensation described in many studies has been assumed to follow from the husband's successful treatment. Three factors other than the need for a "sick" spouse could account for the same behavior: (a) the stress of divorce; (b) the stress associated with the risk of reinvolvement; and (c) the phenomenon of assortative mating.

Divorce. Rae (1972) found that serious psychiatric sequelae (most often of a depressive nature) in the wives of alcoholics were significantly influenced by the issue of divorce. The incidence of disturbance was significantly less in wives of alcoholics with intact marriages at time of follow-up than in wives with an impending or actual divorce. Rae concluded that psychiatric disturbance was more likely to be a function of the stress of divorce rather than a direct function of alcoholism treatment.

Risk of reinvolvement. It may be difficult to appreciate the fear, anxiety, tension, and apprehension of the spouse during the early months of the recovering alcoholic's sobriety. Apprehension about further drinking greets each moment of renewed hope. The relief engendered when the alcoholic enters a treatment program and the "time-out" provided by his or her safe absence from home is all too soon succeeded by the return to the household of the recovering alcoholic. The family may have been through this before and have become skeptical or, more likely, cynical. Coldness, indifference, and aloofness may greet the alcoholic's return to sobriety.

Usually the wife finds it difficult to return control of certain household functions. To consult with her husband, to trust his judgment, and to develop realistic rather than idealistic expectations of the spouse's sober personality are psychological and behavioral chores put upon an often beleaguered spouse. Further, the children may resent the resumption of authority on the part of the recovering parent, or the nonalcoholic spouse may resent the children's return of affection and attention toward the previously psychologically absent alcoholic parent.

Just as divorce has been shown to be associated with symptomatology in the spouse, so may the ambivalence associated with renegotiation of the marital relationship induce symptoms. The spouse, now freed from the daily distracting crises associated with active alcoholism, reflects on the abuse, the lost time, and the wasted opportunities. The recovering husband or wife seems strong enough to endure and sufficiently attentive to perceive the recriminations accumulated over the years. Previously these recriminations may have fallen on drunken deafness or been suppressed out of fear of retaliation. But now the spouse is sober and rational. An explanation may be angrily demanded. The equanimity which the recovering alcoholic must learn in the face of such demands may only aggravate the spouse further.

The spouse does not know if it is "safe" to reinvest emotionally in the marriage. By necessity, he or she may have achieved a greater sense of autonomy during the years of drinking than existed earlier in the marriage. Reestablishment of the marriage may represent an unwanted regression to earlier states of dependency.

Finally, resentment of the sober spouse's newly found peace of mind and beginning success may add to the guilt and confusion of the period. Attention is directed toward the marvelous gains and renewed confidence of the recovering alcoholic. The spouse is given little credit for any of these successes, and her or his ordeals during the years of drinking are little thought of by others (and certainly are not appropriate to the moment). The ambivalence associated with the decision to reinvest in the marriage may provide sufficient stress to produce the symptomatology earlier attributed to decompensation.

Assortative mating. A third potential explanation for the "decompensation" hypothesis is that of assortative mating. Husband-wife similarity is substantial for variables such as race, social class, age, religion, education, interests, and attitudes; but less so for personality variables (Orford, 1975). The psychiatric literature, however, provides evidence of concordance for mental disorders in husband-wife pairs at a rate greater than that expected by chance (Orford, 1975). Penrose (1944) found that the frequency of both a husband and wife's being admitted for psychiatric treatment in Ontario within the same year exceeded by 9 times the expected level. A Danish study (Nielsen, 1964) found a 40% increase in husband-wife referrals for psychiatric services, with approximately a 50% diagnostic concordance. Nielsen (1964) further documented that husband and wife could not necessarily be considered to "infect" one another as in *folie a deux*, since most cases of *folie a deux* occur among nonmarried pairs, particularly sisters. Nor was there evidence that the illness in one partner was a reaction to the breakdown in the other. Common environment and common sources of anxiety did not seem to be explanations for the concordance rates.

More recently, Rimmer and Winokur (1972) provided data supporting assortative mating in alcoholics. Their data indicate that the majority of alcoholics come from disturbed families and tend to marry someone with a disturbed family background. The family history of both the alcoholics and the spouses had higher rates of alcoholism and suicide than would be expected in a normal population. Lower socioeconomic status alcoholic women marry alcoholic men one third to one half the time, a rate in excess of the approximately 10% male alcoholic population (Lisansky, 1957). The chances of having an alcoholic spouse increase with the number of remarriages (Schuckit & Morrissey, 1976).

The stress theory. An alternative to the disturbed personality and decompensation theories is the "stress theory," first advocated by Jackson (1954). The commonly observed somatic, anxious, and depressive symptoms are viewed as a consequence of the recurrent crises and chronic stresses that characterize the alcoholic marriage. Over a 3-year period Jackson studied the wives of alcoholics who attended Al-Anon as well as wives of hospitalized alcoholics. The data are limited because only wives seeking help were studied and only the wives' perceptions recorded. Extensive observations led her to the conclusion that the behavior of wives was an attempt to meet a crisis and regain stability and was largely a function of changing patterns of interaction. Personality types or presence of personality disturbance shaped individual responses but did not obscure a characteristic familial progression (Table 6-1).

Although studies by Lemert (1960) and James and Goldman (1971) failed to confirm the specific stages outlined by Jackson (1954), their work lent credence to the concept that the spouse's behavior changes as a function of the alcoholic's drinking. A variety of coping styles may emerge; all wives used more than one style; and the more severe the alcoholic's problems the greater the variety of coping styles (James & Goldman, 1971; Orford et al., 1975). Withdrawal (arguments about drinking, avoidance of sex) and protection (throwing away bottles) were nearly universal (James & Goldman, 1971).

Orford (1975) writes cogently on the dangers of focusing only on the alcoholism in the alcoholic marriage. He argues that marriages stressed by alcoholism should not be construed as unique. Changes in sexual behavior, anxiety, role reversal, social isolation, and other features of the alcoholic marriage may be manifested in a variety of crises, including hospitalization for mental illness, periods of unemployment, war separation, and bereavement. Orford's critique has merit, but at the clinical level it has been necessary to emphasize the special contribution of alcoholism to marital dysfunctioning, in part, to counter the commonly observed denial of alcoholism by either patient or therapist (Nace, DePhoure, Goldberg et al., 1982). Further, the identification of a marital

TABLE 6-1
Stages of Adjustment to Alcoholism*

1. Attempts to Deny Problem: need to create illusion of "perfect marriage"; wife feels she may be overreacting; friends are reassuring.
2. Attempts to Eliminate the Problem: family withdraws from social contacts and relatives; wife throws away the bottles; behavior is now organized around the drinking.
3. Disorganization: wife gives up trying to control drinking; she questions her normality; children increasingly disturbed.
4. Attempt to Reorganize in Spite of Problems: spouse assumes control of family; alcoholic left with no familial role.
5. Efforts to Escape Problem: spouse separates with children, needs considerable confidence to take this step; marriage may terminate at this point.
6. Reorganization of Part of the Family: spouse and children reorganize themselves as a family.
7. Recovery and Reorganization of the Whole Family: alcoholic is now sober; spouse and alcoholic renegotiate family roles; acceptance of sober personality undertaken.

*Reprinted by permission, from *Quarterly Journal of Studies on Alcohol*, Vol. 15, pp. 562–586, 1954. Copyright by Journal of Studies on Alcohol, Inc., Rutgers Center of Alcohol Studies, New Brunswick, NJ 08903.

partner as "alcoholic" does not imply a one-sided view or assignment of blame. When the term "alcoholic" is properly understood by patient and therapist it is not a form of approbation but a signal for a course of constructive action.

Husband

The literature on husbands of alcoholics is remarkably sparse. The literature is conflicting regarding age differences, with some studies finding the husbands to be considerably older than their alcoholic wives, and others finding no significant age differences (Busch, Kormendy, & Feuerlein, 1973). Middle-class female alcoholics seem to have husbands more amenable to cooperating with research efforts. In studies using the Freiburg Personality Inventory (Busch et al., 1973) and the Interpersonal Perception Technique (Rand, Kulchan, & Roblins, 1982), male partners were seen to have a less masculine and a more feminine self-assessment.

Rimmer (1974), in an interview study of 25 husbands of alcoholics, found 8 to have a depressive disorder, 5 to be alcoholic, 1 a sociopath, and 1 an "undiagnosed" psychiatric condition. Two other husbands were described as "excessive drinkers," and 2 of the husbands with a psychiatric diagnosis were also alcoholic. Thus, 9 of 25 husbands had serious alcohol problems. Two of the alcoholic husbands were alcoholic before the development of alcoholism in their wives, and 3 husbands developed alcoholism at about the same time as their wives.

As more women alcoholics are identified in our society this neglected area of marital and alcohol studies should be developed further.

Children

As described earlier, children of alcoholics may be affected even prior to birth by defects resulting from the fetal alcohol syndrome. Far more common are the effects following birth.

Currently there are about 600,000 cases of child abuse and neglect reported yearly, and underreporting, especially of sexual abuse, is a certainty. More reliable data on child abuse are likely since the establishment of mandatory reporting laws. It is estimated that one out of three adult perpetrators had been drinking prior to an abusive incident and that about 17% of abuse cases involved alcoholism (*Fifth Special Report*, U.S. Department of Health and Human Services, 1983).

Minimal brain dysfunction (MBD) in children has been associated with alcoholism. Children who exhibit symptoms of hyperactivity have been found on follow-up to be drinking more as teen-agers than their peer group (Blouin, Bornstein, & Trites, 1978; Mendelson, Johnson, & Stewart, 1971).

A history of hyperactive symptoms in childhood has been reported for some groups of alcoholics. Tarter et al. (1977) found that the "primary" alcoholics (those with an early history of severe alcoholism) reported more symptoms characteristic of MBD and hyperactivity occurring before age 12 than did "secondary" alcoholics, psychiatric controls, or normal controls. Similarly, Goodwin et al. (1975) found that alcoholics who had been reared away from their biologic parents reported more symptoms of hyperactivity than controls. Along the same lines, family studies of hyperactive children have found a strong association between hyperactivity and parental alcoholism (Cantwell, 1972). The implication from these studies is that alcoholism and hyperactivity share a common genetic basis with hyperactivity serving as a predisposing factor for later alcoholism. The latter association must be considered hypothetical at this time because much of the data has been obtained from the retrospective reports of alcoholic patients (Tarter et al., 1977).

At the same time, other studies have not supported the above association. For example, Vaillant (1983b) found a correlation of only .10 between a measure of childhood hyperactivity and future alcoholism. A study from a child psychiatry private practice (Morrison, 1980) compared the parents (N = 140) of hyperactive children with the parents (N = 91) of nonhyperactive child psychiatric patients. Alcoholism was found to exist in 14% of the mothers and 22% of the fathers of hyperactive children. In the psychiatric control group 9% of the mothers and 16% of the fathers were alcoholics. This difference was not statistically significant, but the percentages for alcoholism in the parents of both groups exceeded that of the general population.

More common than the syndromes of birth defect or hyperactivity is the emotional gauntlet run by the children in an alcoholic's home. Often the victim of the alcoholic's projections, the child absorbs guilt, shame, and self-loathing, unshielded by the adult ego's capacity for observation and differentiation. Unpredictability and inconsistency on the part of the alcoholic parent curb the capacity for trust. Internalization of stable, enduring values is delayed, and the endurance to maintain standards and work toward goals is severely compromised. The parental model(s) transmit destructive ways of gaining attention and faulty means of problem solving. Often torn between two parents, the child suffers a lack of emotional support, yet assumes a premature role of responsibility for family stability.

There are no specific diagnostic outcomes predictable from this experience, although depression may occur more frequently in daughters of alcoholic parents and the risk of alcoholism is increased for sons and possibly for daughters as well (Winokur, 1979).

The concern for children growing up in a home where one or both parents are alcoholic has prompted the consideration that each family member has a "disease" referred to as "codependency." This concept enjoys a certain popular appeal as it attempts to characterize and caricature the different coping styles members of an alcoholic family may acquire, for example, "scapegoat" and "family hero" (Wegscheider, 1983).

More serious evaluations of the children of alcoholics suggest similarities between "codependency" and personality disorders as described in DSM-III-R. The spouse or child of the alcoholic, that is the codependent, is believed to develop inflexible, maladaptive patterns of behavior which interfere with personal relationships and cause significant subjective distress. Cermak (1984) describes similarities between the dynamics of codependency and DSM-III categories of Dependent Personality Disorder and Post-traumatic Stress Disorder, but argues that adult children of alcoholics require a new diagnostic code of "codependency" in order to emphasize the dynamic similarity to the functioning alcoholic. That the child of an alcoholic grows up in a home with adults who exhibit immature mechanisms of defense, such as acting-out, projection, passive-aggressiveness, and denial, is a certainty. Less certain is the proposition that either the child or the spouse of an alcoholic has a unique syndrome not adequately conceptualized by current diagnostic classifications.

The concept of codependency assumes a common experience among children who live close to an alcoholic, but, in fact, a variety of variables must be considered when evaluating the impact of parental alcoholism on a child. A review of the literature on the children of alcoholics identifies several areas that are usually overlooked when discussing the familial impact of alcoholism (Wilson & Orford, 1978).

First, the pattern of drinking must be considered. Does the parent drink at home or away from home? A mother who begins drinking in the late afternoon may adequately carry out dinner time duties and pass out later in the evening. The impact of such a pattern may differ from that of the father who drinks outside the house, but comes home drunk, belligerent, and aggressive. Fear of the latter and concern over the former are common responses.

Second, parental separation and conflict are common in the alcoholic marriage and have a pronounced impact beyond the drinking which causes it. One study (Cork, 1969) reported that 98 out of 115 children from alcoholic families said "parental fighting and quarreling" was their main concern. Marital conflict prompts some children to intervene or to adopt a placating role. Others respond largely by withdrawal, staying in their rooms or avoiding home as much as possible.

Third, has violence occurred? Violence affects children whether they are the direct recipients or not. In a study of 11 families (Wilson & Orford, 1978), 4 families reported violence toward children, 2 toward property, and 2 others reported aggressive arguments with threats of violence. Developmental disorders have been reported as occurring more commonly in boys with a violent alcoholic father (Keane & Roche, 1974).

Fourth, there is no simple characteristic parent-child relationship in the alcoholic family. Some children are angry only when the parent is drinking, but feel affectionate during periods of sobriety. Others remain detached or sullen regardless of the parent's condition. Commonly, children take on increased responsibilities to compensate for the alcoholic's nonfunctioning.

Age and gender of the child play a major role in the nature of the relationship. Older children may distance themselves from the alcoholic parent by joining peer groups. Coalitions with the nonalcoholic parent are common, especially when the father is alcoholic. The impact of alcoholism on a 6-year-old born into an alcoholic family would most likely be different from the impact on a 16-year-old where alcoholism in the parent is of recent onset.

Fifth, has parental alcoholism interfered with the child's ability to form friendships? Typically, children of alcoholics feel restricted in having friends to their home because of the potential embarrassment. The visibility or public awareness of the alcoholic parent's drinking may be a major factor determining "stigmatization" of the child. Most children try to keep their parents' drinking problem a secret from peers and school personnel.

Finally, the impact of extended family should be considered. Wilson and Orford (1978) describe several families where uncles or stepbrothers played vital fatherly roles in the lives of children from alcoholic families. Having an extended family to turn to, to live with, or to confide in may make the difference between depression, chronic anxiety, school failure, delinquency, or the host of other problems children of alcoholics may encounter.

These distinctions have received very little attention in the study of children of alcoholics. In the meantime, the National Association of Children of Alcoholics (NACoA) was founded to serve as a resource for children of alcoholics (COA's). NACoA is devoted to the concept that COA's have unique problems. Evidence of this phenomenon is the growth of Al-Anon groups specific for COA's from 14 in 1982 to 194 by the end of 1983 (Cermak, 1984). Whether a diagnostic entity of "codependency" will be validated by research and whether it is unique to the children of alcoholics remain highly uncertain. Nevertheless, the problems of COA's are real for many, and the formation of groups such as NACoA highlight the increasing concern for "the other victims of alcoholism" and the potential adjustment problems they experience.

Family Dynamics

Resulting from alcoholism. Evaluation, education, and counseling of the alcoholic's family begin with an understanding of certain dynamics that may advance morbidity and mortality if not dealt with. These dynamics can hinder a constructive response to the crisis of alcoholism, but are not necessarily "needed" by the family unit as a homeostatic mechanism. They derive from alcoholism and differ from the psychodynamics of the family unit during the prealcoholic stages of family life. With recovery of the alcoholic member and restoration of a functional family unit, these specific dynamics have little or no continuing impact.

The first to be considered is the stigma associated with alcoholism. Few other family crises (e.g., other illnesses, death, divorce) are burdened with the stigma that accompanies alcoholism. Efforts to contain and disguise the alcoholism drain the family's emotional resources. The need to disguise the source of stress adds to the weight already being borne by the dysfunctional family unit and simultaneously isolates the family from external support systems. Often the denial of alcoholism by the family is a defense against the stigmatizing aspects of this disease.

The spouse needs to refuse to believe it is happening. The stigma of alcoholism fosters a family response of increasing *social* isolation, in contrast to the emotional isolation described next.

The second dynamic is emotional withdrawal. Repeated disappointments over the alcoholic's inability to adhere to promises to change yield waves of despair and anger. The family often responds as if the person had died, but is deprived of the emotional cleansing provided by the finality of death. Involvement is avoided. Hope must not rise again, lest the inevitable disappointment be reexperienced. The result is a further distancing of the alcoholic from potential sources of intervention and support.

Third, guilt and shame. Families experience guilt and shame under many circumstances and in the face of illnesses other than alcoholism. Alcoholism, however, shapes the family experience of guilt and shame in three characteristic ways: First, many spouses who have had an alcoholic parent struggle to resolve (unconsciously) that relationship within the context of their marriage. Inevitably, such an effort rekindles and deepens a sense of earlier failure and disappointment. Second, independent of the above, it is characteristic of family members to attempt to "rescue," control, or prevent the drinking of the alcoholic, a second contribution to failure. Finally, the alcoholic frequently displaces the blame for his plight onto the spouse or other family members. The family is led to believe that they caused the problem. All too often they accept the blame, at least in part, and their guilt intensifies.

Fourth, family members (and the alcoholic) commonly misinterpret symptoms of the disease for consciously determined value choices. The constructs of psychological primacy and craving as discussed in Chapter 5 are two manifestations of alcoholism that confuse the family and add to the discord and stress. In regard to psychological primacy, it is important for the family really to understand that while the alcoholic member is drinking, considerations other than procurement of alcohol and the attendant relief upon consumption are secondary. Typically family members feel devalued and become angry and rejecting. When they understand that the alcoholic member's behavior is governed by his addiction rather than by his values, they may be able to minimize hostile responses.

The alcoholic continues to experience a desire for alcohol long after drinking has ceased. Craving can occur when the alcoholic is reexposed to stimuli associated with alcohol use. If the family is aware of the alcoholic's prolonged struggle with the urge to drink, they may more readily play a role supportive of sobriety. Failure to appreciate the inevitability of desires to drink may lead to accusations, disappointments, and despair.

Contributing to alcoholism. This chapter has emphasized the impact of alcoholism on marital and family functioning. The converse must be considered; family or marital dynamics may evoke or maintain alcoholism. As indicated in Chapter 1, no single factor can be considered etiologic for alcoholism, but marital or family conflict may precipitate the process in the family member who is genetically or developmentally vulnerable to develop alcoholism. Common examples include the "empty nest syndrome," wherein one (usually a woman, but males may also be affected) experiences a loss of role and meaning when the children have grown and left home. The marital relationship may have grown distant, but not invariably so. Self-doubt, anxiety, or depression lead to the onset of pathological drinking. In other instances, a wife drinks to assuage emotional conflict or the emotional void of a troubled marriage. By illustration, Mrs. S. continued with her career after her husband retired, but resented the combination of his leisure time and his continuing dominant role. His retirement led to their being together considerably more than when both were working, and the conflict was exacerbated. She developed a dual dependence on diazepam and alcohol. Eventually a job-related crisis led to treatment. In another example, a woman with several young children felt bored and resentful about staying home. When she resumed her career her husband ignored the stress which a dual role provided and offered neither emotional support nor the assistance of domestic help. The wife's alcohol abuse led to an array of medical symptoms and gained the attention from a previously distant spouse.

Such examples are straightforward and are often seen clinically. More complicated is the family situation where pathological use of alcohol serves a "purpose" for the family and, as such, provides a homeostatic function. A family systems view, as put forth by Bowen (1978), Shapiro (1977), and Steinglass, Weiner, and Mendelson (1971), postulates that alcoholic drinking produces homeostasis in the family and establishes patterns of interaction which are complementary and circular. It is further postulated that the family system resists a change in the status quo (i.e., in the pathological drinking and its effect on the family) as a precaution against the stress of disrupting a presumed state of equilibrium. This viewpoint is extended to the conclusion that a modification in the family relationship system will alleviate the alcoholic drinking.

An alcoholic's drinking pattern may unconsciously serve an adaptive function for some families, but these are in the minority. The "chaotic family" as described by Lewis (1986) may prove to be the type of family structure in which alcoholism serves a homeostatic function. In the chaotic family pathological attachment serves to ward off a perceived hostile world. Pathological alcohol use may be a means for avoiding separation and individuation.

Increasingly sophisticated research on families is enhancing our understanding of the reciprocal relationships between family functioning and pathological drinking. For example, Steinglass (1981), in a study conducted in the homes of alcoholics' families, found that families in a "dry" phase were characterized by flexibility in behavior. When a family entered a "wet" phase (that is, the alcoholic member had resumed drinking), patterns of behavior became increasingly rigid. Distance among members clearly was influenced by the presence or absence of alcoholic drinking. Steinglass hypothesizes that the shift toward increased rigidity of family behavior during "wet" phases is in the interest of maintaining family stability in the face of an actively drinking alcoholic member. This interpretation is quite different from assuming that the drinking itself stabilizes the family unit.

Taking a different tack, Wolin et al. (1980) report data that demonstrate the generational transmission of alcoholism is strongly influenced by the stability of family rituals. If the drinking of an alcoholic parent disrupted such family rituals as dinner time, holidays, and vacations, the "transmission" of alcoholism to the children was more likely than in families where parental drinking did not alter the family's rituals. The most consistent finding in this preliminary study was the relationship between holiday functions and intergenerational transmission. Holidays had remained intact in the large majority of families where alcoholism was not passed on. The converse was true for families with intergenerational alcoholism.

CONCLUSION

Alcohol abuse and alcoholism contribute to many of today's social problems. No institution in our society bears a greater brunt of these pathological conditions than the family. In a 1982 Gallup survey, one of three families reported problems secondary to alcohol use (Gallup, 1982). Sophisticated statistical analyses detail alcohol's economic costs to society, and medical technology provides details of the pathophysiology of alcoholism at the molecular level. In contrast, our understanding of the impact of alcoholism on the family is primitive. The family often "transmits" the disease through some undetermined combination of genetic and psychosocial factors. The family is then left to recoil from the insults of premature death, divorce, abuse, and the emotional burden of stigmatization. With even rudimentary understanding of the effect of alcoholism on the functioning of family members, it should be apparent that treatment planning for the alcoholic patient needs to include family participation. Treatment priorities for the family and steps to successful involvement of the family will be described in Chapter 11.

CHAPTER 7

Beginning Treatment

Treatment begins with the physician's preparations: First, awareness and adoption of functional attitudes, such as curiosity, concern, flexibility, persistence, and optimism, as well as avoidance of dysfunctional attitudes, such as indifference, anger, rigidity, pessimism, and resignation; and secondly, understanding the disease of alcoholism.

Once one is so prepared, it becomes possible to assume either of two styles: 1) collaboration within the context of the doctor-patient relationship; or 2) a particularly challenging form of confrontation. Either of these styles allows the physician to assist the alcoholic patient in accepting treatment for alcoholism, but they are distinctly different. The former technique is most familiar to practicing psychiatrists; the latter is usually used by a counselor, often a recovered alcoholic, who instructs or coaches families or employers on the process as used in dealing with alcoholics. There is no reason a psychiatrist or other physician could not undertake the procedures, but one needs to work with a counselor or other professional skilled in this technique before attempting it. There are excellent films available which demonstrate the specialized technique of confrontation (for example, "I'll Quit Tomorrow," produced by the Johnson Institute, 510 First Avenue North, Minneapolis, MN 55403).

Which approach a physician chooses may be determined to a great extent by personal comfort and interest. Aside from these considerations, the circumstances of the patient shape the choice. Since confrontation depends in large part on the threat of a loss to the patient if treatment is refused—for example, job loss or divorce—this technique is impractical in situations where a specific reprisal from the environment will not be forthcoming or is unnecessary. The patient has to have something to lose, and the significant others in the patient's life must be willing and able to effect the loss. The spouse or other family members should not threaten separation or divorce unless they are prepared to follow through. When angry and frustrated, families may talk about leaving, but usually they are not emotionally prepared to do so. Exploration of their situations and their feelings with a therapist is recommended. Among the issues to be faced is the acceptance of the possibility that separation from the alcoholic member may not change his or her drinking behavior. Family members must see any separation as an attempt to improve their own lives and not as manipulation to change the alcoholic. Those close to the alcoholic are advised to seek help for *themselves*, not just for the alcoholic family member.

For the physician to try to establish a therapeutic relationship may prove futile with the patient who has no "problem," needs "no help," and is generally defiant or blocked by denial. Figure 7-1 is a rough approximation of when one approach is better applied than the other.

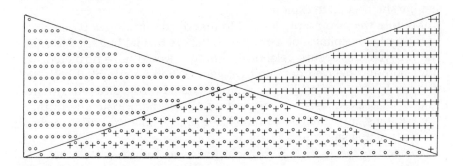

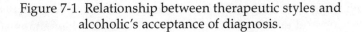

Confrontive   Collaborative

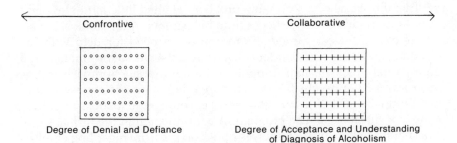

Degree of Denial and Defiance   Degree of Acceptance and Understanding
                                              of Diagnosis of Alcoholism

Figure 7-1. Relationship between therapeutic styles and alcoholic's acceptance of diagnosis.

The patient who has largely accepted the fact of his or her alcohol dependence and a need for help will be served best by a therapeutic approach designed to establish participation in additional specific alcoholism treatment programs. The defiant, denying patient may require and be best served by an approach in which confrontation of behavior is put forth in an effective manner.

Often one has to start with confrontation. For example, a 31-year-old married woman sought treatment for addiction to propoxyphene and codeine. Alcohol abuse was also part of the history. She wanted to be hospitalized for detoxification, but delayed obtaining help from her in-laws who were willing to care for her young child. She continually sought additional medication, threatening to obtain scripts for larger amounts from other doctors until help arrived. I prescribed small amounts of a benzodiazepine on two separate occasions and then refused further prescriptions. She was angry, but did enter a hospital for detoxification 36 hours later, having at last made arrangements for her in-laws to assist. She then followed up with an intensive partial hospitalization program for alcoholism and drug treatment. She remained angry at me, but found another psychiatrist to help her with the many areas of her life she needed to explore.

My role was necessarily limited to that of administrative psychiatrist in the partial hospitalization program. I believe that if I had tried to work out a psychotherapeutic relationship only, I would have furthered her addiction and delayed definite treatment. When I confronted both her and her husband about her continued demand for medications (he frequently made requests for her) and refused to participate any further, the patient's anger helped to mobilize her to follow the earlier recommendation that she enter a hospital.

In another instance, a 27-year-old musician addicted to alcohol and marijuana was uncertain he had a problem or needed any help. He presented with a complaint of depression. He had lost a job as well as a girlfriend because of his drinking problem. He had little left to lose and was supported by weekly checks from his parents. After about six interviews over a 5-week period, he recognized a need for help with his drinking and drug abuse. It took an additional 4 weeks for him to enroll in a partial hospitalization program. The appropriate approach in this case was for the psychiatrist to develop a therapeutic relationship and, within the context of that relationship, encourage the patient to participate in a substance abuse program. A confrontation in the formal sense was not feasible as the patient was under no pressure regarding employment or family involvement.

Commonly, the therapist will need to shift back and forth between a confronting and an empathic mode. The therapist's dilemma is always the uncertainty as to "where to be." This dilemma can be managed, in part, by addressing affective issues empathically. At the same time, the therapist must be prepared to use confrontation when faced with behavior which involves drinking or which seems to be leading to drinking. For example, the therapist can empathize with the grief of a woman recently widowed. Yet, if the widow is alcoholic, empathy cannot be allowed to communicate permission for a return to pathological drinking. Confrontation regarding potential consequences of alcohol use may be necessary. The futility of attempting to reach a resolution of loss by drinking can be introduced into the therapy.

The inclusion of group therapy in the treatment plan provides another means for addressing the dilemma of the need for both empathy and confrontation. A group often can be more confronting than an individual therapist without rupturing the therapeutic alliance since usually within any group can be found a blend of support and confrontation.

At times the therapist may do best to share his or her dilemma with the patient. For example, the therapist can acknowledge the pain and conflict a patient currently presents. Yet, he or she can also explain to the patient the concern about possible use of alcohol. By doing so the therapist is communicating a need to think beyond the immediate crisis of the patient and is conveying hope by introducing an interest in the future.

Confrontations may range from the "routine" to the "heroic" (Corwin, 1973). With alcoholic patients, routine confrontations are in the nature of questioning the patient about why AA meetings are no longer being attended or why an Antabuse prescription has not been filled. In heroic confrontations (reserved for those situations which present an emergency), the therapist is willing to risk his or her relationship with the patient. The patient must make some change, or the therapist will not continue the relationship. An example is found in a male alcoholic who I had learned was physically abusing his wife. Therapy sessions, both group and individual, did not lead to a revelation of the behavior, nor to the drinking with which it was related. My concern was presented directly to the patient. I said that I did not wish to participate in a therapy that seemed to be largely a sham. The patient agreed to include his wife in our sessions and to intensify his efforts to maintain abstinence.

Lewis has emphasized that the timing and manner of a confrontation are of paramount importance (Lewis, 1978). A crisis or a therapeutic stalemate often determines the timing. The manner and range of a confrontation must take into consideration the unique concerns of each individual as well as his or her personality structure. The most common error is to make a heroic confrontation before a working relationship is established or without appreciation of the patient's psychopathology.

The following vignettes are examples of a *heroic* approach that pushed the patients away from treatment instead of creating an alliance and fostering their acceptance of help.

An alcoholic male, employed by a state agency, was confronted by the employer as a part of the agency's employee assistance program. The patient was quickly admitted to an alcohol program. It soon became apparent that he was paranoid and delusional. He refused to sleep in his room or take medication. Within 72 hours he signed out against medical advice and lost his job. A more careful and thorough preparation of the patient for treatment may have enabled the patient to accept help and possibly preserve his job.

A 48-year-old divorced woman consulted the medical director of a general hospital substance abuse unit. A mixture of alcohol abuse and benzodiazepines was impairing her ability to work. In addition, she was depressed, anxious, and distraught over a recent 50-pound weight gain. The physician bombarded her with a description of her "addictive behavior" and viewed her symptoms as manipulative. Her fear of losing her job and the social stigma of treatment were not appreciated. She felt misunderstood and "bad." Months later she sought other sources of help and agreed to a psychiatric evaluation. She became fully cooperative in discontinuing prior medications, abstaining from alcohol, and in accepting a brief hospitalization.

In other words, an understanding of and sensitivity to each patient's unique circumstances are essential. Social and personal concerns, as well as the ego strengths of the individual, require assessment. As these aspects are factored into therapeutic planning, the confrontation can proceed safely and effectively.

The two approaches are not mutually exclusive. To be effective confrontation must communicate concern and a genuine interest in the patient's welfare. As Tiebout (1963), one of the first psychiatrists to work extensively with alcoholic patients, puts it, "My ability to be of help has improved from zero. I find patients welcome my firmness" (p. 3).

The rest of this chapter describes the collaborative doctor-patient relationship and the role of confrontation as applied to alcoholism. Although these topics are dichotomized, the reader will appreciate that a subtle blending of the two may occur.

COLLABORATION WITHIN THE DOCTOR-PATIENT RELATIONSHIP

In the treatment of alcoholism the psychiatrist-patient relationship may differ from that encountered in many other clinical situations, but first I will establish the general framework of such relationships. The doctor needs to communicate regard, support, and a willingness and ability to understand the patient's experience in a nonjudgmental manner. Prior information about the patient from the family, employer, or other sources needs to be kept in mind, but must not interfere with receiving the patient's perspective. In the face of the patient's denial, it is sometimes tempting to blurt out facts you know to be true that contradict the patient's story. To know these facts is vitally important, and they can be put to good use, but only after some confidence in the viability of the relationship has been established.

The Rogerian triad of accurate empathy, genuineness, and nonpossessive warmth are qualities the physician needs in order to establish a working relationship. Respect for the patient is vitally important. Typically alcoholics expect to be rejected or condemned. A physician's respect, courtesy, interest, and understanding have a powerful positive effect on the doctor-patient relationship. Because they feel they deserve rejection, alcoholic patients sometimes attempt to provoke rejection by derisive comments about psychiatry or an arrogant assertion that they really have no wish to change. The well-trained clinician does not take the bait, but continues to be warm, empathic, and genuine.

The physician should seek the active collaboration of the patient, thus establishing a sense of shared control in the therapeutic situation. Many alcoholic patients expect to be railroaded into the hospital or forced to attend meetings before they have a chance to object. The psychiatrist's willingness to individualize treatment and respect the patient's feelings about treatment options will enhance the patient's compliance and sense of responsibility for treatment (Docherty & Fiester, 1985).

One psychiatrist refused to accept alcoholics into his clinic unless they would take disulfiram. Another physician, a nonpsychiatrist in charge of a large rehabilitation center, accepted only those patients who agreed to stay at least 4 months. This degree of rigidity and dogmatism in treatment planning may help some physicians tolerate the anxiety associated with the crises and relapses common to alcoholic patients. Unfortunately, such arbitrariness deters many patients from undertaking treatment. Another variation on this theme is the program that accepts only those alcoholics who have been sober for a month prior to treatment and who have an intact family willing to participate in the treatment program. These conditions of treatment may improve a program's success rate, but they do not help many patients find and sustain motivation for the long process of recovery.

Collaboration and individualized treatment do not mean that the physician allows the alcoholic patient to "call the shots." The alcoholic is defensive, guilt-ridden, angry, and perhaps feeling hopeless. Health has been neglected, typically, and there may be some features of organic brain disorder. Such an individual is not in a suitable condition to judge what is best, but the therapist must gain a foothold and align himself quickly with the healthy part of the patient's ego. This often has to be done with multiple appointments in a brief period, often involving family or relevant others. For example, the alcoholic whose physical condition is deteriorating rapidly but who refuses hospitalization may comply when the doctor insists on seeing him or her daily. Such a schedule communicates the physician's concern and recognizes the degree of severity. When the physician shares the urgency and rationale behind a particular course of treatment patiently and persistently, often the alcoholic's initial resistance dissolves.

Because some patients, including many alcoholics, do not trust psychiatrists or other physicians, corrective experience with the doctor-patient relationship may be necessary. Havens (1978) refers to this as "offsetting the projections." We are expected to be critical, unsympathetic, or, perhaps, dangerous. The task for the physician is to replace the moralistic, rejecting image with one of understanding and acceptance. To fail at this task results in concealment on the part of the patient and prolongs the illness.

Guilt also reinforces the alcoholic patient's concealment. To counter the guilt and distrust, certain guidelines are useful:

- *Avoid direct questions.* The therapist, in anticipation of the patient's defensiveness, can minimize the number of direct, probing questions. For example, rather than immediately attempting to determine how much one drinks and when, explain to the patient that most people, at first, feel embarrassed when talking about the use of alcohol. Typically, they expect to be judged or criticized.
- *Emphasize your helping role.* It is sometimes useful to point out that alcohol often has an effect on one's confidence; it may bolster courage initially, but after awhile one begins to question whether he or she can get along without it. Let the patient know that you think he or she is showing good sense to be willing to examine the issue of alcohol use, because that is the only way any possible serious problem can be prevented.
- *Illustrate with positive examples from other patients.* For instance, one patient, a "self made" man, was a leading union official and later became a top manager. All his life he did things on his own, his own way. Somehow, when alcohol started gaining control over his life, he recognized he was going to need help. He followed a treatment program, went to AA, and recovered fully. This example points out the importance of accepting help from others as distinct from "I have to do it myself."

In another case, a middle-aged woman came for treatment after nearly dying twice before from gastrointestinal bleeding. She had been unable to stop drinking. Her family didn't understand her alcoholism; they were angry with her, and they largely ignored her. After finding someone to talk to (therapist) she gained the confidence to beat her addiction to alcohol. At that time she accepted an inpatient treatment program. The latter example points out that recovery can occur even in the patient with advanced medical complications and an unsympathetic family.

- *Express open, nonjudgmental interest.* Inquire whether they or someone who knows them well has been worried about the effects of alcohol on their functioning. As the patient senses the physician's concern, the tendency to conceal or deny lessens.

The general framework of collaboration within the doctor-patient relationship emphasizes three principles: 1) adoption of the basic Rogerian triad of accurate empathy, genuineness, and nonpossessive warmth; 2) active participation of the patient in planning as an understanding of treatment needs unfolds; and 3) provision of a corrective experience to offset the rejection and criticism that are expected. (These principles are not unique to the treatment of alcoholism. They are part of most clinical situations.)

On the other hand, there are some important guidelines of the doctor-alcoholic patient relationship which deviate from traditional psychotherapeutic approaches.

1. *Establish a real relationship,* not one based on the goal of working through transference. As Lewis (1978) emphasized, transference is ubiquitous. It need not be encouraged by adopting a *neutral* stance. Lewis cautions that to foster the transference neurosis deliberately is a technique appropriate only for formal psychoanalytic treatment; then, only for carefully selected patients. Quoting from Lewis:

   He or she must be able to care about the patient as another human being and, in the process, must not be afraid of letting some personal human needs show. There must be respect for the patient's ego boundaries as reflected in his idiosyncratic feelings, thoughts, and fantasies, as well as a belief in his potential for change and growth. A therapist also must not be afraid to communicate genuine responses to that which transpires between therapist and patient. The clear feedback that this provides the patient is instrumental in helping the patient gain a sense of his or her impact upon at least one other human being. (Lewis, 1978, p. 75)

Avoid aloofness; as I was once advised by a minister skilled in working with alcoholic patients, "get down in the mud with them."

2. *Become comfortable with the process of self-disclosure.* Self-disclosure will be influenced by the goals of treatment, the level of psychopathology of the patient, the nature of the disclosure, and the circumstance of the moment (Lewis, 1978). For example, in working with alcoholic patients it is common to be asked if you drink or have ever been drunk. Tell the truth. If the therapist does drink, a sense of relief sometimes accompanies the understanding that the therapist's concern is not based on moral prohibition and that the therapist can understand something of the pleasurable aspects of drinking. But do not equate your pleasure in the use of alcohol with the experience of the alcoholic, whose need for alcohol far exceeds ordinary social drinking.

3. *Model self-care ideals.* Alcoholic patients demonstrate a decrease in the capacity for appropriate self-care. Emphasize attention to diet, hygiene, and health.

4. *Order a physical examination and conduct a careful medical history.* Appropriate laboratory and radiologic studies should be carried out.

5. *Establish priorities.* The first priority for the alcoholic must be continuing attention to their alcoholism and the steps necessary for recovery. Do not allow other therapeutic issues to usurp this principle.

6. *Be consistent.* Once the diagnosis of alcoholism is established do not waiver under the influence of endless denials. The patient expects you to remain sane.

Up to this point we have reviewed general principles and stratagems useful in forming a working relationship with alcoholic patients. It is essential to recognize that a primary goal in forming a relationship with the alcoholic patient is to motivate that patient to participate in specific alcoholism inpatient or outpatient treatment programs and to utilize AA. Ongoing psychotherapy is a secondary consideration until a firm grip on sobriety has been obtained. Establishing a therapeutic relationship with the alcoholic patient often provides the leverage whereby acceptance of the necessity for a rehabilitation program and utilization of AA become a reality. There are two circumstances, however, where reliance on the therapeutic relationship falls short: 1) when the patient refuses to accept the need for evaluation, thereby providing no opportunity to establish a relationship; and 2) when the patient is willing to keep appointments with a therapist, but either has not stopped drinking (or using drugs) or has not indicated that an understanding or acceptance of his or her addiction is being gained. Under these circumstances the use of a formal confrontation should be considered.

Formal Confrontation

Confrontation refers to the presentation of reality to the patient as seen by those in a meaningful relationship. Confronting a person is telling them how you see them, how you feel in reference to their behavior (Johnson, 1973).

A formal confrontation is often necessary to break through the denial of the patient and to enable the patient to accept help. It is a specific, extended process that is carried out by arranging a meeting between the patient and those who are in a meaningful relationship with him or her. The latter include family members and may include employer, co-workers, clergy or friends. The "significant others" are counseled prior to the meeting and guided during the process by a trained counselor or other therapist.

A typical sequence is as follows:

1. A family member or employer calls and asks what to do about the alcoholic person, who is denying the illness and defiant about going for help.
2. The therapist meets with the person concerned about the alcoholic's behavior and assesses who in the alcoholic's life would be helpful in the confrontation. The family and any others close to and concerned about the alcoholic are included in a preconfrontation meeting and instructed as follows: 1) Write a list of specific behaviors you have observed. Be data-oriented and provide times, places, and details. For example, "Mother, when I came home last Friday the dinner had been burned. The oven was on, but you were asleep in the bedroom. The vodka bottle was on the kitchen counter. I could tell you were drinking by how you looked and when you tried to speak." Or, "Jack, I wanted to go shopping with you last Saturday, but I was afraid. The last time we drove together you nearly had an accident, you swerved in and out of lanes. I smelled alcohol on your breath." 2) Do not be intimidated by threats from the alcoholic ("I'll cut you off without a penny.") or get into arguments ("You've overspent our budget every year of our marriage.") during the confrontation.
3. Be confident that the alcoholic patient will agree to a meeting. Don't be put off by anger. When the alcoholic sees that the family is serious, that the meeting will go on with or without him or her, the decision to attend is usually reached.

Two other matters need to be attended to prior to the formal confrontation of the alcoholic person. First, the participants must understand that their participation is the result of their concern and interest in the welfare of the alcoholic person. Any guilt, reluctance, or ambivalence about confronting the alcoholic needs to be addressed. "I don't want to

hurt his feelings or embarrass him" is a common response. The participants are reminded that the alcoholic behavior is potentially much more
embarrassing and harmful than is a genuine act of intervention in the
destructive reality.

Second, a plan of treatment should be agreed upon. A bed should be
reserved in an inpatient program or an appointment made with the staff
of an alcoholism program before the intervention session.

A 68-year-old man was brought to my office by his wife and two
daughters. I had met with the daughters in order to explain and
prepare them for the confrontation. They, in turn, explained the
process to their mother. The alcoholic father/husband was surprised with the detailed accounts of his family's concern. He was
even more surprised by the revelation that his bags had been
packed and were in the trunk of the car. Although barely convinced
that it was that serious, he was impressed with the family's seriousness and good naturedly accepted their "putting one over on me."
He entered an inpatient alcohol program that morning and with
the continuing support of his family responded favorably.

Of course, the optimal treatment plan is not always accepted so readily. It is necessary to have "fall-back positions" in mind: 1) schedule a
meeting with all the participants several days later to continue the discussion; 2) an agreement to start AA may be reached; 3) a decision to
quit drinking may be offered by the patient.

If the patient has never tried to quit drinking before, a trial of attempted sobriety may be warranted. The agreement should be made that
if any of the above plans are not carried out, more definitive treatment
approaches, such as hospitalization, will be pursued.

When the formal confrontation occurs, it almost always provokes anger and anxiety in the alcoholic person. It can be highly emotional. The
other participants need advice and support so that they can hold firm to
their convictions (which should be based on experience and presented in
a data-oriented manner) and not be demoralized by the denial of the
alcoholic. When an employer is involved who makes further employment contingent on getting treatment, compliance runs very high. When
this leverage is not available, the family must be supported and encouraged to get help for themselves.

If the alcoholic refuses help, the family will be maximizing the eventu-
al possibility of change by seeking help for themselves. Such help could
include Al-Anon, individual, group, or family therapy. Many substance
abuse programs offer seminars or groups for family members who are
struggling with alcoholism in their families. As a change begins to occur
in the family members, as they no longer make excuses for the alcoholic,

and as they begin to carve out a life for themselves rather than always being dominated by the drinking behavior of the alcoholic, a chance arises for the alcoholic to change. As families learn that they cannot control, cure, or cause alcoholism they begin to act differently, and the alcoholic member begins to look at his or her behavior differently as well.

Use of Crisis

Sometimes a spouse separates from his or her partner who drinks. This creates a crisis for the alcoholic, which often leads to acceptance of treatment. The spouse should make his or her return contingent on the alcoholic's receiving adequate treatment. The employer is in an excellent position to create a crisis by not tolerating poor job performance, but instead linking preservation of employment to effective treatment. When naturally occurring crises such as employment problems, medical illness, marital strife, or legal difficulties have not emerged, the process of a formal confrontation is used to "create a crisis," a crisis of reality.

Constructive coercion is a phrase used to describe acting on a crisis in the alcoholic's life so that treatment is accepted. The crisis, whether occurring naturally or created by a formal confrontation, catches the individual with his or her defenses down. The impact of the crisis allows the reality of the alcoholic's life to penetrate the rational part of his or her mind, and appeals to the healthy part of the ego become possible. The crisis can be used to get the alcoholic to treatment. It then becomes the task of treatment to restore the alcoholic to health.

CHAPTER 8

Inpatient Treatment

Inpatient treatment refers to treatment in a specialized alcoholism or substance abuse unit which is either part of a psychiatric hospital, part of a general hospital, or a freestanding rehabilitation unit. If the alcoholic patient has major medical or psychiatric problems, a medical facility such as a general or psychiatric hospital should be utilized. A rehabilitation center may be utilized if medical or psychiatric problems are not present. In either case, services for a thorough medical evaluation should be available as well as the services of a psychiatric consultant.

In this chapter, inpatient treatment does not refer to the treatment of alcohol withdrawal syndromes, other alcohol-related organic brain disorders, or the treatment of alcohol-associated medical conditions. Such conditions may require treatment in a medically based facility and must be attended to prior to the inpatient rehabilitation experience which is the focus of this chapter. Some inpatient alcoholism programs are capable of managing the associated medical or psychiatric disorders resulting from alcohol dependence or which have developed independent of the alcoholism. Other inpatient alcoholism programs may require that the medically or psychiatrically ill alcoholic patient be treated for those conditions prior to admission. For example, hepatic coma or gastrointestinal bleeding would be treated on a medical floor, and a manic or suicidal patient would need to be stabilized in a psychiatric unit before attempting rehabilitation.

WHEN IS IT MANDATORY TO HOSPITALIZE
THE ALCOHOLIC PATIENT?

The following outline* describes the conditions which should mandate hospitalization. These conditions warrant management in a medical or psychiatric unit with plans for transfer to an alcoholism program as soon as stability is attained.

1. Acute alcohol withdrawal syndrome with hallucinations (visual, auditory, or tactile) or confusion.
2. Active or signs of impending delirium tremens.
3. A history of recent convulsions or a poorly controlled convulsive disorder.
4. Disulfiram—alcohol reaction with hyperthermia, chest pains, arrhythmia, or hypotension.
5. Fluctuations in level of consciousness that are prolonged or unexplained, or a comatose or stuporous condition.
6. Depression with suicidal ideation or expressed hopelessness.
7. Trauma to the head, chest, or abdomen necessitating serial observations.
8. An infectious disease that is likely to go untreated or be aggravated by further drinking.
9. Systemic disease of unknown etiology with fever of 101° F (38.3° C) or greater, with hypothermia below 95° F (35° C).
10. A metabolic problem that is out of control, such as diabetes mellitus.
11. Alcoholic hepatitis or acute pancreatitis that is likely to progress in severity with continued alcohol use.
12. Active gastrointestinal bleeding; significant vomiting or dehydration.
13. Significant degree of anemia.
14. Alcoholic myopathy with or without myoglobulinuria.
15. Congestive heart failure or significant hypertension, tachycardia, or arrhythmia.
16. Inability to initiate treatment in an outpatient or nonhospital setting because of continued drinking.

---

*This outline was constructed by the Physicians Task Force on Alcohol-Related Problems in cooperation with the Governor's Council on Drug and Alcohol Abuse (Commonwealth of Pennsylvania; Jasper G. Chen See, M.D., Chairman, 1979).

THE VALUE OF INPATIENT TREATMENT

The importance of inpatient treatment is obvious when one is faced with the conditions outlined above. Apart from these acute medical and psychiatric indications, there are, however, other reasons for the use of inpatient facilities in the treatment of the alcoholic. These reasons include:

1. "Revolving Door" syndrome in which there are many hospitalizations, limited functioning, and little awareness as to what precipitates drinking. If awareness does exist, there is an incapacity to translate such awareness into meaningful action that would help prevent recurrence.
2. Repeated acting out behavior with threat to the safety of the patient, others, or property; behavior not tolerable to the patient and/ or family.
3. Repeated disruptions and crises in environment.
4. Repeated abortive outpatient treatment experiences; inability to establish a therapeutic alliance; inability to tolerate the tension of the treatment situation without serious acting out.
5. Very poor work or educational performance where evidence indicates the patient's capacity is at a significantly higher level of achievement.
6. Absence of geographically accessible outpatient treatment facility.
7. Concurrent treatment and rehabilitation of physical or psychiatric illness (including personality disorders) which complicate the alcoholism.
8. Patient's illness is such as to need an environment with specific therapeutic modalities to augment individual and group psychotherapy.

Inpatient facility, in this sense, refers to a structured program of therapeutic modalities that focus specifically on alcohol dependence or abuse. One of the strongest reasons for advocating inpatient treatment for the alcoholic man or woman is protection from continuing alcohol use. Treatment cannot be effective as long as the alcoholic continues to drink.

Second, inpatient treatment enables the patient to be removed from his or her usual environment and responsibilities and, as a consequence, be in a position to attend exclusively to his or her problem with alcohol. The usual distractions of everyday life that may support the alcoholic's denial are eliminated by hospitalization.

Third, inpatient treatment can provide a more concentrated and intense treatment experience than can be attained in an outpatient setting. Such intensity is often necessary to break down the denial of the alcoholic and enable the alcoholic to gain understanding of the disease concept of alcoholism.

Last, inpatient treatment provides the conditions necessary for the task of ego strengthening. The alcoholic patient is regressed. He or she is functioning with limited impulse control and a diminished capacity for adequate self care. The inpatient milieu provides an auxiliary ego. The alcoholic patient needs these external controls until the internalization of self-care processes is accomplished. A well designed and well functioning inpatient program will provide consistency, instill a sense of responsibility, modify impulsivity, discourage passivity, teach the ability to delay gratification, assist the patient in gaining a sense of patience, offer healthy modalities for relaxation and normal regression, and provide a model for self-care behaviors. The external controls in a hospital environment enable the patient to avoid alcohol or drugs. The support provided by the staff enables the patient to learn that feelings of frustration and acute need for relief can be tolerated, delayed, and directed into healthier forms of expression than that provided by the immediate gratification of alcohol. As one begins to learn that he or she can tolerate not drinking and in fact *enjoy* not drinking, confidence in an alcohol-free lifestyle develops. Success depends on an inpatient program that provides the right balance of therapeutic structure, individualized treatment, confrontation, and support (Nace, Saxon, & Shore, 1986). The following section describes the components of an optimal inpatient program. An example of a patient's weekly schedule is shown in Table 8-1.

STAFFING

The *sine qua non* for any program is a highly motivated, well-trained staff. The most effective staff are part of the treatment team because they choose to work with alcoholics, not because they were assigned on a rotating basis or by administrative fiat.

It is vital to have some staff who are recovering alcoholics. The recovering* alcoholic who is professionally trained can bring his or her personal experience with alcoholism and recovery to the patient and serve as a role model. Trained recovering people are acutely sensitive to nuances of denial, and they are freer generally about confronting the alcoholic patient. What they say is usually more acceptable to patients be-

---

Recovered and *recovering* are used interchangeably. Some prefer to always use the term "recovering" to emphasize the ongoing process of maintaining sobriety and personal growth.

Table 8-1
Substance Abuse Program: Model Schedule for Patients†

TIME	MONDAY	TUESDAY	WEDNESDAY	THURSDAY	FRIDAY	SATURDAY	SUNDAY
6:45 AM	Wake Up	Wake Up	Wake Up	Wake Up	Wake Up		
7:15–8:00	Exercise	Exercise	Exercise	Exercise	Exercise		
8:15–9:00	Breakfast	Breakfast	8–8:30 Breakfast	Breakfast	Breakfast	Breakfast	Breakfast
9:00–9:30	Community Meeting	Community Meeting	8:30–9:30 Education	Community Meeting	Community Meeting	9:00–10:00 Education	See Current Week Activity Calendar
9:30–11:00	*+ Occupational Therapy	Activities Therapy / Unit Meal Preparation	9:30–12:00 Personal Reflection Papers, Assigned Readings, Fourth Step Inventories	Occupational Therapy	Activities Therapy	See Current Week Activity Calendar	See Current Week Activity Calendar
11:00–12:00	Education	Education		Education	Education		
12:00–1:00	Lunch	Lunch	Lunch	Lunch	Lunch	Lunch	Lunch
1:00–2:30	Activities Therapy Group A / Group Therapy Group B	Occupational Therapy—Women / Group Therapy—Men	Occupational Therapy / Combined Groups	Activities Therapy Group A / Group Therapy Group B	Group Therapy / Combined Groups	See Current Week Activity Calendar	See Current Week Activity Calendar
2:30–4:00	Activities Therapy Group B / Group Therapy Group A	Occupational Therapy—Men / Group Therapy—Women	Group Therapy / Combined Groups	Activities Therapy Group B / Group Therapy Group A	2:30–3:30 Free Time / 3:30–5:00 Occupational Therapy Combined Groups		
4:00–5:00	Individual Meetings	Individual Meetings	Individual Meetings	Individual Meetings			
5:30–6:30	Supper	Supper	Supper	Supper	Supper	Supper	Supper
Evening Schedule	#Outside AA & NA Meetings	NA Meeting 8–9 P.M.	Outside AA & NA Meetings	Outside AA & NA Meetings	Outside AA & NA Meetings	Outside AA & NA Meetings	Outside AA & NA Meetings

*Individual cooking evaluation or relaxation therapy available in this time frame by Occupational Therapy Staff.
+Individual assessments in this time frame by Recreational Therapy Staff.
#When not attending evening meetings, patients are expected to work on Personal Reflection Papers, Assigned Papers, and Fourth Steps.
†Table constructed by John J. Sheehan, M.H.S., C.A.C., Davie, FL.

cause recovering alcoholism counselors share their own past experiences with patients so they do not feel put down. The staff person who has recovered is also useful for the morale of the treatment team. Here is a colleague who may have failed several attempts at rehabilitation, signed out of hospital against medical advice, and denied his or her alcoholism for a long time, but has eventually found sobriety and kept it. The recovering person also provides "backbone" to the treatment team in the sense that mental health professionals are trained to be understanding and supportive but may not be, at first, very comfortable saying "no" to patients. Because they know from experience that the alcoholic has to be stopped, recovered personnel are more comfortable and more vigorous in setting limits and keeping treatment priorities focused on the alcoholism.

> A group of patients in an inpatient alcoholism program had been complaining that not enough morning newspapers were being sent to the unit and the eggs were watery at breakfast. The counselor, a man who had been recovered for over 2 years, brought the group back on target in a morning meeting by reminding them that a few months earlier they had been drinking their meals and hadn't cared one way or another about current events.

The recovered person seeking a counselor position should have a well-established record of unbroken sobriety as well as abstinence from drugs. Two years of sobriety has been a standard length of time before considering one eligible for a professional role. Specific training in addictions, counseling, and psychology leading to state certification in alcohol and drug abuse counseling are essential. The recovered person who aspires to a career in counseling may have to overcome undue rigidity in regard to personality style and ideational "set" and be able to accept that his or her clients may find sobriety easier to attain than he/she did, or that they obtain sobriety through different means than that which was effective for the counselor. An acceptance that some alcoholics have psychiatric disorders other than alcoholism and that medication may be necessary is also essential.

Recovering staff members should be active in AA or NA (Narcotics Anonymous). Their visibility in the AA community helps to give a program credibility in the eyes of some AA groups. Further, continued attendance at AA reinforces their sobriety and provides a good role model in aftercare.

Most recovered people working in programs are counselors or members of the nursing staff. Occasionally the medical director of the program or other professionals are also recovered alcoholics. The most effective programs do not have a staff made up entirely of recovered alcoholics, nor the entire staff nonalcoholics. Balance is necessary in order to provide a broad view of treatment options. I prefer about a 1 to 1 or 1 to 2 ratio of recovered alcoholics to nonalcoholic staff.

Staff members who come from a family with alcoholism are also very useful. The exception is the staff person who is still living in a family with an active alcoholic. For example, a female nurse currently married to an active alcoholic husband may be too vulnerable to displacing her feelings into the work environment to be effective. The experience of having grown up in an alcoholic home or having once been in an alcoholic marriage, however, may enable the staff member to appreciate and be especially sensitive to and supportive of the family's or spouse's needs. Such a staff person may also have had an Al-Anon experience which can be shared with families struggling to make changes.

Program Director

A psychiatrist with interest and experience in addictions provides the optimal staffing for program leadership. A psychiatrist can lead the team in planning individualized treatment and provide psychiatric differential diagnosis and medical supervision. The psychiatrist is also in a position to supervise the clinical work of the counseling, social work, nursing, and psychology staffs. It is unfortunate that relatively few psychiatrists have the training or experience to assume this position, but many other professionals perform effectively as program directors, including recovered alcoholic counselors, psychologists, social workers, and other medical specialists.

Alcoholism Counselors

Unless they are specifically trained in other techniques, counselors focus on the disease of alcoholism and its attendant defenses in their work with patients, rather than dynamically oriented psychotherapy, sex therapy, or other treatment processes. Many nonalcoholics can function well as counselors, and a balance should be found in the proportion of recovered to nonalcoholic staff. An optimal case load for an inpatient counselor is 6 to 8 patients. Counselors are expected to provide didactic lectures—for example, explaining the steps of AA, discussing the role of emotions in recovery, and conducting group psychotherapy that places special emphasis on confronting pathological defenses, understanding alcoholism as a disease, and continuing care.

Nursing Staff

Nursing staff are chosen for their interest in alcoholic patients and their ability to relate in a consistent yet not overly authoritarian manner. Nursing personnel with an interest in milieu and group dynamics are essential. Many nurses serve as co-therapists in group therapy and may be counselors with some patients as well. Nurses sophisticated in psychiatric nursing are essential, yet they must also retain awareness of acute medical syndromes because of the many medical problems which alcoholics may present. A willingness to be available to families is important: They must be able to meet with families during visiting hours and respond to family telephone inquiries. The nursing staff can play a vital role in aligning the family with the treatment team and providing support to the family when the patient presses for a premature discharge. Most important, the entire tone or atmosphere of the inpatient program is reflected by the nursing staff. Optimistic, yet serious and dedicated to their task of furthering treatment goals, each member of the nursing staff touches the lives of the patients in important ways that often go unacknowledged. A kind word, time to listen, a sympathetic touch, a cheery good morning, willingness to share a laugh, and continuing personal interest may well contribute as much to the patient's recovery as the formal treatment sessions on a patient's schedule.

Social Workers

The primary function of the social work staff is to conduct an evaluation of each patient's family, to provide educational and group-process experiences for family members, to facilitate the family's participation in support groups such as Al-Anon, and to conduct family therapy. The evaluation of the family must determine whether other family members are chemically dependent and whether the family is denying or facilitating in some other way the patient's substance abuse. No program should be considered suitable that does not emphasize family participation. Some features of the family program will be described later; typically, these are managed by the social work staff.

In addition to working with families, I think it is advisable to have each social worker serve as the primary counselor for one or two inpatients. Although this leads to some role blurring with other members of the treatment team, it keeps the social worker in touch with the dynamics of the alcoholic patient and lessens the likelihood of overidentification with the family. One social worker for each 15 inpatients is a workable ratio.

Activities Therapist

Activities therapists play a vital role in addressing specific needs of alcoholic patients. They offer the patient something to do that is independent of, and apart from, the drug and alcohol culture. They arrange graded tasks that assist in building confidence and restoring self-esteem. Whatever the activity, patience and perseverance are tested. The patient's capacity to endure frustrations, ability to follow complex directions, and control over impulses can be evaluated. New experiences are provided, and former pleasures can be reexperienced in an alcohol-free state. Activities such as camping, hiking, photography, yoga, and jogging allow the patient to experience a sense of mastery and well-being without chemical assistance. A minimum of two activities therapists are required for a 30-bed unit.

Psychologist

The addition of a psychologist to an inpatient alcoholism treatment program adds substantially to the depth of patient evaluations and to treatment planning. The psychologist needs to be sophisticated in neuropsychological testing because assessments of organicity and cognitive deficits are especially important in the alcoholic population. In addition, the psychologist should be skilled in group therapy and be qualified as an individual therapist. Research skills are highly desirable for designing follow-up studies or other clinically relevant research projects, supervising data collection, and carrying out statistical analyses.

Attending Psychiatrist

The services of an attending psychiatrist trained in addictions provides the opportunity to ascertain whether other psychiatric disorders, including personality disorders, complicate the recovery process for the patient. The need for medication can be determined, and the psychiatrist can provide individual or marital/family therapy as indicated. Of equal importance is the psychiatrist's treatment of the alcohol dependence and his or her ability to guide the staff in this undertaking.

Treatment programs in psychiatric hospitals often have alcoholic patients work with a psychiatrist during their inpatient stay and as part of aftercare treatment. In some settings, the psychiatrist for each patient is in charge of treatment planning. This model is satisfactory if the psychiatrist cooperates with the program staff of the alcoholism unit. Strong leadership by a psychiatrist who is program director will often be necessary for this model to reach its potential. However, when each psychiatrist goes about his or her own way in terms of prescribing, setting limits, or granting privileges, independent of the program's goals and policy, chaos results. Such a program does a disservice to patients.

On the other hand, when an attending psychiatrist collaborates with the program staff, a strong program emerges. This model works when the attending psychiatrist "prescribes" the alcoholism program in its entirety for his or her patient. That is, the patient participates in all the structured activities and is not excused from, for example, group therapy because it is "too stressful" or from occupational therapy because it isn't "interesting." The program staff can assist in determining if a particular activity is unsuitable for any given patient. In other words, staff splitting is a risk with the attending psychiatrist model, and such splitting must be avoided at all costs.

In another model, one that has the advantage of minimizing splitting, the staff psychiatrist (director) for the alcoholism program is in charge of all aspects of patient care, and the therapist (psychiatrist, psychologist, or other trained mental health professional) meets one-to-one with the patient for the purpose of psychotherapy. The therapist establishes a confidential therapeutic relationship which can be sustained after hospitalization is completed, but plays no direct decision-making role in day-to-day matters during the inpatient period.

I would like to emphasize that the availability of an individual therapist is extremely valuable for many alcoholic patients. Few programs outside a psychiatric hospital have the resources to provide this particular service. The structure of individual therapy with alcoholic patients will be discussed in a subsequent chapter, but the need of such services provided by a psychodynamically trained mental health professional has been underemphasized in the field of alcoholism treatment.

PROGRAM COMPONENTS

Before describing the essential components of an inpatient alcoholism program, it may be instructive to contrast a general psychiatric unit with an alcoholism rehabilitation unit (Table 8-2).*

The program described in this section, component by component, represents a blend of these two models. The psychiatric unit model in Table 8-2 is inadequate because it lacks focus on alcoholism; the alcohol rehabilitation model falls short because the focus is too narrow for many

---

*I am indebted to Kent Neff, M.D., of Portland, Oregon for his analysis of the differences presented in Table 8-2.

TABLE 8-2
Contrast Between Psychiatric Units and Alcoholism Programs*

Psychiatric Treatment Program	Alcoholism Treatment Program
Primary DX = Psychiatric	Primary DX = Alcoholism
Medication Orientation	Medication-Free Orientation
No Alcoholism Counselors	Alcoholism Counselor Very Important
No Peer Pressure/Support for Alcoholics	Strong Peer Pressure/Support
	Significant Education for Alcoholics
No/Little Education for Alcoholics	Family Involvement Important
No Minimum Family Involvement for Alcoholics	Follow Up of Alcoholism by "Team," AA
Follow Up of Patient (by Psychiatrist)	

*Reprinted with permission from Kent Neff, M.D., Portland, OR.

patients. Psychiatric assessment and a complete diagnostic evaluation are essential. Medications are life-saving for some patients. By adding the strengths of skilled alcoholism counselors, family involvement focused on alcoholism, and extensive use of AA and peer support for abstinence, an integrated program emerges which can meet the needs of a diverse group of patients. The blending of these two models has been documented to produce highly favorable outcome (Saxon et al., 1983).

The essential components of an inpatient alcoholism program are described below.

1. *Complete medical evaluation.* Each patient is examined and evaluated by a physician upon admission to the inpatient program. An assessment of physical and emotional status includes a history of acute medical, emotional, or social problems. In addition, the family or an interested person is interviewed at the time of admission by the nursing or social work staff to provide additional collaborative data. Appropriate laboratory studies, X-ray studies, and specialized medical consultations can be arranged if indicated by the initial evaluation. Continuing medical needs are met by the attendance of a staff physician while the patient remains in the inpatient program.
2. *Detoxification.* Accomplished under the care of a physician, detoxification constitutes the initial phase of treatment for an individual in need of such services. Appropriate medications are used on an individual basis. The medications are tapered or discontinued as the patient's condition warrants. The detoxification process is modified according to the substance abuse patterns of the patient. Details regarding detoxification from alcohol will be found in Chapter 12.

3. *Orientation*. Each patient is oriented to the program, the hospital, the policies and procedures, and their rights and responsibilities by a member of the nursing staff as soon as possible after admission. The patient receives procedures, schedules, and policies and rights in writing.
4. *Therapeutic community meeting*. Each patient is introduced at a daily morning meeting that includes all patients and staff. This meeting enables each patient to participate in a forum where concerns common to all patients and staff can be discussed and grievances or requests presented.
5. *Individual counseling*. Each patient, at time of admission, is assigned an alcoholism counselor who is a member of the staff. The purpose of this assignment is to provide each patient an individual to whom they can turn for advice, assistance, and regular counseling. A social-psychological history is to be obtained, and progress notes which reflect the counseling transactions are included in the patient's chart. Counseling sessions focus on the impact of drinking on the patient's life, the process of denial, and the means to achieve recovery.
6. *Group psychotherapy*. Each patient enters the inpatient group psychotherapy program. Group psychotherapy is held on at least a daily basis and serves as a forum for each individual to express his or her feelings. Personal experiences are shared in order to enhance each patient's understanding of alcoholism as a disease. Strong emphasis is put on the group approach so that each patient may overcome the feelings of isolation, guilt, and shame which are common in alcoholism. Better understanding of one's individual route to alcoholism and potential for recovery is obtained through sharing personal experiences with others.
7. *Educational program*. Each patient participates in an educational program which meets on a daily basis and includes lectures and discussion groups by the staff. A series of films relevant to an understanding of alcoholism is presented; topics include the medical aspects of alcoholism and a better understanding of the dynamic factors that lead to alcoholism and to recovery. The educational program helps each patient understand more fully the concept of alcoholism as a disease and the steps furthering recovery that they can take while in the hospital and after discharge. Discussion of the educational hour's content is held by the patients and staff at the conclusion of each session.
8. *Activities therapy*. Activities therapy is provided daily. Each patient participates in an activities therapy program designed by the activities therapist to help him or her develop a stronger repertoire of constructive activities to replace the consumption of alcohol and the drinking-related behaviors. An active physical program that is suited to each person's needs also serves a rehabilitative function. In addition, occupational therapy provides a forum for

the expression of cognitive skills and personality characteristics. Characterological problems and emotional reactions can be utilized for greater personal growth and understanding. In addition, cognitive skills can be assessed and recovery from alcohol-related deficits followed.

9. *Alcoholics Anonymous.* Each patient attends Alcoholics Anonymous meetings daily while in the hospital. The purpose of this is to help them gain a better understanding of AA and eventually to build a bridge to AA meetings in their local communities. Obtaining a sponsor and excursions to AA meetings close to the patient's home are arranged on an individual basis.

10. *Dietary services.* A hospital dietician is assigned to the program and arrangements are made for a special diet when necessary. The dietician is available for consultation with any patient should particular dietary problems be presented.

11. *Social work services.* Each patient and his or her family are assigned a social worker. Social work services may include arrangements for housing, assistance in obtaining employment, and financial counseling. The major part of the social work staff's responsibility is in the area of family evaluation, education, and treatment as described below.

12. *Family program.* The primary focus of the family program is educational. Psychotherapeutic intervention may follow. The cognitive structuring of the experience of alcoholism coupled with group support often yields a degree of stabilization sufficient either to bring about crisis resolution or to establish conditions for more intensive intervention. Below is an outline of a family program which emphasizes a cognitive or psychoeducational approach.

Family group. A weekly group for family members during the inpatient phase and for 4 weeks postdischarge is designed to help identify their emotional, physical, and behavioral reactions to living with an alcoholic.

Transition group. This group is also held weekly during the inpatient phase of treatment and continues for the first 4 weeks after discharge. The group meeting provides a forum where the inpatient alcoholic and his/her family join with the recently discharged alcoholics and their family members to express specific concerns related to adjustment at home following hospitalization.

Family education hours. Two hours per week consist of a film followed by discussion led by staff. Patients and families participate together. A third hour, for families only, is usually an informal lecture or discussion presented by members of the staff. It may deal with such issues as medical or psychological aspects of addictions.

Children's education seminar. This program entails a series of weekly sessions for latency children and young adolescents. Although attendance of any child above age 8 in the weekly group for family members is encouraged, children have special needs. They may not feel free to speak up when a parent is present. There are often loyalty issues and other conflicts for the child in an alcoholic family. The group is both didactic and therapeutic in its encouragement and support for the children to express how they have been affected by a parent's addiction and how they view the problem. They see films, meet with Al-Ateen representatives, and have a chance to share thoughts and feelings. Some teen-agers may use the group to examine their own use of alcohol and/or drugs. Thus, there is a preventive thrust to the group and a chance to refer for further intervention.

The social worker plays a key role in building an alliance between the inpatient program and the family. Stewart (1981) has described the importance of the family-institution alliance wherein the family receives understanding and support as clarity, acceptance, and commitment to the goals of inpatient treatment are established. If this alliance between the family and the goals of the inpatient program is not satisfactorily established, the potential benefit from a family program is seriously compromised.

13. *Weekend excursions.* After the patient has been in the hospital at least 2 weeks, brief passes home should be arranged. These passes may be for only 6 hours the first weekend and increase to 8 to 12 hours on subsequent weekends if the patient tolerates the experience well. The excursions serve several purposes: (a) Re-exposure to the home environment. This experience helps counter the false confidence many patients acquire in the hospital, where they experience relatively little craving for alcohol and, therefore, think that they have the problem solved. (b) Being around family members or friends helps the patient appreciate the work that needs to be done to improve relationships and enables the patient to assess the feelings of his or her family better now that he or she is in a sober state. A realistic appraisal of who can be supportive now becomes possible. (c) The ability or willingness to follow a plan can be assessed.

Each excursion should be carefully planned to further recovery following inpatient treatment. For example, attendance at an AA meeting is often part of the plan. Does the patient follow through with his or her stated intentions? It is important for the alcoholic to have the experience of leaving his or her home and going to an AA meeting rather than simply attending AA meetings from the hospital where he or she is usually accompanied by other patients. Can the patient stay with a schedule of weekend activities without being prodded by the staff? Can the regressive pull of the home environment be countered in the interest of establishing and continuing sobriety?

Planning for weekend excursions is often instructive. Does the patient think he or she can stop by the taproom, shoot darts, and drink coffee? This, of course, should be discouraged. Does the patient try to do too much and then set himself/herself up for failure? Is there little capacity to structure time? What will the patient do if he or she experiences a strong urge to drink? All of these questions make explicit the steps necessary to negotiate the social milieu outside the hospital. Developing an aftercare support system, learning to avoid high-risk drinking situations, and gathering a realistic appraisal of relationships and aftercare needs are the goals of weekend excursions.

In conclusion to this chapter on the structure of inpatient treatment, I would suggest that a well-designed, well-staffed inpatient program is the treatment of choice for most alcoholic patients. I recognize that this point is subject to argument but advance the preference for inpatient treatment on the basis that so much can be offered in a relatively short period of time. The intensity of the approach affects the disease process in a way that rarely can be accomplished by outpatient treatment. Further, the comprehensiveness of inpatient treatment allows the alcoholic patient an opportunity to be restored to maximum physical, emotional, and social health at the least risk.

Most inpatient programs are structured for lengths of stay of approximately 28 days. There is no magic in the 28-day stay. Many patients could benefit from longer stays, depending on their cognitive functioning, the presence of other psychiatric disorders, the complexity of their family and social milieu, and the tenacity of their denial. Still others can make significant gains in less time.

The importance of inpatient treatment has been emphasized. I would add that outpatient follow-up is essential and complementary to the inpatient experience. Without outpatient aftercare services, the inpatient gains are unlikely to be sustained. The next chapter reviews outpatient treatment from the point of view of an alternative to inpatient care as well as its importance for recovery following inpatient treatment.

CHAPTER 9

Outpatient Treatment

As indicated in the last chapter, inpatient treatment offers substantial advantages and is the treatment of choice for most alcoholic patients. On the other hand, treatment in an outpatient setting is a reasonable consideration for some alcoholics. The patient's willingness to participate in outpatient rather than inpatient treatment and his or her ability to finance treatment are two major factors which often influence the choice. There are sounder reasons for deciding on outpatient or inpatient treatment, and the circumstances listed below suggest outpatient treatment as a viable option:

1) *Motivation.* If the patient is highly motivated to comply with a treatment regimen, outpatient treatment may be successful. For example, a 28-year-old single male was threatened with a jail sentence after he received a second driving while intoxicated (DWI) arrest. He understood that he was an alcoholic but didn't know what to do about it. His attorney and family urged him to seek treatment, and he began a three-phase outpatient program (described below) and agreed to take disulfiram.

2) *Ability to stop drinking.* Some alcoholic patients can stop drinking without hospitalization. When this is possible, outpatient treatment can be considered. The course of treatment will lead, hopefully, to commitment to abstinence, a fuller understanding and acceptance of the disease, and the utilization of a support system such as AA. When cessation of drinking is not possible or is frequently interrupted by drinking, inpatient treatment should be recommended.

As an example, a man was unable to refrain from drinking after he left work. He either drank at a bar before he got home or bought alcoholic beverages on the way home. He had been sideswiping cars parked in his neighborhood as a result of his drinking. It was unsafe to consider outpatient treatment for this patient, and he accepted hospitalization.

Another patient, a 53-year-old manufacturer's representative, shared his wife's concern about his progressive loss of control over alcohol. They removed alcohol from their home and he entered an outpatient treatment program. He was able to refrain from alcohol use throughout the course of outpatient treatment.

3) *Social support*. Is there encouragement in the patient's environment to stop drinking? If the patient has a family—spouse, parents, children—who offer support and encouragement and who value the patient's efforts to benefit from treatment, an outpatient setting may be feasible. If the patient lives by himself or lives within a family which is indifferent to his or her alcohol use, the chance for success in an outpatient setting is minimal. If the patient lives with another alcoholic, inpatient treatment should be used. If the patient's family doesn't really think there is much of a problem or if hostility dominates the relationship, there will not be enough support to sustain the motivation necessary for outpatient treatment.

A middle-aged woman, employed but living by herself, could not afford inpatient treatment. She had a long history of unipolar affective disorder which was being treated. Her alcoholism was beginning to interfere with her work performance as well as with her treatment for depression. Although not an ideal candidate for outpatient treatment, the situation became manageable because the patient's sister provided support and encouragement. The woman was able to function in and benefit from a program which included family members. The sister of the patient participated in an outpatient program and offered the moral support the woman so badly needed. In other instances a network of friends—not drinking buddies—may be utilized to encourage and support efforts to avoid alcohol (and other drugs) (Galanter, 1984).

A young man addicted to both cocaine and alcohol had no healthy support from his divorced parents. The parents competed with each other for his loyalty and attention and were inclined to offer financial support in situations where his own initiative would have been the better alternative. To his credit he sought out both NA (Narcotics Anonymous) and AA sponsors and called each daily. He also changed his taste in women, avoiding former girlfriends who were oriented to clubs and the "fast lane" party circuit. He began to develop relationships with women in AA or NA or those who accepted him when he explained, "I don't drink or get high."

4) *Employment.* If the alcoholic patient has been able to remain employed and the alcoholism has not yet interfered with job performance, it would be reasonable to consider an outpatient approach. For example, a banking executive had become aware of a progressive pattern of increasing alcohol use. Morning drinking, tremors, and blackouts were now occurring. He had not sought treatment before, had never seriously tried to stop drinking, and was carrying major responsibilities. In this instance an attempt at outpatient treatment seemed indicated. He preferred not to be hospitalized, and his wife was very supportive of his efforts to seek treatment. On the other hand, employers sometimes prefer inpatient treatment for their employees out of concern for job safety if drinking continues or because of confidence in a particular treatment facility.

5) *Medical condition.* As the medical condition of the patient is assessed, three considerations are important: 1) The potential severity of withdrawal symptoms; 2) the presence of secondary medical complications (e.g., alcoholic hepatitis, cirrhosis); and 3) the presence of other medical conditions (diabetes, heart disease, for example).

If the patient has a history of withdrawal seizures, alcoholic hallucinosis, delirium tremens, or other pronounced withdrawal symptoms, hospitalization should be recommended to accomplish a safe detoxification. Similarly, if the patient does not seem reliable in regard to following an outpatient detoxification regimen, inpatient treatment should be used.

The patient with significant medical complications, such as cirrhosis, esophageal varices, pancreatitis, or evidence of organic brain damage, should receive inpatient treatment. Other medical problems may render outpatient treatment relatively unsafe, and the physician must evaluate the severity of such conditions, the risk of further aggravation if drinking continues, and the capability of the patient to comply with the relatively unstructured setting of outpatient treatment.

6) *Absence of associated psychiatric disorders.* The presence of severe personality disorders (e.g., borderline or antisocial), major depression, psychotic conditions, or severe anxiety disorders indicate the need for inpatient rather than outpatient treatment. If the patient is suicidal, outpatient treatment is contraindicated. A history of poor impulse control, fights, drinking while on disulfiram, and quitting previous treatment programs would also indicate inpatient treatment.

7) *Prior treatment experiences.* If the patient is early in the course of alcoholism and has never sought treatment before, a trial of outpatient treatment should be considered in the absence of absolute contraindications. However, if the patient has failed to follow through or benefit from previous attempts at outpatient treatment, he or she is likely to have cycled through a variety of inpatient

programs and have exhausted insurance coverage or other financial resources. In such instances, the clinician has little choice. Sometimes, even if support for additional inpatient treatment is available, the chronically relapsing patient may do better to avoid the potentially regressive attractions of inpatient care and try something different—namely outpatient.

To summarize, outpatient treatment should be considered for the alcoholic patient who is early in the course of the illness and free of medical or other psychiatric disorders. Other factors which support a decision for outpatient treatment include motivation which seems well in place, whether internally derived or socially determined, employment, support of family or other social networks, and ability to discontinue alcohol and other drug abuse outside a protected environment.

Even with the favorable factors listed above, some patients will prove to need inpatient treatment. As mentioned earlier, choice of treatment is often dictated by patient acceptance and financial considerations.

Next, an optimal outpatient treatment program will be described, one which offers a chance for success even when some of the favorable conditions listed above are missing. A spectrum of outpatient services will be outlined which can be tailored to a patient's needs as they change over time.

AN OUTPATIENT APPROACH

Duration. A minimum of one year of treatment in an outpatient setting is a suggested guideline. This would apply whether or not treatment began with an inpatient stay. If so, follow-up care (outpatient) should be expected for at least one year. Some programs emphasize two years of outpatient treatment, but many patients will not comply. Those who are doing well will usually be involved in AA and gradually wean themselves from more formal therapies after one year. Nonrespondents will go through one or more inpatient treatment programs or will get discouraged and drop out of treatment or seek treatment elsewhere.

A specific program designed for an outpatient setting includes three phases:

Phase 1. Evaluation

This phase consists of an interview with a psychiatrist wherein the patient's history is reviewed, mental status assessed, and the diagnosis of a substance abuse disorder or other psychiatric disorder is determined. A family member or the entire family is interviewed by a social worker, and an assessment of the impact of the addiction on family functioning and the apparent effect of the family on the addiction is made. The family's understanding of the problem is evaluated, and their capacity to be supportive is assessed. The possibility of addictions or other psychiatric disorders in family members is considered. The need for family members to receive help is explained, and involvement in Al-Anon strongly encouraged. Finally, an alcoholism counselor meets with the patient and evaluates his or her acceptance of the need for treatment. A detailed explanation of the treatment program is provided, and attitudes toward AA explored.

Following these three interviews the counselor, social worker, and psychiatrist meet to discuss their experiences with the patient and his or her family. A decision to initiate outpatient treatment or to refer to an inpatient setting is then made. In some instances, the patient refuses any treatment and in others a psychiatric disorder such as mania, major depression, or suicidal preoccupation necessitates immediate psychiatric hospitalization. At other times a prompt referral to an internist is necessary as acute medical needs are paramount.

If the patient is assessed to be a candidate for outpatient treatment, a physical examination by the patient's family doctor or an internist who consults to the program is required before starting Phase 2.

Phase 2. Evening Program

This phase involves an intensive 6-week program of psychoeducational treatment combined with group and individual therapies. Part of the treatment plan involves having a co-participant with each patient. This typically is a spouse, parent, sibling, or child, but could be a friend. The patient and his or her participating "significant other" attend the program 4 hours per evening, 3 evenings per week, plus 2 hours on Saturday mornings. The content of the program is similar to that described in the chapter on inpatient treatment. Films, lectures, and discussion of readings on substance abuse are used. During part of each evening the patients and family members separate and meet in their own groups, enabling family members to feel free in asking questions or expressing concerns about their family member or themselves. Individual counseling sessions are held with each patient by a counselor on a weekly basis. A vital part of the program is the dinner hour during each evening session. The informal mingling of patients, family members, and staff enhances a sense of camaraderie and common purpose.

Some programs meet four or five times a week, but this may prove exhausting for employed patients and family members. A program as described above is typically scheduled for a range of 4 to 8 weeks. Six weeks has seemed optimal with the opportunity for a patient to continue on an individual basis.

Phase 3. Recovery Group

After completion of the Evening Program (Phase 2), each patient is encouraged to participate in a weekly group therapy session ("recovery group") for the next 12 months. This group will confront any tendency to deny alcoholism. Emphasis is placed on continuing sobriety, recognition of feelings, and coping with affect appropriately and without use of alcohol or drugs. Family members are offered a separate group therapy experience, and a recovery group for married couples is often very useful. These groups are in addition to the strong recommendation that patients be attending several AA meetings each week and that family members be involved in Al-Anon.

OFFICE MANAGEMENT OF THE ALCOHOLIC PATIENT

If a structured outpatient program such as that described above is not available, office management of the alcoholic patient may be necessary. As the initial phase of treatment, office management is very difficult and should focus on helping the patient accept more definitive inpatient or outpatient programs as described earlier. Every effort should be made to introduce the patient to AA. Schedules of local AA meetings should be kept in the office and given to each patient. The physician should know several recovered men and women active in local AA who are willing to meet with a new patient, share their experiences, and take the patient to an AA meeting. I've frequently had an AA member meet with my patients after our appointment. They would share a cup of coffee and plan to attend an AA meeting that evening or the next day.

If the patient refuses referral to programs specific for the treatment of alcoholism or other forms of substance abuse, it is necessary to obtain past medical records, do a physical examination and relevant laboratory tests, and obtain a collaborative history from relatives. Prescribing should be avoided except for the guidelines offered in Chapter 11. If the patient is withdrawing from alcohol, a three-to-four-day supply of benzodiazepines is appropriate (see Chapter 11).

It will be essential to establish a therapeutic relationship with the patient, explain the disease concept, recognize and point out the dynamics of the disease, and consistently urge the patient toward abstinence. Should the patient be able to stop drinking under these circumstances, a further diagnostic evaluation becomes possible and any concomitant psychiatric disorders addressed. It is important to interview the spouse or other family members to determine whether or not they can be supportive of abstinence and treatment. The family will need education regarding alcoholism. Literature can be provided to them and Al-Anon should be recommended. Often martial or family therapy may be helpful.

The important thing to remember is to keep the issue of alcoholism in the forefront of treatment and emphasize the necessity for abstinence. Other therapeutic issues are necessarily given lesser priority until the latter goal is obtained. A particularly helpful adjunct to office management of the alcoholic is the use of disulfiram (discussed in Chapter 11).

Thus far we have discussed office management from the perspective of the patient who is just beginning treatment for alcoholism. Office management for those patients who have successfully completed an inpatient or outpatient program as described above is a different situation and is an opportunity to support recovery and facilitate a growthful sobriety. Many of the above principles apply: strongly encourage AA attendance; try to help the patient enroll in a recovery group as described above; involve spouse and family as appropriate; and utilize disulfiram when indicated. As sobriety becomes more secure, dynamic issues may be explored through psychotherapy.

The following clinical example illustrates office management:

A 45-year-old woman expressed concern to an internist about her drinking. She asked him for help and was referred for an evaluation. Although not clearly alcohol dependent, she reported an escalating pattern of abuse over the past two years. Socially embarrassing episodes and a relatively harmless flirtation with an old friend alarmed this usually reserved and shy woman. She refused an outpatient program and did not require inpatient treatment. She quickly reversed her drinking pattern and seemed able to limit alcohol to wine at dinner during social occasions outside her home. In the course of the outpatient appointment over a 3-month period she recognized that her college-age son had a serious alcohol and drug problem. She took the initiative to arrange for his treatment. She refused AA and group therapy as personal revelation of most any kind was unusually painful for her. I saw my role to be supportive of her efforts at altering her alcohol use and supportive of her concern for her son. In addition, I provided an educational role for her and her husband (he was seen once) and remained available for further appointments if her current stability was lost.

A more difficult patient was an attorney in his early sixties and prominent in community activities who had been hospitalized for "anemia" and whose wife had left town until he quit drinking. He agreed to try AA but felt a disdain for their "self-pity." He begged not to be sent to an inpatient program. He preferred to take disulfiram and to meet with me individually. After 6 months he stopped the disulfiram without discussion with me. He has continued to remain sober and our appointments terminated after 10 months.

My work with him was largely directed toward helping him guard against relapse and providing him with an understanding of the effects of alcohol. I also served as a reminder for him of the benefits he had gained by giving up alcohol. For example, his relationship with his wife improved and he was able to be very supportive as she experienced several deaths in her family. In addition, he experienced renewed interest in former community activities. Early in treatment I met with his wife several times to encourage her to give him a chance, to help her cope with her anger, and to educate her about alcoholism as a disease.

As mentioned above, a most potent use of office-based outpatient treatment is in the context of aftercare following the patient's treatment in a formal substance abuse program.

A 52-year-old consulting engineer was referred by a treatment center in another state. The patient had moved from the city where he was treated and was within weeks of completing an inpatient program. It would be several months before his wife and children could join him. He was sober but depressed. His new job was at a staff level and a distinct decline in status. His alcoholism had led to the loss of his previous job and had put severe strain on the family's financial condition. He joined AA and used the meetings as a social outlet by going out to dinner with members after meetings. An antidepressant was prescribed and yielded a good result as manifested by improved concentration, renewed energy, and a better sleep pattern. He was also able to understand that his current position of lesser responsibility was an advantage for him in his early months of sobriety. The guilt this man felt about the trials of his family and the need to moderate his expectations of himself and of others were major themes in therapy.

To conclude, outpatient treatment offers a viable option for the carefully considered alcoholic patient. An agreement with the patient to accept inpatient treatment if an outpatient approach fails should be made as treatment options are considered. Although family involvement and support should be sought in any treatment setting, results of outpatient treatment depend most clearly on a supportive interpersonal environment which backs up the efforts of treatment personnel.

CHAPTER 10

Psychodynamic Considerations

The psychiatric treatment of alcoholism necessitates an awareness of three spheres of clinical concern: (a) *Organicity*. Organic changes in brain functioning secondary to acute and chronic effects of alcohol may interdigitate with treatment efforts at any stage of the disease (see Chapter 12). (b) *The Disease of Alcoholism*. These subjective experiences and the associated defenses operate dynamically to influence the patient's relationship to himself or herself and the environment. Breaking through the denial of the alcoholic patient and establishing an acceptance and understanding of the disease concept is a major task of rehabilitation programs. A successful recovery, manifested by sobriety, improved personal relationships, and improved work performance is unlikely if the pathological defenses are not removed and the fact of one's disease accepted. Once this occurs, a satisfactory result is obtained for many alcoholic patients. (c) *Psychodynamic Considerations* that predispose one to alcoholism, precipitate alcoholism, or modify one's ability to recover from alcoholism. The complex interrelationship between these spheres of clinical concern is illustrated in Figure 10-1.

The psychodynamic issues most relevant to substance abusing patients (including alcoholic patients) do not imply specific diagnostic entities as found in DSM-III-R. The relationship between alcohol dependence and other psychiatric disorders will be reviewed in Chapter 12. Psychodynamics is a theory of human behavior and motivation that emphasizes the functional significance of emotions, conflicts, defense mechanisms, interpersonal relationships, and other vectors that influ-

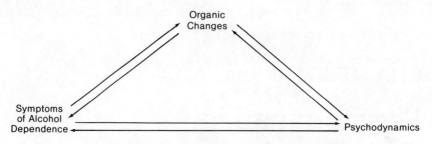

Figure 10-1. Three spheres of clinical concern.

ence behavior. Psychodynamics describes learned patterns, largely unconscious, of affective and cognitive responses to internal and external stimuli and proposes that behavior is determined by past experience, genetic endowment, and current reality (American Psychiatric Press, 1984).

GUIDELINES FOR THINKING ABOUT PSYCHODYNAMICS

- Psychodynamics need to be considered carefully in the assessment and treatment of the alcoholic patient. Recovery may hinge on skilled recognition and management of these emotional forces. No single psychodynamic pattern is common to alcoholism or other substance use disorders. Recognizing the role which psychodynamic factors may play in the development of alcoholism or in the patient's struggle with recovery does not imply the existence of an "addictive personality." The concept of addictive personality has not proved to be clinically useful as neither psychological testing nor clinical interviews demonstrate traits unique to and consistent in all alcoholic patients.
- Recognition of psychodynamics does not imply an etiological role in a singular sense. The cause of alcoholism is unknown, but it is best thought of as multidetermined.
- Most alcoholics who have recovered have done so without formal therapeutic attention to their particular psychodynamics. This does not mean that psychodynamics were not modified during the course of the disease. The stresses and crises associated with the disease may lead to psychodynamic shifts which enable healing to occur. For example, a defensive stance of self-sufficiency may bend as repeated failures to control drinking occur. The psychodynamics of alcoholism and recovery seem to have been intuitively sensed by Bill Wilson and the other early founders of AA (Kurtz, 1979). The genius of AA may be the creation of a program that allows psychodynamic forces to operate in the interest of, rather than against, recovery.

- The psychodynamic forces operating in the patient should be understood by the therapist. It is a matter of extremely sensitive clinical judgment how this understanding is utilized. There are times when the patient's capacity to recover depends upon or is greatly facilitated by a deeper understanding of his or her behavior.

A young woman, the wife of a physician, was admitted following an overdose of amitriptyline. Apart from depression and dependence on alcohol, her drinking commonly was initiated by the anger and frustration she felt toward her husband. Her drinking was a source of anguish for him, and he felt "impotent" whenever a drinking bout began. She drank "at" him when she became angry. Understanding the relationship between drinking, anger, and retaliation toward her husband assisted this patient in removing alcohol from the power struggle intrinsic to her marriage. She recognized that alcohol was life-threatening for her and was able to begin working on sobriety and her marriage in parallel.

Another example where an understanding of dynamics proved helpful occurred in a physician:

A surgeon in his mid-fifties had become alcohol dependent at least 10 years prior to seeking treatment. His wife distanced herself by developing her own career. This in turn frustrated his increasing demands for attention and appreciation. More blatant and severe drinking resulted. During inpatient treatment he was able to appreciate, through a review of his recent behavior and his current interactions with the staff, how regressed (impatient and demanding) his behavior had become. The regressive effect of alcohol, combined with his long history of denial of personal needs, led to a breakthrough of infantile demands. He could see that much of his frustration evolved from his expectation that he should have what he wanted when he wanted it. This realization was contrary to the way he usually thought of himself, and he began to value sobriety as a symbol of renewed maturity.

- Focusing on psychodynamics only can be potentially harmful in two ways: One, the patient and/or the therapist may assume that insight or an understanding of one's emotional vulnerabilities will cure alcoholism, that as self-understanding grows, the patient will either be able to regulate his or her drinking safely or will decide not to drink at all. Such an unfounded assumption has often compromised dynamic psychiatry's contribution to the treatment of alcoholism. Many alcoholic patients are comfortable exploring their reactions and responses in therapy and expect that when deeper self-understanding occurs the drinking will take care of itself. Therapists of any persuasion need to avoid this trap.

Gus, a middle-aged homosexual man, had been in intensive analytically oriented therapy for over 8 years. Conflicts regarding homosexuality, aggression, and passivity had been addressed and this aspect of treatment was important to his growth as an adult. Regrettably, his drinking began progressing over a 4 to 5 year period and was ignored. Eventually, he developed a peripheral neuropathy and alcoholic hallucinosis and was admitted to an alcoholism treatment program. He responded very well with a good long-term outcome. In addition, he worked through the disappointing ending of his prior therapeutic relationship.

Second, some patients, alcoholic or otherwise, cannot work with uncovering, psychodynamic approaches. They may not be able to tolerate the anxiety or other strong affect and retreat to drinking.

An alcoholic nurse wished to repair her relationship with her two grown sons, who had been alienated by her alcoholism. As she explored her guilt, strong feelings about the parenting she had received as a child began to surface. A brief psychosis ensued, then a "slip," and finally therapy was structured toward a greater acceptance of the past and the necessity to let the wounds heal. The patient had no further hospitalization coverage, was on probation in her job, and had used all her sick leave. Any further uncovering of dynamic material would have seemed to jeopardize this patient's emotional and social stability.

With these guidelines we can proceed to a review of psychodynamic formulations and pay special attention to the evolution of dynamic thinking as applied to patients with alcohol dependence.

PSYCHODYNAMIC FORMULATIONS

For several decades psychodynamic formulations have been de-emphasized in the etiology of alcoholism for three reasons: (a) The search for an "addictive" personality or prealcoholic personality was discredited because no measure or assessment of personality functioning could be found that consistently predicted alcoholism or was consistently associated with alcoholism; (b) early instinctual theory emphasizing oral gratification (Rado, 1933) was an oversimplification and not verified by clinical experience; and (c) data from genetic studies have stimulated a strong interest in predisposing biological variables. Recently, Peele (1986) has addressed the limitations of current genetic models.

Despite the low profile assumed by psychodynamic theory in the alcoholism field, there are at least three models which are helpful in organizing clinical data. The first model, the dependency conflict model, was the earliest viable formulation (McCord & McCord, 1960).

The model illustrated in Figure 10-2 emphasizes maternal determinants of dependency needs. Blane (1968), in a variation on this model, describes the "counter-dependent" alcoholic who is motivated to disguise underlying unmet needs by a pseudomasculine independent image. Humiliation over feeling "needy" necessitates a defensive facade which overvalues personal independence, denial of emotions, and self-determination. The individual influenced by this dynamic pattern is usually angry. The anger has a distancing effect, which reinforces the independent facade, which betrays the pain of an unmet need to be cared for.

A second model can be described as a "power conflict" model (Mc-Clelland et al., 1972). This model emphasizes adult situational factors as well as childhood experiences. The essence of this formulation is that alcohol produces increased feelings of personal power, a subjective experience which is compelling for males who feel their masculine role is undercut by social or interpersonal processes. This model (Figure 10-3) has been used to explain the high rates of alcohol consumption among inner-city black males. The young black male is expected to be "macho" but finds himself frequently cut out of the job market. The ensuing

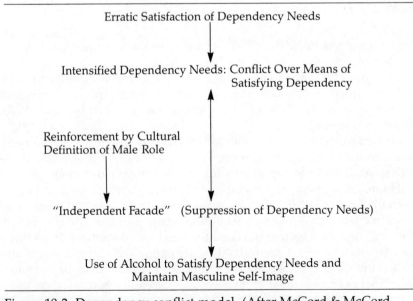

Erratic Satisfaction of Dependency Needs

Intensified Dependency Needs: Conflict Over Means of Satisfying Dependency

Reinforcement by Cultural Definition of Male Role

"Independent Facade"   (Suppression of Dependency Needs)

Use of Alcohol to Satisfy Dependency Needs and Maintain Masculine Self-Image

Figure 10-2. Dependency conflict model. (After McCord & McCord, 1960. *Origins of Alcoholism*. Reprinted by permission from Stanford University Press.)

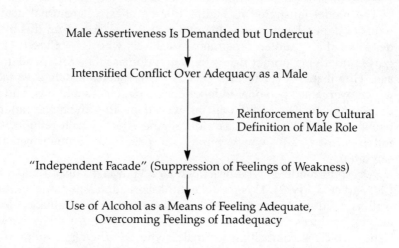

Figure 10-3. Power conflict model. (Reprinted with permission of the Free Press, a Division of Macmillan, Inc., from *The Drinking Man* by David C. McClelland, William N. Davis, Rudolf Kalin, and Eric Wanner. Copyright © 1972 by David C. McClelland, Willian N. Davis, Rudolf Kalin, and Eric Wanner.)

conflict over feeling inadequate as a man is resolved by the pharmacologic effect of alcohol.

Wilsnack (1973) has found alcohol to have a similar capacity for conflict resolution in females. With women alcohol increases feelings of femininity and was "useful" for those women in conflict and doubt about their feminine role.

A third model is derived from self-psychology (Kohut, 1971) and emphasizes the role of early distortions in one's sense of self and how these repressed distortions impact on adult functioning (Figure 10-4).

Figure 10-4 attempts to simplify complex developmental concepts from the field of self-psychology. It is assumed that the child requires an empathic relationship with a parenting figure and that the parent will "mirror" or reflect back to the child the need for admiration. From this a healthy sense of self is derived. Also, the parent will need to accept and be worthy of idealization by the child. This matrix of empathy established between the infant and parent is a necessary psychological environment just as, physiologically, the respiratory system requires an agreeable mixture of oxygen and carbon dioxide.

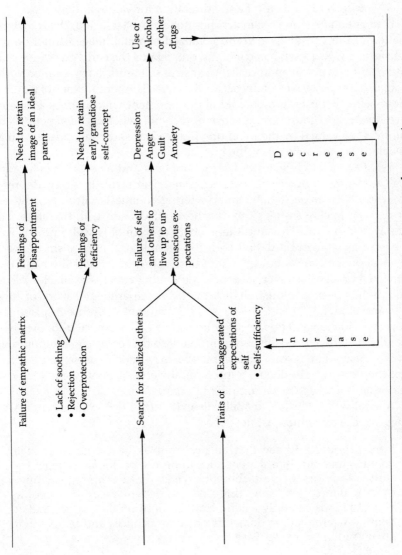

Figure 10-4. Self-psychology developmental concepts.

A healthy sense of self will develop as the early "grandiose self" and "idealized parental image" characteristic of childhood are gradually transformed from, for example, "I'm superman" to "I'm worthwhile" and "you're God" to respect and admiration for values and ideals.

If an adequate empathic matrix has not been established, the transformation of the grandiose self and idealized parental image cannot occur satisfactorily. Regression occurs, and one retains the early grandiose self and goes on to adopt an unrealistic sense of self-sufficiency coupled with unrealistic expectations of oneself and others. The continuance of a grandiose self constitutes a pathological development which serves a defensive function to counteract a sense of incompleteness. The experienced failure to be valued by the parenting figures leaves the individual with a deficiency in the ability to value himself or herself.

Reality will surely lead to disappointments and a sense of failure in regard to these unconscious expectations. The result is anger, depression, guilt, or anxiety. Enter mind-altering chemicals: alcohol or other drugs will quickly assuage the dysphoric affects and will, therefore, be highly reinforcing. This anesthetic effect of alcohol is well known. For the man or woman burdened with the pathological narcissism derived from the retention of the early grandiose self-concept and the need for idealized others, however, a second reinforcing effect is available. Alcohol, as has been demonstrated through the experimental work of McClelland et al. (1972) and Wilsnack (1973), promotes a sense of personal power or adequacy. Thus, alcohol not only can be expected to anesthetize the pain of depression and guilt, but also to reestablish, temporarily, the defensive grandiosity and self-sufficiency which has served to protect the person from deeper sources of anxiety. Alcohol works too well and, therefore, becomes a compelling experience.

A letter written in 1953 by Bill Wilson (Kurtz, 1979), cofounder of AA, suggests the dynamics just described:

> I am beginning to see that all my troubles have their root in a habitual and absolute dependence upon my personal prestige, security, and romantic attachment. When these things go wrong, there is depression. Now this absolute dependence upon people and situations can only lead to conflict. Both on the surface and at depth. We are making demands on circumstances and people that are bound to fail us. (p. 214)

Psychodynamic models serve as cognitive "maps" useful in the organization and the conceptualization of clinical data. This chapter has highlighted three formulations; overlap amongst them is apparent. The most useful dynamic formulations are those that capture in a cognitive sense that which exists at the intuitive and experiential levels. Bill

Wilson's letter and the formulations of self-psychology illustrate this relationship. As we learn more about the development of self-esteem, initiative, empathy, and ambition—in other words, about the process of normal narcissistic development and its pathological offshoots—we may understand and possibly predict vulnerability to many pathological states better.

Ego Psychology

Parallel with the developing concepts from self-psychology, useful advances in the area of ego psychology have emerged from classical psychoanalytic thinking. Of particular importance has been the description of ego deficits in alcoholic patients. Khantzian (1981) has specified two major areas of ego deficiency:

Impairment in recognition and regulation of feelings. Alcoholic patients may have difficulty recognizing their feelings. Unable to detect the discrete feeling states which serve as signals for initiative, the alcoholic person often experiences a vague state of discomfort which is difficult to express. Affect may become deverbalized or somaticized (Wurmser, 1974).

Alternatively, when feelings are experienced there may be difficulty with regulation. Anxiety may seem terrifying, and anger can become overwhelming. Considering the range and variety of discomfort associated with affects in alcoholic patients, it is not surprising that the rapid, predictable, and pleasurable effect of alcohol is highly valued. It has been assumed that the defect in affect recognition and regulation precedes alcohol dependence, but this assumption awaits empirical verification.

During the first year of recovery from alcoholism, many alcoholic patients experience difficulty not in recognition of feelings, but rather with the awareness of their emotional states. It is as if they have come out from under a state of emotional anesthesia which resulted from drinking and are now exposed to the range of human emotions. It is useful to explain this to patients using a physical analogy: One is emotionally "out of shape." Just as muscles become sore and ligaments ache when one undertakes a physical conditioning program, so will the alcohol-abusing patient feel bombarded with emotion as he or she turns aside from alcohol as a source of comfort. The most common problem is recognizing normal feelings. There is concern that one's emotions are abnormal—too anxious, too angry, too relaxed. A major therapeutic task is to assist the patient in recognizing the normal variations in affective states and to support them as they learn to endure affect without succumbing to the temptation to change feelings by using drugs or alcohol.

Impairment in self-care. A second major ego deficit, observable in alcoholic patients and believed to precede the development of alcohol dependence, is self-care. Alcoholic patients often have shown deficiencies in judgment and in anticipation of consequences of behavior. A failure to anticipate danger or a lack of attention to cues that usually serve as warnings leads to a history of minor accidents, medical problems that could have been prevented, financial problems, or legal difficulties (Khantzian, 1981). Possibly, this deficit in capacity for self-care enables the use of alcohol in an excessive and ultimately harmful manner.

In addition to the impulsive, stimulus-bound, or reckless range of behavior and the relative inattention to cues that characterize the deficit in self-care, a second facet warrants attention. This second facet in the self-care deficit is a sense of helplessness or inability to take initiative. It is as if the individual feels that if someone else doesn't do it for me it can't be done.

Some clinical examples may illustrate this point:

A 55-year-old physician clearly recognized his alcoholism and the need for long-term aftercare treatment. He was enthusiastic about attending AA meetings while in the hospital. Staff and fellow patients encouraged his use of AA, and a van provided transportation to the meetings. At time of discharge he was given names of recovering physicians in his community who had offered their support. It was at this point that he struggled over following through. It seemed difficult for him to make the calls and to initiate these contacts. He was not denying his need for the support and had been relieved to know help from colleagues was available. He had difficulty in taking the initiative in carrying out self-care behaviors on his own. A combination of prodding and patience by the staff finally broke through this barrier.

A young woman with extensive prior treatment described her most recent relapse. She had recognized the signs of impending relapse (thus showing some capacity for recognizing cues): withdrawal from family and friends, isolation, and failure to attend AA meetings. Despite her cognizance of impending danger, she was not able to initiate steps (for example, call her AA sponsor) to interrupt the inevitable binge. At this time she is working on the need to develop behaviors that promote self-care.

Self-care deficits are believed to reflect a failure in the internalization of care-taking behavior of the parents. It is obvious that the alcoholic's capacity for self-care is diminished once alcohol abuse is underway. It remains to be determined to what extent defects in self-care precede the development of alcoholism and how specific such ego deficits are to substance abusing patients.

Attention to the ego function of self-care is essential in the treatment of alcoholism. As patients become aware of the defect they often are able to make corrections and lessen the chance of relapse.

This review of psychodynamic considerations in the treatment of alcoholism emphasizes that an understanding of dynamics is vitally important to effective management of alcoholism. Second, it is equally important to apply this understanding of dynamics very judiciously so that recovery is enhanced and the establishment and maintenance of sobriety are not compromised. With this background, specific therapies will be addressed.

CHAPTER 11

Specific Therapies

In this chapter the application of specific therapies to the treatment of alcoholism will be addressed. The therapies to be discussed are individual psychotherapy, group psychotherapy, family therapy, and pharmacotherapy. Each of these therapeutic approaches will be presented in the light of their use in the treatment of alcoholic patients. A discussion of these techniques in a generic sense is not intended.

INDIVIDUAL PSYCHOTHERAPY

If one were to visit alcoholism rehabilitation centers (Stuckey & Harrison, 1982) or AA meetings, it would be apparent that individual psychotherapy is held in low esteem as a treatment method for alcoholics. Historical factors help us to understand this assessment. First, individual psychotherapy has traditionally meant psychoanalytically oriented therapy, which made use of interpretations and development of insight. Alcoholism was seen as a symptom of underlying psychopathology and, as such, was expected to abate entirely or be brought under control as insight developed. This approach has proven to be largely unsuccessful (Tiebout, 1982; Zimberg, 1982). Second, the influence which an alcohol dependence had on the thinking and behavior of the alcoholic was not widely appreciated. The concept of alcoholism as a disease was neither accepted nor understood, and the impact of the physiological and psychological dependence on alcohol was underemphasized. Third, abstinence was not emphasized. Attempting to do psychotherapy while the patient continues to drink, especially if the therapy is not focused on drinking, is of little benefit. In fact, it may do harm since the patient may interpret the therapist's passivity about alcohol use as legitimizing continued drinking.

These criticisms remain cogent today. For example, a prospective study (Vaillant, 1981) of males who had developed alcoholism revealed that, of those who obtained psychotherapy, only 1 of 13 men would relate remission to psychotherapy. Further, the therapy experience was often seen to deflect attention away from the drinking problem. Consider this addicted physician's published account (Rogers, 1985):

> During the 70s I saw two psychiatrists at different times because of my depression. I told each of them during the course of therapy I thought I was "taking too many drugs." The first of them said: "You're taking too many drugs because you are depressed. I'll have to treat your depression before we can get you off drugs." He put me on Mellaril and Tofranil.
>
> The second psychiatrist said: "You're depressed because you have too many unresolved conflicts. We need to talk about these. Cut down on those other drugs you're taking." He put me on Elavil.
>
> Surely they would have told me if I were a drug addict.
>
> I spent hundreds of hours and thousands of dollars on psychiatrists, and I only got worse. My drug-taking and my drinking increased.
>
> For a long time I carried with me resentments against the psychiatrists I had asked for help. They didn't know, apparently, that my depression was a direct result of my alcoholism and drug addiction. Why didn't they know I was crying for help? Why didn't they know about denial? Why didn't they know that alcoholism and drug addiction are primary diseases? Why didn't they encourage me to join Alcoholics Anonymous? For a long time I wanted an apology from them.

Does all of this mean that individual therapy has no role in the treatment of the alcoholic? No, but the role of psychotherapy needs to be redefined and is subject to variation depending on the patient and what phase of treatment he or she may be in. But first, certain behaviors on the part of the therapist need to be emphasized.

The Behavior of the Therapist

1. *Active.* The therapist should be prepared to ask questions, provide answers, and intervene by involving family members or by utilizing a hospital. A passive stance in the interest of an unfolding of dynamically

related material is called for only under specific circumstances, such as when the patient is not endangering his health by drinking or when the patient can tolerate the frustration of relatively little feedback from the therapist.

2. *Educative.* The therapist should be able to explain the disease of alcoholism to the patient. The characteristic responses, resistances, and experiences of alcohol dependent people should be taught to the patient as therapy proceeds. Literature on alcoholism should be available to distribute to patients for reading between sessions. The patient's reactions to and understanding of the reading material can be explored in therapy sessions.

3. *Confrontational.* The therapist will need to be open with the patient about his observations. Patients who are drinking pathologically but keeping therapy appointments will need to be told of the risks to health and social functioning that their behavior entails. They cannot be allowed to assume that they will get better simply by keeping appointments.

4. *Countertransference openness.* The therapist needs to retain awareness of his or her feelings toward the patient. If advice and treatment efforts or recommendations are ignored or devalued by the patient, the therapist should explain his concerns, first within himself or herself, and then with the patient. The therapist needs to avoid a buildup of anger, disgust, or derision toward the patient. He or she should strive to communicate countertransference responses as tangible expressions of caring. Such openness helps patients appreciate their effect on others in a nonjudgmental setting. It also reveals the therapist as a real person who is comfortable with his or her feelings and who is accepting of himself or herself as a less than omnipotent and less than perfect being.

To summarize, this discussion puts forth a group of behaviors which have as their purpose the termination of drinking and the consolidation of a relationship. The therapist is asking, indeed insisting, that the patient deprive himself or herself. It is necessary to be explicit about this: "The therapist must not sidestep his depriving role; instead he must freely acknowledge it and let therapy begin right there" (Tiebout, 1973, p. 6). With experience, therapists become more aware that alcoholics will accept limitations, including abstinence from alcohol (Dodes, 1984). Active, open concern expressed by the therapist serves as an auxiliary form of self-care, temporarily complementing the deficit in self-care described in the last chapter.

Treatment Phases*

These phases of treatment refer to the stages of recovery which a patient passes through during treatment. The role of the therapist varies according to the patient's phase of recovery and according to the amount of prior treatment received. As progress occurs, the therapist's focus shifts from the dynamics of the addiction to the dynamics of the individual. In general, therapy is directed toward achieving abstinence and strengthening the ego in the areas of affect tolerance, self-care, and self-esteem regulation.

Recognition phase. This phase begins with the patient's first treatment contact that implies an admission of a problem.

A 45-year-old building contractor had been told a year earlier by his family doctor that he had a "drinking problem." A year later this man recognized that his physician might be right and called for an appointment. He admitted alcohol was a problem and promptly stopped drinking. Thus, at age 44 there was a treatment contact (family physician), but it took a year for the patient to "admit" or acknowledge that the problem existed.

Admission of the problem is the essential feature of this first phase of recovery (Johnson, 1973). The admission can be prompted by outside forces (employer, court, family, or friends). Similarly, internal recognition may occur as the person assesses declining health, change in work performance, or the concerns of family and friends.

What is the role of the therapist at this stage? All efforts should be put into helping the patient accept the need for an alcoholism treatment program. This involves being active with the patient—confronting and educating the patient—all in the interest of forming a relationship that can be used as leverage toward acceptance of the need for a treatment program.

The building contractor referred to recognized and admitted to a problem, but would go no further. He stopped drinking, but refused to enter an outpatient or inpatient program and saw no need to have appointments with me because he had stopped drinking and he was feeling better.

What did I do in this case? First, I acknowledged his alcoholism, that is, I told him he was alcoholic. Second, I explained what is meant by

---

*The phases to be described are similar to Johnson's (1973) phases of treatment as described in *I'll Quit Tomorrow*. This section is modeled on his original work with some modification.

alcoholism and how it affects one's thinking and behavior. I met with his wife and him on one occasion to assess her understanding and to provide further education. I strongly reinforced his efforts to quit drinking because this reflects a step toward better self-care. I tried to stay on good terms with him and create a relationship that he could return to as necessary.

What was not done? No attempt was made to approach the patient's need to appear self-sufficient or his carefully guarded reactive grandiosity. He denied the need for AA or therapy. I was in no position to confront the obvious denial of his long-standing dependence on alcohol. He had admitted a problem and had stopped drinking, but was not ready to explore dynamic themes.

I left the door open for further treatment, which seems likely to be necessary eventually. At that time a progression to additional phases of treatment might occur.

Compliance phase. This is a very difficult phase of treatment. The patient superficially recognizes or admits to alcoholism. He or she participates in a treatment program and perhaps attends AA as well. But when the program has been completed, or others are not there to encourage or prod the continuation of treatment or attendance at AA, the need to deal with the disease is dropped. Compliance is sometimes revealed in treatment by the patient's failure to carry out plans. In Chapter 8, the use of weekend passes was described. The patient who carefully plans a well-structured weekend, but is then unable to follow through (e.g., found other things more important, felt too tired, "forgot," or any number of other excuses) is likely to be in the compliance phase.

Tiebout (1953) cogently describes this phenomenon. Compliance is a "going along" but without wholehearted acceptance. There is cooperation, but it is a skeptical act where one is unconvinced of the necessity, but not about to argue. Tiebout describes compliance as a form of submission wherein the patient superficially acknowledges his or her condition (but does not have a deeper understanding of the implication). When the pain of one's alcoholism becomes acute (a medical crisis occurs, a job is threatened, or spouse leaves home) the patient cannot explicitly deny the problem. He or she accepts (complies with) the need for making a change. As the pain recedes (the pancreatitis subsides, the spouse returns), the need for change subsides. It is as if the acute pain that forces the alcoholic to see the reality of his or her condition also stimulates the underlying reactive grandiosity, which of course contributes to the defense of denial.

Tiebout (1949) describes the process as follows:

Patients express less concern about their drinking, complain that they were rushed into seeking help, that they're not worse than anybody else, that the worry of others is silly and a gratuitous invasion of their rights, until finally, memory of their own acute period of anxiety is swallowed up by the defiance and the grandiosity and thus loses its effectiveness as a stimulus to create suffering and a desire for change. This cycle will go on repeating itself as long as the defiance and the grandiosity continue to function with unimpaired vigor. (p. 53)

How does the therapist respond during the phase of compliance? First, the therapist continues to work with the patient, avoids discouragement, and accumulates data that document the patient's loss of control over alcohol use. Keeping the reality of the patient's relationship with alcohol in the forefront is essential. Poignant moments of regret and grief revealed during the acute crises which led to treatment are recalled for discussion. The recollection of painful experiences is not used to induce guilt, but to serve as an antidote for the glib dismissal, the minimalization, and the denial of the pathological drinking. The complications of drinking are re-presented to stimulate the development of self-care behaviors. The facts are reviewed to help the patient counter the momentum that is building for a return to alcohol use.

It is also important for the therapist to work with the family and/or employer during this phase in order to help them sustain the effort to stick with their expectations of change in the alcoholic. It provides them with support and information which will forestall their tendency to deny the seriousness of the illness and will dissolve the veneer of "wishful thinking" that everything may be all right this time.

Compliance, therefore, represents a superficial adaption to the painful consequences of alcoholism. The conscious mind is appeasing the environment, but acceptance of powerlessness over alcohol at the deeper unconscious level remains to be achieved. The defense of reactive grandiosity is operating unconsciously.

A young woman, during group therapy for alcoholism, expressed unintentionally—but well—her feelings about treatment. "I've started something I don't want to finish—I mean, I do want to finish!" Her "slip of the tongue" revealed her ambivalence about treatment, and she quickly attempted to cover it up.

For stable recovery to occur, the compliance phase must be surpassed. The next phase, the acceptance phase, is a giant step forward. Specific events (crises) or actions (confrontations) may be necessary for the shift from compliance to acceptance to occur.

Acceptance phase. In the acceptance phase of recovery, the therapist recognizes that the patient admits defeat as far as being able to continue drinking. This is different from only admitting that alcohol has caused problems as it occurs in the recognition phase of recovery. The first step of AA expresses it as follows: "We admitted we were powerless over alcohol—that our lives had become unmanageable."

The key advance in this phase of recovery is the acceptance of power-lessness over alcohol. The patient is now open to reality; the defensive grandiosity described earlier has subsided. The therapist is now in a position to consolidate a therapeutic alliance. Confrontation (see Chapter 7) can now be set aside. The patient is able to listen and to learn. This phase provides the therapist with an excellent opportunity to help the patient recognize events in his or her life that stimulate the urge to drink. The patient is also more accepting of recognizing rationalizations and forms of denial as they occur. The former defensiveness is not there. It is crucial, however, that the therapist be aware that the pathological defenses (e.g., denial and reactive grandiosity) can again appear and impede recovery.

During this phase the patient may begin to develop greater tolerance for affect. Frustration is handled with greater ease. Feelings of guilt and shame can now be recognized and can be discussed in therapy.

> A young professional athlete was mandated to receive treatment for cocaine abuse and alcoholism. Modest and personable, he cooperated fully. He was polite, said all the right things, and enjoyed the affection and admiration of his fellow patients and staff alike. There was very little to confront.
>
> In retrospect, it became apparent that little self-revelation took place while he was in the alcoholism treatment program. After discharge he immediately began drinking. He frightened his wife, but for the first time she was able to avoid being intimidated. She prepared to leave him. He became angry and frustrated over his inability to control events.
>
> After several weeks of turmoil, he returned to treatment. He felt "stopped" by alcohol, was frightened and depressed. The seriousness of his condition now colored his affect. He had accepted defeat by alcohol in a deeper sense, and the facade of past compliance was replaced by greater openness.

How does one effect a shift from the phase of compliance to one of acceptance? There is no easy answer to this. Two paths seem apparent. They do not represent so much a choice on the part of the therapist, but rather sets of conditions which can be used to mobilize a healthy shift in defense. On the first, least common path, the therapist has a strong commitment to doing therapy and develops a firm therapeutic alliance with the patient.

> A psychiatry resident was asked to treat a hospital employee, an alcoholic nurse who had exhausted her resources for private care. She was "hopeless." All efforts to curb her alcoholism had fallen short. The resident took his assignment seriously. Although he was very inexperienced with alcoholic patients, he wished to please his supervisors (the source of this referral).
>
> The resident was able to uncover and respect the one kernel of self-esteem this woman had left: her pride in being a registered nurse. Building on this, the nurse gradually transferred her interest in caring for others to an interest in self-care. Against a background of frustration and failure with all other treatment attempts (including AA and rehabilitation programs) the relationship with the resident enabled the patient finally to accept her "powerlessness over alcohol." Sobriety followed, but not without a variety of other concerns that necessitated continuing treatment.

Sometimes a therapeutic relationship formed in the context of past treatment failures leads to remarkable success. I have wondered if success occurs in part because the therapist feels he has nothing to lose. Expectations are low because no one else has ever been able to do anything. This position has an advantage over one in which the therapist's narcissistic needs for success are pitted against the patient's grandiosity. In the latter case, the therapist loses, as does the patient.

More commonly, acceptance is reached by the alcoholic's being "stopped," particularly when external circumstances impinge on all sides. The spouse, the employer, friends, and physician are unanimous and united in no longer accepting the alcoholic's attempts to control, avoid, or evade treatment. When the alcoholic realizes he is stopped, that manipulation no longer is effective, acceptance, rather than simply recognition and compliance, has a chance to occur.

> A very successful civil engineer more or less agreed that he was alcoholic. He had been agreeing for 10 years. Yet, he said to look at his high salary, his kids were in fine schools, and so on. Finally, he was fired. It was clean and neat. His drinking had made him unfit for the task at hand. The impact of this crisis led to a major depression, but also to an alcoholism treatment program. Soon he was able to express gratitude that someone had "blown the whistle" on his drinking. His being fired saved his life as it led to his acceptance of being powerless over alcohol and to an acceptance of a need for treatment.

Finally, a fourth phase of recovery may be observed. This phase allows for much greater choice in therapy. Not the choice of whether to drink or not, but the choice as to what areas to explore.

Integration phase. The achievement of sobriety does not usually depend on reaching this phase. Most alcoholics gain sobriety by virtue of the Acceptance Phase. It is desirable for the Integration Phase to develop, and individual therapy is the treatment of choice during this stage. The alcoholic at this time can be approached psychotherapeutically like nonalcoholic patients. The issues to be addressed in therapy is a decision between patient and therapist.

The alcoholic has now fully accepted his or her condition and acquired stable sobriety. The organic effects of alcohol have abated to the maximum possible. (Patients with permanent brain damage, if only moderate, can still be expected to benefit from psychotherapy.) The patient understands the disease concept of alcoholism and its various manifestations, for example, craving. It is now optimal to attend to individual dynamics or to other specific disorders.

> An employee of the telephone company had over 5 years of sobriety when he sought therapy. He had been experiencing anxiety attacks with increasing frequency. Issues of control and dependency vis-à-vis women were involved. He was able to explore these areas effectively. He was at peace with a life of abstinence. Although he missed some good times he had had during his drinking days, the idea of further alcohol use was out of the question, and he was free of conflict about alcohol even during the times when he was symptomatic with an anxiety disorder.

In contrast to the Acceptance Phase, the Integration Phase is free from conflict over alcoholism. The person is able to dismiss urges to drink without experiencing a "close call" over a slip. Shame and guilt about being an alcoholic have been replaced with a self-respect rooted in recovery. Guilt over the past is put into proper perspective. It serves as a reminder for continuing to practice good self-care and to value sobriety. The rigidity of personality functioning (Butts & Chotlas, 1979) that often characterizes early sobriety is lessened, and flexibility and patience emerge.

On the other hand, the alcoholic in the Integration Phase of recovery remembers that he or she is vulnerable to a return of alcohol dependence.

After 10 years of sobriety, John retired from his original career and entered the field of alcoholism counseling. Having acquired a masters degree in psychology, he took tough jobs which involved tact, patience, and perseverance. His career in the field of alcoholism treatment ranged from working with corporations and industry to devise policies for alcoholic employees to counseling with addicted adolescents. He balanced the ability to confront with patience and understanding. Although he attended AA infrequently he was able to remind himself on a daily basis that his success rested on remaining sober.

To conclude, individual therapy is the optimal treatment for the alcoholic in the Integration Phase and can be vital during the Acceptance Phase. Individual therapy in the Recognition and Compliance Phases is largely focused on confronting denial, assisting the patient to understand and accept that he or she has a disease, and motivating the patient to participate in an alcoholism program and/or AA. As the patient moves into the Acceptance and Integration Phases, the focus can shift from the dynamics of the disease to the dynamics of the individual. Regardless of phase of recovery, a therapist does well to remain alert to a possible resurgence of pathological defenses and should be prepared to confront any manifestations suggestive of relapse.

GROUP PSYCHOTHERAPY

Group psychotherapy is the most commonly used psychotherapeutic approach in the treatment of alcoholism (Zimberg, 1982). It is the mainstay for most alcoholism rehabilitation programs as well as for out-patient programs and aftercare. According to anecdote, group psychotherapy has received wide support as the treatment of choice for alcoholic patients (Kanas, 1982). Empirical support for this belief is sparse, but a few controlled studies indicate that therapeutic goals are more readily achieved, self-concept improved, and re-admissions fewer for alcoholic patients treated in insight-oriented groups (Ends & Page, 1957) (Yalom, Bloch, Bond, Zimmerman, & Qualls, 1978).

In this section, the discussion of group psychotherapy for alcoholic patients is applicable to groups in a variety of settings: inpatient, aftercare, outpatient, and couples groups. Variations on group technique such as encounter groups and psychodrama are not discussed (see references [Blume, 1977; Lieberman, Yalom, & Mills, 1973] for further information).

Structuring Group Psychotherapy for Alcoholic Patients

A desire to achieve and maintain abstinence from alcohol and other mind-altering chemicals is a necessary prerequisite to entering group psychotherapy. Mixing patients who intend to try controlled drinking with those who clearly need to abstain can compromise the efforts of patients seeking abstinence. The members accepting controlled drinking may become the focus of group hostility, or their example may encourage other patients to try a return to drinking and, in turn, lead to disastrous consequences.

A male/female cotherapy team is optimal for facilitating group process. A group can be led by one therapist if the therapist has extensive experience in working with alcoholic patients.

The therapists may be psychiatrists, nurses, or other mental health professionals. Regardless of professional background, training in both addictions and group therapy is necessary. Recovered alcoholism counselors need training in group therapy techniques in order to be effective. Unless the recovered counselor has specific training, the group tends to become modeled after an AA meeting, and the group leader (counselor) assumes the role of "speaker."

A commitment from the patient to at least 1 year's participation in weekly group therapy is recommended. Some treatment centers recommend 2 years but, in fact, very few alcoholic patients continue group psychotherapy for that length of time. The size of the group may vary from 6 to 12 persons; the length of sessions should be from 1½ to 2 hours.

Rules should be presented at the first session and discussed with new members as they enter the group. Such rules might include not coming to therapy under the influence of alcohol, the need to start on time, the avoidance of romantic involvement with other group members, payment schedules, and the confidentiality of disclosures.

There is an advantage in having patients pay monthly in advance. For example, if four group sessions are scheduled during a given month, payment for all four would be expected by the time of the first monthly session. Attendance is improved, thereby, and the patients tend not to let other activities interfere with their coming to therapy.

The patient who arrives intoxicated may remain in the therapy session if he or she is not disruptive. The drinking should not be denied by the group, but the rules should be restated. The intoxicated patient should not be the focus of that therapy session. When he or she returns at subsequent session, an exploration of his or her behavior is essential. If the patient is disruptive, he or she should be asked to wait outside until the group therapist(s) can meet with him or her. It may be necessary to notify a family member or in some other manner arrange transportation.

The therapist(s) must always be prepared to shift group focus to a member who is close to or actually having slips. As the group develops cohesion and members achieve increasingly stable sobriety, drinking tends not to be a prominent part of the group's focus. Interpersonal relationships, feelings, family, and work concerns prevail. This is desirable and highly preferable to any tendency for comparing "bottle" stories. However, the process of the group will need to shift on an as-needed basis back to the basic issue of sobriety, adequate support systems, denial, or any other issue that emerges as a threat to abstinence from alcohol or drugs.

What about the patient who continues to have slips? Hospitalization, disulfiram, or an intensification of treatment efforts must be planned. The patient should feel support from the group, be encouraged to stay in treatment, but not be given the message that it is acceptable to continue to drink. Patients who are having frequent slips often drop out of therapy. Every effort should be made to contact them, review a treatment plan, and encourage them to return to the group or arrange other treatment. If a patient who is absent cannot be reached by phone, a letter should be sent to him or her. The patient who has dropped out or is attending infrequently often expects that the therapist and/or the group will be angry. A letter expressing the concern, interest, and willingness of the therapist to be of assistance may enable the patient to reestablish the therapeutic effort. If no response is obtained from the patient, the spouse or other appropriate family member may be contacted, and the offer of help extended. A meeting with the family is often very effective in bringing the patient back into therapy.

General Advantages of Group Psychotherapy

Yalom (1975) identifies eight elements intrinsic to group psychotherapy which account for the efficacy of this technique. The relationship of these elements to group therapy with alcoholics is detailed as follows by Galanter and Pattison (1984):

- *Information*—concepts of alcoholism, family dynamics, behavioral alternatives, and other forms of help are made available.
- *Hope*—positive expectations are formed that problems can be solved, needs met.
- *Universality*—patients find that they are not unique in their wretchedness ("Stinkin' Thinkin'") or feelings. On the other hand, those striving for perfection become more mellow about being "just human."

- *Catharsis*—patients learn that feelings (even strong ones) can be expressed and handled, rather than turned into anxiety. They find these experiences are likely to bind people to you rather than drive them away if done in a relatively constructive way.
- *Altruism*—reciprocal helping relationships increase a person's sense of value and power.
- *Imitation and learning new social skills*—patients model and practice coping behaviors, new identities.
- *Cohesiveness*—a sense of solidarity, identity, perhaps give a sense of a "new family." The alcoholic finds people in caring relationships oriented toward positive change and coping without alcohol.
- *Interpersonal learning*—patients find out how they are perceived by others, how they largely create or maintain their own problems, how they can become responsible for their feelings and lives without self-perpetuating, self-destructive games.

The specific advantages of group psychotherapy for the alcoholic patient include a greater capacity to recognize denial. The tendency to minimize, rationalize, or deny one's dependence on alcohol is often apparent to the group as a fellow member describes his or her alcohol experience. Patients see such defensiveness more easily in others than in themselves, but gain greater self-awareness through these observations.

A second advantage is the ability to "keep the memory green." This expression refers to the importance of remaining aware of the consequences alcohol has had in one's own life. Sharing experiences related to alcohol use in a group provides a reminder of one's own past and reinforces current commitments to treatment.

Third, alcoholic patients have a reputation for being skilled manipulators. A group of alcoholics, therefore, can detect a manipulative process in a fellow member very quickly.

Confrontation provides a fourth advantage. Alcoholics can talk to each other in a way that is difficult for the nonalcoholic to do. One alcoholic can confront another with more vigor and certainty because his or her comments can be paraphrased by "I know, I've been there myself." "I did the same thing myself." "I learned I had to do things differently if I wanted to stay sober."

Fifth, the intensity of group therapy allows a wide display of feelings to unfold. The alcoholic patient is in a setting where recognition of his or her feelings may be facilitated, and there is sufficient support to help one another tolerate strong affect.

Sixth, a group may enhance the development of trust. Each group therapy session should add to the sense of trust which is vital for therapeutic work to proceed. Group therapy with alcoholic patients allows a modification of the characteristic reactive grandiosity to take place. A therapeutic breakthrough occurs when the chemically dependent patient takes the risk (trust) to share his or her ambivalence about drinking or drugs. By trusting the group with this information ("I still want to get wasted"; "I did get drunk last week.") the air of self-sufficiency begins to evaporate. Acknowledgement of one's feelings or behavior is tantamount to an acceptance of help, information, or guidance from others and thus lets go of pathological narcissistic defenses.

As with individual therapy, the phases of recovery described earlier in this chapter are recognizable in the group setting. One of the advantages of a group approach is the power of example that the group can provide. The patient just recognizing his or her alcoholism or in the compliance phase feels the contrast between himself or herself and the patient who has accepted his or her dependence.

In summary, by its intrinsic process and dynamics group therapy lends itself to the treatment of alcoholism. Its acceptability by alcoholic patients is also worth noting. The less intense transference to a therapist avoids premature exposure of emotions connected to competition, envy, dependency, or projection which may interrupt a therapeutic alliance. Group therapy is also less costly, and its acceptability may be enhanced further by the patient's experience of peer support as gained through AA.

FAMILY TREATMENT

Alcoholism is commonly referred to as a "family disease," meaning that family members living with an alcoholic are affected by the alcoholism. They may be anxious, depressed, irritable, withdrawn; somatic symptoms may develop; acting-out behaviors or co-addiction may occur. *Family disease* also refers to the possibility that a family member's behavior may perpetuate (enable) the drinking of the alcoholic. An example is the wife who still calls into work for her husband, explaining that he won't be in because of the flu, when he has a hangover. The wife is protecting her alcoholic husband from taking responsibility for his alcohol-related behavior. This is referred to as *enabling* because the spouse's behavior facilitates the continuation of pathological drinking. In addition, a family may intentionally contribute to the development of alcoholism.

A physician, despite his daughter's history of drug and alcohol abuse, insisted on ordering drinks for her when they were together. She was able to refuse, but remained confused and angry over her father's behavior.

Lewis (1986) describes two general tasks for the family: "The production of children who can separate and lead lives of autonomy, and the provision of a social milieu in which the parents' personalities can be stabilized and continued psychological growth can occur." Obviously, a family with an alcoholic member could be compromised in either or both of these general tasks.

Because of the circular relationship between the effect of alcoholism on the family and the family's effect on the development, maintenance, or recovery from alcoholism, an adequate treatment plan for the alcoholic patient includes participation of the family in treatment. Family therapy typically refers to treating more than one member of a family simultaneously in the same session. In this chapter, treatment for the family is given a much broader scope and includes a spectrum of services. These services may range from the psychoeducational, to insight-oriented therapy for a family member, to group therapy for family members, to the more traditional conjoint family therapy.

An Approach to the Family

The first therapeutic approach to the pathological functioning of the alcoholic family should be toward termination of the alcoholic's drinking. As a general rule, if the alcoholic gains sobriety, the family usually is able to restructure itself and function at a previously achieved healthier level. Reiss (1981) describes the possibility of growth as one potential family response to a crisis. The crisis of alcoholism could, theoretically, lead to reintegration at a higher level of functioning than had existed during earlier periods.

> An accountant ran his family in a characteristic dominant/submissive style. After he lost a job because of alcoholism, he began to take treatment seriously. His wife became very active in Al-Anon and no longer accepted a submissive role. She broke from the pattern of being a "narcissistic object" for her husband. He noted the changes in her and accepted his need to change in their relationship. As a result, the family shifted from a dysfunctional mode to a more functional level. This had a positive effect on the couple's adolescent children and was of great benefit to the alcoholic husband, who has now learned that it was unnecessary and impossible to control everyone in his environment.

One may also see families who remain in chronic conflict whether or not the drinking ceases and, in some instances, the attainment of sobriety leads to a breakup of the family. In the author's experience, the latter is more likely in the marriage that was entered into while one or both of the partners was actively alcoholic.

Termination of the alcoholic's drinking may depend on a skilled education of the patient's family and the development of a working alliance with the family. Even when both are achieved there is no certainty that the alcoholic member will recover, but there is a distinct possibility that the rest of the family can learn to distance themselves from the alcoholic's drinking and not be left with guilt, hopelessness, and anger. In other words, the spouse, parents, or children who are living with the alcoholic have a chance, should treatment for the alcoholic fail, to escape the conflict or chaos themselves. This is so important that the clinician is obligated, I believe, to help the family, independent of the response of the primary patient. In some instances when the family gets help and begins to make changes, the alcoholic member finds it within himself or herself to make an effort also (Bowen, 1978).

Thus, there are two reasons for involving the family: One, it may facilitate recovery for the alcoholic patient; and two, the family needs help with the crisis atmosphere of living with alcoholism.

The first step in the process is *outreach*. A sustained, vigorous pursuit of the family is an essential factor in developing family involvement in alcoholism treatment. Clinicians must be prepared to confront the resistance to involvement of family members, just as they are forced to confront the alcoholic's denial. Family members should be evaluated early in the course of treatment and be present if the patient is being admitted to an inpatient facility. It may be necessary to follow-up with phone calls or letters to the families who are resistant.

The alcoholic's resistance to having the family members involved must be faced. This is sometimes the result of guilt and the desire not to burden the family on his or her behalf. At other times, the alcoholic knows that contact with a family member may reveal previously denied manifestations or his or her alcohol-related behavior. Similarly, family members may resist contact because of anger, guilt about their role in drinking, or fear of remaining with an alcoholic. The request for family involvement should be considered even more serious than a request made to families for blood donations when a member is facing major surgery, because what they can contribute cannot be bought or supplied by anyone else.

Family Evaluation

The evaluation has two basic purposes: The first is to obtain an account of the patient's drinking history. The spouse, for example, although not an independent observer in the fullest sense, can usually provide a more objective picture than the patient. Interviewing the family separately from the patient is important for this purpose. Family members are more relaxed and better able to be objective when they know that the alcoholic has begun treatment, e.g., entered a hospital program.

From the spouse or other family members the *evolution* of the drinking should be obtained. Details such as escalation of drinking after the death of a parent may emerge. Job-related disappointments not emphasized by the alcoholic patient may be very apparent to the spouse. *Current drinking patterns* and the *problems* the family sees as resulting from alcohol use should be explored. How each member of the family has *coped* with the drinking behavior is of particular importance. Is the family intimidated by the alcoholic? Do they verbally (or physically) attack each other? Do they withdraw, placate, or do they take constructive steps to help themselves and/or the alcoholic member?

The second purpose of the evaluation—making an assessment of the family's structure and functioning—has less to do with rounding out the history of the alcoholism and more to do with treatment itself. From this treatment needs and planning can be formulated.

Lewis (1986) defines family structure as repetitive patterns of interaction that are usually out of the awareness of the family members but which have become routine. Structure is believed to develop from the resolution or lack of resolution of marital issues such as commitment, division of power, and the balance between attachment and separateness.

Research from the Timberlawn Foundation (Lewis, 1986) has led to a classification of family structure and functioning that is empirically derived and clinically useful. To summarize briefly, the continuum of family functioning ranges from the well-functioning (competent family) to the dysfunctional (dominant-submissive family or chronically conflicted family), to the severely dysfunctional (chaotic family). Several points on the continuum may be described:

The well-functioning family. A strong parental alliance with shared power; feelings and opinions are listened to and respected; solutions to problems are negotiated. Communication is clear and spontaneous; differing opinions are acceptable; the family is flexible, warm, and optimistic. Families within this range are seldom seen clinically.

The dysfunctional family. (a) The dominant-submissive family: characterized by one spouse who rules the family; the other spouse is submissive and may be child-like in his or her passivity and dependency; the family is rigid with little spontaneity; control is all-important and emanates from the dominant spouse. If submission is acceptable to the other spouse, little conflict may emerge. If not, depression, tension, anger, and rebelliousness can be expected. (b) The chronically conflicted family:

the parents compete with each other for power; each strives to dominate; the children are drawn into the conflict. A fear of closeness is believed to underlie this chronic and repetitive struggle. This family fosters distrust and manipulation of others.

The severely dysfunctional family. These families lack defined leadership, are unable to solve problems, and are characterized by chaos. The family members band together against an outside world that is hostile, identities of individual members are not well established, and sameness rather than differentiation is the norm. The individual's best chance of survival is felt to be to cling to the family.

Alcoholism may develop in any of the types of families described. Thus far research has not identified specific family systems that distinguish alcoholic families from nonalcoholics families (Steinglass, 1980).

Kaufman and Pattison (1981) describe four patterns of family reaction to alcoholism. These are "the functional family system," "the neurotic enmeshed family system," "the disintegrated family system," and "the absent family system."

The first, "the functional family system," corresponds closely to Lewis' well-functioning family. The parents are successful as parents, and the children are well adjusted. Drinking in this family does not evolve from family stress, but may develop in response to personal neurotic conflict or social stresses (Kaufman, 1984). This type of family is competent enough to contain the alcoholic member without disintegrating into a dysfunctional or chaotic state. The family responses to the alcoholic would be in the helping rather than the rejecting mode.

The "neurotic enmeshed family system" is that most commonly described in the alcoholism literature (Kaufman, 1984). These families seem to be a blend of (or vacillate back and forth between) the first two dysfunctional types described by Lewis. In this system drinking may be related to family structure. For example, the dominant-submissive dysfunctional family may contain a spouse (usually the wife) who is angry about being controlled and "rebels" through use of alcohol.

A cold, successful sales executive dominated his family and his foreign-born wife. Criticism and sarcasm were the coin of communication. As years passed and the children left home, the wife's tolerance for his controlling nature lessened. Passive and dependent, the daughter of an alcoholic herself, she "learned" that lifting a glass of bourbon to her lips was the symbol for a shift in power. When she was drunk her husband was at a loss. He was humiliated and impotent to control his wife. He divorced her rather than tolerate the uncertainty of her response to a recovery program.

The dominant-submissive or the chronically conflicted family structure may play a role in the etiology of alcoholism. On the other hand it is important to recognize that, as Lewis (1987) points out, a previously competent family may regress to a dominant-submissive or conflicted structure under severe stress, for example, alcoholism. Longitudinal studies of families prior to the onset of alcoholism are very much needed.

The "disintegrated family system" and "absent family system" of Kaufman and Pattison have essentially extruded the alcoholic from the family. Possibly these two reactivity patterns are derived from the structure of the severely dysfunctional or chaotic family as described by Lewis. According to Lewis, the severely dysfunctional family requires sameness and fusion. Alcoholism may represent an attempt to break from this structure, or the alcoholic may be too deviant for the family to tolerate. On the other hand, some chaotic or severely dysfunctional families protect a member's alcoholism because it seems to keep the family member relatively helpless and, therefore, more dependent and tied into the enmeshed system. In such families it is not uncommon for several members of the family to be alcohol dependent or, at the least, alcohol abusers. Such families are suspicious of the usual helping agencies and aren't likely to go outside the family system for support.

Along this line, Kaufman (1984) has emphasized that separation of the alcoholic in the "disintegrated" system is "pseudo-individuation." A family exists somewhere, but is usually destitute and dependent on relatives. In the case of the "disintegrated" reactivity pattern, if the alcoholic and his or her family are reunited, a chaotic family structure is likely.

The "absent family system," as described by Kaufman and Pattison, is that often found in alcoholics on skid row or involved with bottle gangs. In this instance the alcoholic member seems to have been extruded from a poorly functioning family. The absent family system may be a consequence of the disintegrated system (Kaufman, 1984) or the chaotic system (Lewis, 1986).

Treatment Planning

At this point, it is appropriate to consider how these conceptualizations of family structure in general (Lewis, 1986) and family reactivity patterns to alcoholism (Kaufman & Pattison, 1981) lend themselves to treatment planning for the family. Table 11-1 outlines the recommended approaches to the family according to the family's place in a spectrum of structures. Next, descriptions of the therapeutic approaches will be given.

The well-functioning family first should be provided *education* regard-

TABLE 11-1
Family Structure and Treatment Approach

	Structure	Etiologic Significance of Structure	Potential for Facilitating Recovery	Treatment Approach For the Family	
Lewis	Kaufman & Pattison			Early	Later
Well-Functioning (competent)	Functional Family System	–	+ +	Education	Al-Anon
Dysfunctional: Dominant-Submissive or Chronically Conflicted	Neurotic Enmeshed Family System	+	+ –	Education Al-Anon	Family Therapy Al-Anon
Severely Dysfunctional (chaotic)	Disintegrated Family System Absent Family System	+ +	–	Treatment of individual alcoholic	Education Family Therapy Al-Anon

ing alcoholism, with emphasis on alcohol's effects on the patient and the family. An understanding of the disease concept and the common reactions of family members should be explained. Literature on alcoholism and the family is very useful. Local Al-Anon groups can provide a variety of educational materials useful for families.

A cognitive approach is usually sufficient for the well-functioning family. To reintegrate the family at a level of functioning that existed before the alcoholism, the option to explore dynamic issues in family therapy can be offered. *Al-Anon* attendance is encouraged for its value as an ongoing support system.

The dysfunctional family will need *education* as well. However, the conflicted relationships will require, in most instances, *family therapy* in order to modify conflicts over power and intimacy. Individual therapy for family members may also be indicated. Al-Anon for the dysfunctional family is especially important since its principles assist family members in detaching from the drinking behavior and emphasize help for the family. Thus, the enmeshed, conflicted family is provided a support group through Al-Anon that emphasizes autonomy and individuation.

The severely dysfunctional or chaotic family works against recovery by its suspiciousness, distrust of outsiders, avoidance of change, and attempts to prevent separation from the family. For these reasons, treatment of alcoholism is facilitated by focusing on the individual patient. Inpatient treatment is usually necessary to accomplish sufficient distance from the family so that educational and therapeutic approaches can be more effective. Introduction of the family into treatment needs to be done slowly according to what can be tolerated by the individual members. If an alliance can be gained, then education and family therapy can be utilized. Al-Anon can also be emphasized since it serves as a support group whose dynamics counter the pathological enmeshment of the family.

Forms of Family Therapy

In the treatment of alcoholism it is helpful to view family therapy as a variety of approaches. In Chapter 8 several approaches to family members were described. These emphasized cognitive or psychoeducational approaches, modalities requiring a minimum of services, which can be offered in either an inpatient or outpatient setting.

In this section a brief description of other family therapy approaches will be described. These forms of family therapy will be more psychotherapeutic in contrast to the predominantly cognitive forms described earlier.

Conjoint family therapy may involve the parents as well as children, or it may focus only on the couple. The therapist(s) should have training in family therapy techniques and understand family systems. In addition, an understanding of alcoholism and its impact on the family is essential (Nace, DePhoure, Goldberg, & Cammarota, 1982). It is desirable to use a male/female cotherapy team. A recovering alcoholic co-therapist is an advantage if the person is also sophisticated in family therapy. Many times it is not possible or practical to have a co-therapist, and treatment can be conducted with one therapist.

In conjoint family therapy attention is directed to the nonalcoholic members in regard to changes they may need to make in themselves. This is a shift from their focus on the need for their alcoholic family member to change. Of course, an emphasis on sobriety for the alcoholic needs to be kept in the forefront by the therapist. The alcoholic member should be working on his or her alcoholism in other settings as well—for example, AA, group therapy, or individual therapy.

Typically I raise the issue of whether the family is willing to have a "dry house" (i.e., an alcohol-free home). If both the alcoholic and his or her spouse agree to this idea, progress is being made. If the spouse prefers a "dry house" (thereby showing a willingness to forego the convenience of having alcohol available for himself or herself) but the alcoholic objects, the issue requires exploration. Usually it reflects a form of denial on the part of the alcoholic. Specifically, the alcoholic is denying the attraction which alcohol potentially holds. Often the alcoholic feels conspicuous if alcohol is not around to serve guests, reflecting his or her feelings about being alcoholic, and these feelings need exploration. The family situation is less favorable if the alcoholic prefers a "dry house," but the spouse refuses. This may reflect anger on the part of the spouse ("Why should I have to give up my pleasure?").

More serious, the spouse may also be alcoholic or have an interest in keeping the alcoholic sick. For example, a wife who refused to participate in her husband's treatment considered him hopeless and was trying to preserve a relationship with his family in order that she and their five children could benefit from trust funds established for their benefit. She did not wish to antagonize her treatment-resistant husband in the face of an uncertain outcome. When both the alcoholic and the spouse prefer to keep alcohol at home, the reasons for the decision are important to explore.

It is important for the family to understand the advantages of an alcohol-free home. For example, the alcohol-free home provides an island in daily life where the temptation to drink can be lessened. It also serves a symbolic function by recognizing the commitment to remove something that has the potential to disrupt or destroy family functioning. On the other hand, recovery from alcoholism does not rest solely on this issue. The therapist, I believe, has a responsibility to raise the issue and to assist the family in exploring the affect around this topic.

Conjoint family therapy is also indicated to address chronic conflicts which may have either antedated or resulted from the alcoholism. As indicated from earlier examples, the family may learn to function at a higher level than previously experienced and conjoint treatment provides an excellent opportunity to facilitate that process.

Couples group therapy offers the same advantages as conjoint family therapy by providing the couple the opportunity to explore the dynamics of their marital relationship and to understand the interaction between the alcoholism and the marital relationship better. Four to six couples represent an optimal size for the group, and weekly sessions of $1^{1}/_{2}$ to 2 hours should be scheduled. A particular advantage to group therapy for couples is the opportunity to observe other couples' patterns of interaction and to recognize similar tendencies in their own relationship. In addition, feelings of isolation are diminished for most couples who participate in such groups. The opportunity to model the example of better functioning couples or couples who are developing greater openness with each other is a powerful stimulus for risking new, healthier behaviors.

Couples group therapy has received empirical support through a study by Gallant, Rich, Bay, and Terranova (1970). Of 118 couples studied, 45% were able to make significant improvement in both their alcoholism and marital relationship.

Spouses group therapy enables the spouses or other family members to explore their feelings and to do something for their own growth and development rather than organizing their lives around the alcoholic. This group is particularly useful if the alcoholic family member is still drinking. Under such conditions the use of a couples or family approach is often disrupted. The spouses (or children or parents) need to be strengthened, i.e., need to learn not to be intimidated by the family member's drinking. They frequently recognize that their despair, anger, and guilt are holding them back as much as the drinking behavior of their family member. The courage to change is emphasized. In the group setting models of change unfold, and support for small steps is strongly reinforced.

> Mary had lived with an alcoholic husband for over 20 years. He refused treatment. She began her own therapy after a teenage son became drug-dependent. Through group therapy combined with an occasional individual session, she was able to distance herself from the alcohol and drug use in her family. She succeeded in gaining promotions in her job along the way. Her capacity to func-

tion independently of her husband was secured, and her ability to set limits with her children was much improved. Little apparent improvement in her husband or drug-dependent older son was noted. The benefits of therapy for Mary were sufficiently reinforcing for her to make a financial sacrifice to continue treatment. She developed greater skills at taking care of herself and enjoyed the feeling that she deserved good things for herself.

When the Drinking Continues

If the alcoholic family member continues to drink, a number of possibilities may develop. The family may become discouraged and give up efforts to obtain help. This is a crisis, and efforts must be made to support the family and facilitate their obtaining the help they need. I believe that one of the strongest indications for family therapy is when the alcoholism remains unchecked. Of course, the family therapy may need to proceed without the participation of the alcoholic member. However, if the drinking is less disruptive and the alcoholic can attend therapy appointments sober, then every effort should be made to include the alcoholic in family therapy as well as to reinforce the need for additional specific help for the addiction.

Another possibility is that drinking may continue at a low level. The success of temporarily controlling drinking may reinforce the denial of the alcoholic, and he or she may find the family's continued concern over alcohol use objectionable. The therapist should not be lulled into a position of thinking all is well under these circumstances. Many families will not tolerate such efforts at "controlled drinking" because they have been through it before. Therapy should attend to the family's reponses to the drinking and their efforts to better take care of themselves. Sometimes this involves living apart from the alcoholic member.

If the family feels comfortable about occasional slips or efforts to control drinking, the therapist should stay with them and be alert to any shifts back to a pathological drinking pattern. With experience the family will learn the necessity to make changes, either as a step toward achieving a sober level of functioning or as a necessary step to growing as a family independent of the alcoholism.

To summarize, there are various approaches to treatment for families affected by alcoholism. The specific approaches depend greatly on the level of functioning of the family and the degree to which they have remained involved with their alcoholic family member.

Family therapy can be a powerful tool for intervention, which either enables the alcoholic to avail himself or herself of treatment for alcoholism or enables the family to grow, independent of the destructive impact of alcoholism. Family therapy is also valuable in maintaining the alcoholic's sobriety and facilitating the family's ability to shift from a dysfunctional mode to a functional, competent pattern of relationships.

The family therapist needs to be sophisticated in both the areas of alcoholism and family therapy. A capacity to continue with the family through thick and thin is essential. Persistence and availability will in most instances lead to favorable results for the alcoholic patient and family members.

PHARMACOTHERAPY

In this section the use of psychotropic medications and the use of disulfiram in alcoholic patients is discussed. The reader must appreciate that there is no specific pharmacologic treatment for alcoholism. Although there are alcoholic patients who can benefit from some pharmacologic agents under certain circumstances, severe conservatism in prescribing must be emphasized.

Disulfiram (Antabuse)

Disulfiram should be considered as an adjunct in the treatment of alcoholism rather than a complete program in itself. Patients taking disulfiram should be involved in other forms of treatment as well.

Pharmacology. Disulfiram is a white, odorless powder which is insoluble in water. Although rapidly absorbed from the gastrointestinal tract, disulfiram is fat soluble and takes about 12 hours for plasma-lipid equilibration to occur. After 12 hours full effect from disulfiram can be expected. It is metabolized by conjugation with glucuronic acid, oxidation to sulfate, or decomposition to carbon disulfide and diethylamine. The excretion is slow with about one fifth remaining in the body after 1 week. Most of the drug is metabolized in the liver and excreted in the urine (Ritchie, 1975).

Mechanism of action. Disulfiram is a deterrent drug. The deterrent is the ethanol-disulfiram reaction. This reaction results from the effect of disulfiram on the enzyme aldehyde dehydrogenase. After alcohol is ingested, the ethyl alcohol molecule is metabolized to acetaldehyde by the enzyme alcohol dehydrogenase. The normal conversion of acetaldehyde to acetic acid is blocked by the effect of disulfiram on acetaldehyde dehydrogenase. There occurs, therefore, a rapid increase in serum acetaldehyde at levels 5 to 10 times normal. Acetaldehyde is very toxic and produces the following effects which are commonly referred to as the *Alcohol-Antabuse Reaction* or *ethanol-disulfiram reaction*:

- flushing of the skin, particularly the face and upper chest
- throbbing headache
- nausea (and possibly vomiting)
- sweating
- hyperventilation and respiratory distress
- chest pain
- anxiety
- palpitations
- hypertension

If the reaction is severe, shock and cardiac arrhythmias can occur. The intensity of the reaction is proportional to the amount of alcohol ingested and the dose of disulfiram. The reaction usually lasts 30 to 60 minutes.

When disulfiram is recommended patients often express a fear that "that stuff can kill you." In fact, deaths are very rare. In use in the United States since 1948, disulfiram has been taken by hundreds of thousands of people. The literature reports 20 deaths (Ewing, 1982).

Treatment of the alcohol-Antabuse reaction. Most reactions are mild because the patient quickly stops drinking as symptoms emerge. The symptoms develop about 10 to 20 minutes after ingestion of alcohol. A mild reaction may occur with a blood alcohol level of 5 mg. to 10 mg. per 100 ml. A full reaction can be expected with a blood alcohol concentration of 50 mg. to 100 mg. per 100 ml. and consciousness may be lost if the blood alcohol concentration exceeds 125 mg. per 100 ml.

A severe reaction may require treatment of shock involving use of ephedrine for the hypotension and administration of oxygen. Intravenous antihistamines may abate some of the symptoms. Ascorbic acid (Vitamin C) given intravenously in a 1 gram dose has a beneficial effect, presumably on the basis of ascorbic acid's antioxidant effect. This effect is believed to decrease the production of acetaldehyde by allowing alcohol to be excreted unchanged (Product Profile, Ayerst Laboratories, 1979). A patient reporting a disulfiram-ethanol reaction should be advised to see a physician or, in severe cases, go to an emergency room.

Side effects of disulfiram. Mild drowsiness is a common side effect, which usually subsides in 7–10 days. Since disulfiram is taken only once a day, a bedtime dosage schedule could be used to minimize this effect. A garlic or metallic-like taste may be noted. A lower dose may alleviate this effect. Other side effects include erectile dysfunction, fatigue, headaches, acneform skin eruptions, tremor, restlessness, and allergic dermatitis. Peripheral neuritis and a toxic psychosis with delirium and paranoid or affective features are possible, but uncommon. Rare side effects include hepatic dysfunction and optic neuritis.

Skin manifestations may be relieved by antihistamines, and most side effects respond to a lower dosage.

Tables 11-2 and 11-3 (Product Profile, Ayerst Laboratories, 1979) provide an outline of disulfiram-like drugs and disulfiram-drug interactions. Coumarin anticoagulants and phenytoin (Dilantin) have their metabolism delayed by disulfiram. Therefore, prothrombin time may be decreased and Dilantin levels increased by the use of disulfiram.

Dosage. Antabuse is produced in 250 mg. and 500 mg. scored tablets. Some physicians routinely prescribe 250 mg. daily. Others begin with 500 mg. for 5 days, then decrease the dosage to 250 mg. daily. Disulfiram should not be given until the blood alcohol level is zero. This requires at least a 12-hour interval after the last drink.

The dynamics of prescribing disulfiram. When treating the alcoholic patient, the clinician has the responsibility of explaining the variety of available treatments. Therefore, an explanation of disulfiram and its potential usefulness should be forthcoming. Apart from the ethics of patient participation in treatment planning, there is a second compelling reason for discussing the use of Antabuse with patients, which may be referred to as the "dynamics of prescribing Antabuse." The presentation of Antabuse to an alcoholic patient provides an opportunity for both the therapist and the patient to appreciate more deeply the dependence on alcohol. Consideration of using Antabuse often enables the patient to become aware of his or her lingering doubts and fears of living without alcohol. A clinical example may make this point clearer.

I explain to a patient that there is a medication available which can help a person stop drinking. When the word "Antabuse" is put forth there often is an immediate protest, "not for me"; "I don't like to take pills"; "that's a crutch"; "that stuff can kill you." These vigorous protestations usually are made without any knowledge or understanding of how the drug works or why it might be helpful. I explain that Antabuse prevents acetaldehyde, formed from alcohol, from being removed by the body. The backup of acetaldehyde produces a reaction very soon after any alcohol is ingested. I describe the ethanol-disulfiram reaction. By this time the patient may be thoroughly disgusted with the discussion. Further responses include "I'd have to look out for food cooked in alcohol" (implying an unreasonable burden); "You don't trust me"; or "I wouldn't be able to use aftershave."

The issue at hand is not to persuade, cajole, or browbeat the individu-

TABLE 11-2
Disulfiram-Like Drugs and Chemicals*

Analgesics and Anti-inflammatory Agents:
  Aminopyrine
  Phenylbutazone
  Phenacetin

Anti-infective Agents:
  Cephalosporins (Cefoperazone, Moxalgam)
  Chloramphenicol
  Furaltadone
  Furazolidone
  Griseofulvin
  Isoniazid
  Metronidazone (Flagyl)
  Quinacrine
  Sulfonamides

Industrial Agents:
  Carbon disulfide
  Hydrogen sulfide
  Tetraethyl lead
  Tetramethylthiuram disulfide

Oral Hypoglycemic Agents:
  Acetohexamide (Dymelor)
  Chlorpropamide (Diabinese)
  Phenformin (DBI)
  Tolazemide (Tolinase)
  Tolbutamide (Orinase)

Miscellaneous:
  Glyceryl trinitrate
  Procarbazine
  Ethacrynic Acid
  Cyclothiazide
  Phentolamine (Regitine)
  Dimercaprol (BAL)
  Coprinus atramentarius (mushroom)
  Calcium carbimide (The Canadian equivalent of Antabuse. Temposil)

Calcium Cynamide:
  Animal charcoal
  Butanal oxime

*After *Product Profile: Antabuse (Disulfiram) in Alcoholism,* 1979. Reproduced, 1987, with permission of Ayerst Laboratories.

TABLE 11-3
Disulfiram-Drug Interactions*

Drug	Interaction Effect with Disulfiram
Antipyrine	Inhibits hepatic mixed function oxidase, catalyzed hydroxylation.
Paraldehyde	Metabolism of this acetaldehyde polymer is blocked at acetaldehyde phase.
Anesthesia	Hypotension, possibly by depletion of norepinephrine.
Benediazepines Chlordiazepoxide Diazepam	Decrease clearance leading to drug accumulation.
Coumarin derivations	Prolongs prothrombin time by decreasing biotransformation of coumarin.
Ethylene Dibromide (Volatile liquid used as a soil fumigant in dyes, as a solvent, and as a lead scavenger in leaded fuels)	High levels of carcinogenicity and unexplained mortality of rats.
Metronidazole	Visual and auditory hallucinations.
Phenytoin and congeners	Inhibits metabolism leading to toxicity (as antipyrine).
Primidone	Enhances primidone conversion to phenobarbital.
Isoniazid	Impairs acetylation, leading to neurotoxicity.

*After *Product Profile: Antabuse (Disulfiram) in Alcoholism,* 1979. Reproduced, 1987, with permission of Ayerst Laboratories.

al into accepting an Antabuse prescription. The point is to highlight the concern that emerges when an alcohol-dependent person is offered a treatment that precludes use of alcohol. The contrast between the patient's recitation of the damage alcohol has done and his or her vow to never drink again with the protest against an opportunity to avoid alcohol ingestion is striking. At this point it often becomes obvious that most alcohol dependent patients are ambivalent about not drinking. No, they do not want to drink; they know what it has done, but they know that if things get really bad and the going gets too tough, a familiar "friend" is always nearby. Antabuse represents the final threat to that relationship. When patients are helped to see that Antabuse "cuts the cord" to alcohol use in a very literal sense, they often experience a deeper awareness of their feeling of need for alcohol, of their lingering psychological dependence. They may recognize that their talk up to this time was really in the service of compliance, not a full acceptance of their condition. This can be a humbling but important realization.

How does one respond to the protests against Antabuse? In regard to items such as hair spray, aftershave lotion, and perfumes there is very little risk. Large quantities may lead to inhalation of vapors and produce a mild reaction, usually a slight flushing response at most. Alcohol is not absorbed through the skin, so the concern is with volatile products.

> A hairdresser requested use of Antabuse but was concerned about being exposed to hairsprays all day long. While in the hospital treatment program, she was given the chance to "practice" and use her sprays in a work-like situation. No reaction resulted, and she was discharged taking Antabuse.

A common complaint is that Antabuse is a "crutch." When this concern is presented, it is useful to point out that a crutch is actually a device designed to enable one to stand up and move forward. What is so bad about that? Furthermore, we all have such crutches, that is, something we rely on or lean upon to help at various times.

Concern about food that has been cooked in wine is an interesting one. Actually, in such instances the alcohol has usually evaporated. But this objection to Antabuse is of concern not because of a potential reaction, but because of the alcoholic's attitude. It is necessary to redirect attention to the issue of priorities. If it is too much trouble to pay attention to the way one's food is prepared or to products one buys, there may be too little concern or understanding of the disease or its treatment. It is important to help the patient see that effort is necessary for recovery from alcoholism and that the amount of effort is certainly less odious than the consequences of drinking. In fact, the need to stay alert for alcohol products is good practice because alcoholics need to be mentally active in reference to their recovery. That is, whether or not Antabuse is used, the alcoholics need to remember why they are not drinking and need to remain alert to their vulnerability to relapse. Antabuse may heighten one's consciousness in this regard.*

Indications and contraindications. Alcohol abuse or alcohol dependence is an indication to consider the use of disulfiram, but neither is sufficient in itself to prescribe disulfiram. To a proper diagnosis must be added an appropriate attitude on the part of the patient. Disulfiram is appropriate for an alcoholic patient who can view his or her use of Antabuse as "one additional weapon on my side against a return to alcoholism." If the patient feels positive about Antabuse, its usage may be appropriate. If the patient is willing to take Antabuse only because his or her doctor is recommending it, to please the patient's spouse, or to "get people off my back about drinking," the prognosis is unfavorable. Resentment usually develops, and the patient sabotages treatment. I explain to patients that they should not take Antabuse for someone else's benefit. If they feel better about themselves because they are taking Antabuse, then the drug will truly be an adjunct to treatment.

I also explain one may substitute aspirin tablets for Antabuse, that is, only pretend to use Antabuse. Also, it is simple to push the medicine into one's cheek and later spit it out or even induce vomiting after it has been swallowed. My point in explaining these techniques of sabotage is to encourage the patient not to use disulfiram at all rather than merely pretend to use it. Such pretense is soon followed by a return to drinking. Then, the patient must face the disappointment of his family or employer. That is difficult enough. But when the family or employer had thought the patient was using disulfiram, the obvious deception only further threatens these relationships.

Apart from these attitudinal factors, contraindications are largely relative. The physician must weigh the risk of harm resulting from a possible ethanol-disulfiram reaction against the health consequences of drinking. Allergic reaction to disulfiram, severe heart disease, and psychosis are contraindications. If a patient is taking metronidazol (Flagyl), paraldehyde, or any alcohol-containing preparation, disulfiram should not be prescribed. The antituberculosis drug, isoniazide, may lead to a toxic reaction if given with disulfiram. The suicidal patient should not be

---

*A brochure with a wallet card and description of medications and other products containing alcohol is available from Ayerst Laboratories, 685 Third Ave., New York, NY 10017.

prescribed disulfiram, nor should the patient whose judgment is easily compromised either by organic changes or by an impulsive personality disorder. If the clinician feels that a patient is likely to test Antabuse, forget that he or she is on Antabuse, or curse Antabuse, it is best avoided.

Clinical usefulness. Disulfiram's usefulness is as a deterrent drug (not a form of aversion therapy) (Ewing, 1982). The fear of the ethanol-disulfiram reaction assists the patient in avoiding alcohol use. Many patients are relieved to be on Antabuse. They make their decision not to drink each day when they take the pill. This act frees them to concentrate on other concerns rather than to obsess over whether or not they may take a drink that day.

Some patients find that they experience less craving when on disulfiram. This is understandable on the basis that the more available alcohol is, the more likely one may experience an urge to drink. When one is on Antabuse, alcohol is essentially unavailable.

Antabuse also "buys time." The patient knows that a reaction can occur up to 14 days after the last use of Antabuse. If the patient stops Antabuse in preparation for drinking alcohol, there is a time period (usually 3 to 5 days, but possibly up to 14) of waiting. This interval may lead to a reconsideration.

A warning function is also available for patients taking disulfiram. The patient must be instructed not to discontinue the medication without first consulting the prescribing physician or a therapist who can assess their progress. Therefore, if a patient finds that he or she is forgetting to take Antabuse, this omission can be interpreted as a signal for plans to drink.

An additional clinical benefit is that alcoholic patients taking Antabuse have the opportunity to appreciate that the decision to drink is under their control. When on Antabuse, drinking must be planned. They may gain a fuller development of their capacity to exercise control over the decision to drink or not to drink.

How long does one take Antabuse? I usually recommend 6 months, then review the patient's progress in sobriety as evidenced by continuing treatment, AA attendance, work performance, family life, and leisure satisfaction. Some patients prefer to remain on Antabuse for an additional 6 months or longer. There is no absolute upper limit if the patient is not having any adverse effects, e.g., hepatotoxicity. One patient I knew of has taken Antabuse for 20 years, but this is very unusual. Some patients are able to use Antabuse effectively by taking it only during stressful periods, during certain holidays, or while travelling on business. Some patients don't want to begin Antabuse but want a prescription just in case they feel an urge to drink. This is not the optimal approach to the use of Antabuse but does warrant consideration for some individuals.

Efficacy studies. A review of over 40 studies (Lundwall & Baekland, 1971) indicates that most studies are flawed by poor design features such as lack of controls, heterogenous populations, and inadequate follow-up. Nevertheless, the authors conclude that disulfiram is a valuable treatment method for some alcoholics. One study, noted for its careful design (Wallerstein et al., 1957), found that over a 2-year period patients on disulfiram did better than groups treated with hypnotherapy or conditioned reflex therapy. Overall, it seems that patients with favorable prognostic signs for any form of treatment also do better with disulfiram (Kwentus & Major, 1979).

Specifically, the older patient (>40 years) who is socially stable and has a long drinking history does better on disulfiram than younger patients with a rapid progression of alcoholism and who are not socially stable. Depression and sociopathic features are unfavorable prognostic signs (Kwentus & Major, 1979).

To conclude, the physician should not view Antabuse as a cure for alcoholism, but as a useful adjunct to other treatment approaches for many patients. It is important to inform patients of the availability of Antabuse, how it works, its usefulness, its side effects, and the symptoms and dangers of the disulfiram-ethanol reaction. Further, the patient's response to a discussion of Antabuse is helpful in furthering an understanding of his or her dependence on alcohol.

Psychotropic Drugs

There are no psychotropic drugs specific to the treatment of alcoholism. The use of psychotropic drugs with alcoholic patients is indicated when there is a concomitant psychiatric disorder that is potentially responsive to medication, or when medication can be helpful during the period of withdrawal from alcohol. Extensive reviews (Becker, 1979; Solomon, 1982; Viamontes, 1972) on the use of psychotropic medications are consistent in pointing out the lack of well-designed studies and the failure to delineate any subtype of alcoholism in which pharmacotherapy would improve outcome. The reviewers concur that there is not specific pharmacotherapy for alcoholism (Becker, 1979).

Drawbacks to the Use of Medication

There are, in fact, a number of reasons why the use of medications may be deleterious to the treatment of alcoholic patients.

First, most prescribed medications have their own potential for addiction. They include sedative-hypnotics, especially benzodiazepines. Zimberg (1975) has reported on the increasing occurrence of alcoholics entering treatment with concomitant drug abuse problems. When the associated drug abuse problem is a prescription drug, it most commonly is Valium or Librium and has been prescribed by a physician. Benzodiazepines are potentially addicting (Connell & Berlin, 1983; Greenblatt, Shader, & Abernathy, 1983; Lader, 1983) and have a major role in the treatment of alcohol withdrawal syndromes, but are not indicated beyond short-term conditions.

A 40-year-old male had been arrested for an alcohol-related offense. Humiliated and anxious about the forthcoming court hearing, the patient began Antabuse and obtained a prescription for Xanax. By the time the patient was admitted to an alcoholism program 2 weeks later he had increased the Xanax to 3 times the recommended dosage. He had a withdrawal seizure shortly after admission because the staff were unaware of his pattern of abuse and discontinued his Xanax.

The first drawback, then, is the potential for replacing one addiction (alcohol) with another (pills).

Second, the use of medication may interact with crucial attitudinal factors of the physician or the patient. A physician, hampered in his or her treatment efforts with alcoholic patients, may turn to medication as a distancing maneuver and prescribe for a wide variety of symptoms rather than face (along with the patient) the core issue of dependence on alcohol. On the other hand, the patient may assume that by taking medication he or she is successfully managing the alcoholism and nothing further needs to be done. This, of course, is always a risk with the use of disulfiram as well. In such instances medications seem to reinforce the denial process.

Third, the alcoholic patient has been regressed by his or her experience with alcohol. He or she has come to rely upon instant gratification, has lost tolerance for discomfort, and has become passive in functioning. Recovery depends on active, sustained effort, the development of patience, and acceptance of less than perfection in self and others. New behaviors need to be learned. Taking pills (relying on something that you swallow to make you okay) may reinforce the attitude that one's difficulties are solvable by chemicals. This is not to deny that some alcoholic patients for periods of time require medication for specific psychiatric disorders. The meaning of taking medication for the patient, the possibly unrealistic expectations of the medicine, and the threat of not attending to specific nonpharmacological approaches to alcoholism should be explored if medication is being considered.

Fourth, the risk of drinking while on medication needs to be assessed. Alcohol combined with antidepressants, sedative-hypnotics, benzodiazepines, or major tranquilizers is a potentially harmful (perhaps lethal) combination.

Finally, there is a need to be cognizant of a possible conflict for some patients who are active in AA or are involved in a treatment program that discourages use of any medication. Some patients request that no medications be prescribed, even though an antidepressant seems indicated. They value their newly learned skills in coping without any form of drugs, and it is important to respect that effort.

On the other hand, there are many patients who need to be educated about the use of certain medications. For example, the schizophrenic patient should usually be encouraged to use an antipsychotic medication and should be informed that such substances are not addicting. They may need help in countering recovered people who are not understanding of psychosis and, in a misguided attempt to help with the alcoholism, persuade a patient to throw away his or her pills. I have seen recovering people do well as they were being treated with phenothiazines only to experience a psychotic episode when advised by AA friends to avoid pills. As an organization, AA does not speak against use of medication and does not attempt to practice medicine, but a few AA members lose sight of this fact and offer gratuitous advice.

Patients do need to know that antidepressants, lithium, or major tranquilizers are not addicting. Reassurance about the usefulness of these agents for specific conditions and only for as long as necessary helps to avoid conflict for the alcoholic patient who is trying to learn to free himself or herself from chemical dependence.

A middle-aged physician with a mixed drug and alcohol dependence requested continued use of a decongestant. Should this be of any concern? The decongestant was possibly indicated for a chronic sinus condition. Despite an indication for the use of a nonaddicting substance, I chose to use his request as an opportunity to review drawbacks to continued reliance on medication to relieve symptoms. He needed to know that the use of a nonessential medication might be "a foot in the door" for an increasing reliance on drugs to cope with other symptoms, in particular those symptoms which had earlier paved the way to drug abuse. I wasn't concerned about abuse of the decongestant, but rather his potential failure to learn new behaviors.

Are There Some Alcoholics Who Benefit
From Benzodiazepines or Sedative-Hypnotics?

This question addresses the issue of whether there are alcoholic patients without additional psychiatric disorders whose recovery is enhanced or even depends upon the use of such psychotropic medication. This question does not refer to depressed, manic, psychotic, or anxiety-disordered alcoholic patients, that is, those with dual disorders (alcohol plus a concomitant psychiatric disorder). Those alcoholics with an additional psychiatric disorder need treatment, pharmacologic or otherwise, for the concomitant disorder.

One set of circumstances suggests that benzodiazepines may be helpful beyond the acute phase of alcohol withdrawal. Patients who exhibit withdrawal or withdrawal-like symptoms over an extended period of time (up to 6 months) are highly vulnerable to a return to alcohol use. Kissin (1977) has described better outcomes for such alcoholics when they are given Librium. The judicious use of benzodiazepines during this period may forestall a return to alcohol. The target symptoms in cases of protracted withdrawal are tremulousness, anxiety, insomnia, and depression. This syndrome may be subtle and persist for months after removal of alcohol (Begleiter & Porjesz, 1979).

For the most part, studies that show an advantage in using antianxiety or sedative-hypnotic agents for alcoholic patients are short-term, i.e., 6 weeks or less (Boroman & Thimann, 1966). Continuation in treatment is the variable that commonly stands out favoring a tranquilizer-treated group (Ditman, 1966), but even that advantage fails to hold for more than a few months (Rosenberg, 1974). On the other hand, one of the better controlled studies (Shaffer, Freinek, Wolf, Foxwell, & Kurland, 1963) found the use of Librium to be a disadvantage. More drinking occurred among the alcoholic patients taking Librium than those receiving a placebo.

The use of psychotropic medication of the sedative-hypnotic or minor tranquilizer classes is a strong test of the physician's judgment. The issue should be approached with an understanding that the large majority of alcoholics do not benefit from such medications following the acute period of detoxification (Solomon, 1982). From there the physician determines whether symptoms indicative of a protracted withdrawal syndrome, periods of severe stress (for example, sudden death of a spouse), or specific complaints such as insomnia, somatic symptoms, or anxiety warrant a trial of medication.

If the physician, aware of the drawbacks described earlier, decides that the use of this class of drugs is warranted, the following guidelines (modified after Senay, 1983) are recommended:

1. Inform the patient of the drawbacks described earlier.
2. Set a time limit for the use of the medication. For example, one week for a severe grief reaction.
3. Indicate the drug is being used only until nonpharmacologic approaches can begin to take effect.
4. Monitor whether the drug has any effect on the target symptom(s).
5. Be aware of any abuses, for example, requests for additional prescriptions, procurement of medication from other physicians, unwillingness to do anything but take medications.
6. Don't be blackmailed by threats to go to another doctor for medication.

The Question of Lithium and Antidepressants

The relationship between affective disorders and alcoholism will be reviewed in the next chapter. The issue of antidepressants in the treatment of alcoholism uncomplicated by an affective disorder, however, is straightforward. Controlled studies fail to show any advantage in the use of antidepressants (Viamontes, 1972). If, after the patient is detoxified and a reasonable period of evaluation has elapsed (about three weeks), a major depression or dysthymic disorder is found to coexist with the alcoholism, antidepressants should be considered as they would with any other depressed patient. If no clearly defined affective disorder is present, antidepressants are not indicated.

It is well documented that lithium salts are effective in the treatment of manic episodes and in the prevention of recurrent depression (Coppen, Montgomery, Gupta, & Bailey, 1976; Coppen, Noguera, & Bailey, 1971). Is lithium useful in the treatment of alcoholism? An early report (Fries, 1969) found no advantage in administering lithium to 17 alcoholics. Since most of the patients quickly discontinued use of lithium, the findings are inconclusive. Kline, Wren, Cooper, Varga, and Cord (1974), in another early study, found that disabling drinking episodes over a 48-week follow-up were significantly less in a lithium-treated group compared to a placebo-treated group. These data are based on the 30 of 73 patients who remained in the study.

Since Kline's study, further data support the effectiveness of lithium in the treatment of depressed alcoholics (Merry, Reynolds, Bailey, & Coppen, 1976; Reynolds, Merry, & Coppen, 1979). The number of days incapacitated by drinking were significantly reduced for alcoholics who were depressed and on lithium compared to depressed alcoholics on placebo. It is important to note, however, that alcoholics who were not depressed showed no advantage from lithium in regard to days of incapacitation. These findings are contradicted, however, by the report of Young and Keeler (1977) that all 15 patients in their study with a history of both alcoholism and bipolar affective disorder relapsed in regard to alcoholism within the first year on lithium.

At this stage of our knowledge, the better controlled studies conclude that alcoholic patients with certain affective disorders may be helped with the use of lithium. It is undetermined as to how long lithium should be used in this subgroup of patients. If lithium is used, every effort should be made to engage the alcoholic in nonpharmacologic forms of treatment as well. It is also uncertain how lithium is effective in affective-disordered alcoholics. The study by Reynolds et al. (1979), although showing an improvement in alcohol-related behavior in the depressed alcoholics on lithium, did not demonstrate a significant difference in depression ratings from baseline to the end of the study (approximately 10 months later). This may be due to the relatively small number of depressed alcoholics in the lithium and placebo groups (9 and 7 respectively). The patients in the Kline et al. (1974) study showed less depression with time, independent of lithium. The same held true for Reynolds et al.'s study: all patients demonstrated a trend toward lower scores on the Beck Depression Inventory whether or not they were initially classified as clinically depressed and whether or not they were on lithium.

Judd and Huey (1984) have raised the possibility, through carefully conducted studies, that lithium may alter the subjective effect of alcohol. The alcoholic subjects on lithium, compared to alcoholic subjects on placebo, reported feeling less intoxicated, reported less craving, and less confusion. Judd et al. (1979) are careful to point out that in objective comparisons, such as rater-observed or performance test data, the effect of lithium on performance after administration of alcohol showed no consistent effects. Similarly, in a rating of mood changes after administration of alcohol, the alcoholic sample yielded rating changes that were similar for both placebo and lithium conditions.

Until further data are available it seems reasonable to assume that lithium is not a panacea for the alcoholic population, but that it may be useful for a subgroup of alcoholic patients with a history of bipolar affective disorder or recurrent depression.

Major Tranquilizers

Phenothiazines, haloperidol, thiothixene, or other classes of drugs indicated for psychotic disorders have no specific role in alcoholism treatment. The alcoholic with a concomitant psychotic disorder should receive treatment as would nonalcoholic patients. In the past phenothiazines were used for withdrawal purposes, but the lowered seizure threshold and the availability of more suitable and safer agents such as benzodiazepines render them unnecessary under routine circumstances. The major tranquilizers may be indicated in the alcoholic-related organic brain syndrome. Delirium tremens may be better managed with low doses of haloperidol or other antipsychotic medications if benzodiazepines prove insufficient. Chronic alcoholic hallucinosis may require long-term use of a major tranquilizer in order to control the hallucinations and associated fears. Short-term use of a major tranquilizer may be indicated in severe anxiety states if there is a prior history of medication abuse that precludes the use of other agents; for example, the patient with a history of diazepam abuse is best treated by avoiding benzodiazepines. Short-term treatment and a focus on target symptoms are the key factors in such instances.

To conclude, there is no specific pharmacologic approach to alcoholism. Disulfiram is often a useful adjunct in the treatment of alcoholism, and the psychoactive agents are often indicated in alcohol-related organic brain syndromes or alcoholism complicated by a concomitant psychiatric disorder. Careful diagnosis over a prolonged period of time is essential in making the decisions in regard to the use of psychotropic medication. The next chapter will review the relationship between alcoholism and other psychiatric disorders, a consideration that reinforces the need for careful evaluation and diagnosis.

CHAPTER 12

Alcoholism and Other Psychiatric Disorders

The relationship between alcoholism and other psychiatric disorders is complex. At the simplest level alcoholism has been dichotomized as primary versus secondary or essential versus reactive. The primary or essential form develops without a preceding psychiatric disorder, whereas secondary or reactive alcoholism refers to alcoholism which developed subsequent to a preceding psychiatric disorder. In a more sophisticated vein, Meyer (1986b) has described psychopathology as a risk factor for addictive disease or as a modifier of addictive disease in terms of rapidity of development, symptom picture, and response to treatment.

In this chapter three possible relationships are described between alcoholism and other psychiatric disorders (see Table 12-1).

Model A applies when a patient with bipolar affective disorder, manic type, originally drinks to "come down," but eventually develops a dependence on alcohol independent of its use during a manic episode. Model B, "Primary Alcoholism," applies when one considers the relationship between alcoholism and alcohol-induced organic brain syndromes (psychiatric disorder).

It is important to understand the differences between the two examples just mentioned. In Model B, alcohol use is etiologic in regard to the alcohol-induced organic brain syndrome either by virtue of its direct toxic effect on the neuron (alcoholic hallucinosis) or by associated vitamin deficiencies (alcohol amnestic disorder). In the example of Model A, etiologic significance cannot be assigned solely to the bipolar disorder, but is best considered to be one of a number of variables that contribute

TABLE 12-1

Possible Relationships Between Alcoholism
and Other Psychiatric Disorders

Model A. Primary Psychiatric Disorder:	Psychiatric Disorder Increases the Risk of Alcoholism
Model B. Primary Alcoholism:	Alcoholism Leads to Psychiatric Disorder
Model C. Parallel Disorders:	Psychiatric Disorder Alcoholism

to alcoholism (bipolar patients who drink but do not necessarily develop alcoholism).

For a specific psychiatric disorder to develop after drinking has been terminated is not unusual. The relationship between alcoholism and the additional psychiatric disorder is often unclear. It cannot be assumed that the drinking was an attempt to medicate "symptoms" (Model A). Heavy drinking can mask an additional disorder. Model C (Table 12-1) applies in such a case, as it implies that an individual can have more than one disorder at the same time and that a causal relationship need not be assumed. For example:

A 38-year-old businessman became sober, and within months a series of panic attacks developed. He had never experienced similar anxiety in the past and successfully avoided a return to alcohol. Imipramine curbed the panic disorder, and the patient continued his therapeutic program for alcoholism.

There was no apparent relationship between the alcoholism and the panic disorder. The abuse of alcohol had not been precipitated by anxiety attacks and was pervasive by the time he sought treatment. The clinical approach was to treat each disorder specifically.

For the remainder of the chapter specific psychiatric disorders will be discussed in relationship to alcoholism. The first group of disorders to be considered, the alcohol organic mental disorders, are the most straight-forward as alcohol abuse is responsible for their development.

ALCOHOL ORGANIC MENTAL DISORDERS

Transient Disorders

Alcohol intoxication. This familiar syndrome is characterized by an alteration in behavior consequent to alcohol use. Disinhibition occurs early as manifested by euphoria, loquacity, and excitement. Later, sluggishness and depression may occur. Motor skills and cognitive processes begin to decline at the 50 mg/dl (0.05%) level. This is the level of legal intoxication for driving in some European countries. In the United States, the legal level for drunkenness is 100 mg/dl (.10%) (Cohen, 1984).

A blood alcohol concentration of 10 mg/dl (.01%) percent is metabolized about every 40 minutes. This is equivalent to one drink (e.g., a 12-ounce bottle of beer, 5-ounce glass of wine, or 1½ ounces of 80-proof whiskey). If a 160 lb person consumes 4 drinks in an hour, he or she reaches the legal level of drunkenness (.10%) and remains somewhat impaired for about 4 hours.

The DSM-III-R (American Psychiatric Association, 1987, p. 128) criteria for alcohol intoxication are listed below:

1. Recent ingestion of alcohol (with no evidence suggesting that the amount was insufficient to cause intoxication in most people).
2. Maladaptive behavior effects, e.g., disinhibition of sexual or aggressive impulse, mood lability, impaired judgment, interference with social or occupational functioning.
3. At least one of the following signs: slurred speech, incoordination, unsteady gait, nystagmus, flushed face.
4. Not due to any other physical or mental disorder.

Intoxication can lead to alcoholic coma. A blood alcohol level of greater than 250 mg/dl would usually be necessary for this to occur. If coma occurs at a lower blood alcohol level, other causes are likely (Sellers & Kalant, 1976). These authors list the following possible complicating states of alcoholic coma:

• Other drug ingestion
• Hypoglycemia
• Subdural hematoma
• Meningitis
• Pneumonia
• Upper GI hemorrhage
• Pancreatitis
• Hepatitis
• Portosystemic encephalopathy
• Hypothermia

Alcohol idiosyncratic intoxication. This condition was formerly called "pathological intoxication" and is rare. DSM-III-R criteria are given below:

1. Maladaptive behavioral change, e.g., aggressive or assaultive behavior, occurring within minutes of ingesting an amount of alcohol insufficient to induce intoxication in most people.
2. The behavior is atypical of the person when not drinking.
3. Not due to any other physical or mental disorder. (p. 129)

Edwards (1982) considers the entity "a very uncertain concept," as the amount drunk in cases of violence is often greater than that acknowledged by the drinker, and the EEG findings (temporal lobe spikes or nonspecific findings) are of dubious significance.

Nevertheless, the clinician is obligated to consider this disorder as a possibility when a "paradoxical" reaction or "loss of tolerance" effect to small amounts of alcohol leads to violence and amnesia in an individual with evidence of brain damage.

Treatment of this rare condition is directed toward containment of behavior. Low doses of diazepam may be useful. The reaction is usually over within a few hours.

Uncomplicated alcohol withdrawal. The presence of a withdrawal syndrome is diagnostic of alcohol dependence. In the alcohol-dependent patient symptoms of withdrawal emerge 4 to 6 hours after the last drink and may last up to 5 days. The withdrawal symptoms vary in intensity from patient to patient, depending upon the chronicity and severity of alcoholism and the general nutritional and physical status of the patient.

Withdrawal symptoms are an expression of an excited central nervous system which is rebounding from the depressant effect of ethyl alcohol. The rebound produces hyperventilation and a respiratory alkalosis. In addition, a temporary decrease in serum magnesium has been observed and increases neuronal excitability and the possibility of seizures (Victor, 1973). The two metabolic defects, combined with autonomic nervous system hyperactivity, produce the characteristic signs and symptoms of tremulousness, flushed face, sweating, weakness, anxiety, insomnia, nausea, hyperreflexia, startle reaction, increased pulse rate, and elevated blood pressure.

DSM-III-R criteria for diagnosis of Uncomplicated Alcohol Withdrawal are as follows:

1. Cessation of prolonged (several days or longer) heavy ingestion of alcohol or reduction in the amount of alcohol ingested, followed within several hours by coarse tremor of hands, tongue, or eyelids, and at least one of the following: nausea or vomiting; malaise or

weakness; autonomic hyperactivity, e.g., tachycardia, sweating, elevated blood pressure; anxiety; depressed mood or irritability; transient hallucinations or illusions; headache; insomnia.

2. Not due to any physical or other mental disorder such as Alcohol Withdrawal Delirium. (p. 130)

During the 24–48 hour period of withdrawal, illusions or sensory misinterpretations are common. Visual or auditory hallucinations, as well as the less common tactile and olfactory hallucinations, may occur.

An alcohol withdrawal seizure ("rum fit") is most likely to occur in the 7–48 hour period of withdrawal. The seizure is grand mal and is a single seizure in 40% of cases. It progresses to *status epilepticus* in about 2% of cases. Alcohol withdrawal will also precipitate seizures of ideopathic epilepsy or seizures of posttraumatic etiology. Photophobia during the withdrawal period or a prior history of seizures are the two most reliable predictors of withdrawal seizures. The development of *delirium tremens* (alcohol withdrawal delirium) occurs in about one-third of individuals who have a withdrawal seizure (Bernat & Victor, 1982).

Treatment: The treatment of alcohol withdrawal begins with a careful medical history and physical examination. Mild sedation with benzodiazepines, supportive care, and vitamin and mineral replacement constitute the bulwark of treatment. Fluids should be given orally. Usually intravenous fluids are not necessary and should be given only on an individual basis. In cases of protracted vomiting, severe sweating, or diarrhea, electrolyte monitoring can help determine the need for intravenous hydration or other treatment (Czechowicz, 1979).

Below is an outline for the usual treatment regimen:

- Chest x-ray and other radiologic studies as indicated by history and examination (for example, evidence of trauma).
- CBC; urinalysis; liver function studies such as SGOT, SGPT, GGTP, bilirubin, serum amylase if a history of pancreatitis is suggested; serum MG+ may be useful if recent dietary intake has been poor.
- Vitamin replacement: Thiamine 100 mg, intramuscularly initially, then 100 mg orally for the duration of detoxification; multivitamin daily.
- Benzodiazepines: The dosage must be individualized and determined empirically for each patient. Chlordiazepoxide (Librium) may be given in dosages of 25–50 mg orally every 4 hours. Oxazepam (Serax) in a dosage of 15–30 mg every 4 hours may be preferable to chlordiazepoxide because oxazepam is excreted primarily through the kidneys, therefore is an advantage for patients with marked liver dysfunction. As needed (PRN) doses should be available on a 1 hour basis for agitation. Benzodiazepines are usually not necessary after 4 or 5 days.

- Usually mineral deficiencies can be corrected by dietary replenishment. If there is evidence of magnesium deficiency, magnesium sulfate 2 ml (50% solution) can be given intramuscularly every 6 hours for 24 hours.
- Anticonvulsant medication is not given routinely. If there is a history of prior withdrawal seizures or a history of other seizure disorders, prophylactic anticonvulsants are indicated. If the history is insufficient to determine the above and extreme sensitivity to light (photophobia) is noted, anticonvulsants are advisable.

Phenytoin (Dilantin) or phenobarbital is the most commonly used agent. Phenytoin can be given prophylactically in a loading dose of 300 mg three times a day for the first 24 hours, 200 mg three times a day for the next 24 hours, then 100 mg three times a day. Phenobarbital may be given orally or intramuscularly 130 mg initially and then 60 mg four times a day for the first 24 hours, 60 mg three times a day for the next 24 hours, and then tapered off over the next 2 to 3 days (Novick, 1984).

Throughout the period of detoxification, observation for associated medical problems is carried out and encouragement for enrollment in an alcoholism treatment program is emphasized.

Alcohol withdrawal delirium (delirium tremens). This disorder is much less common than uncomplicated alcohol withdrawal. Less than 5% of alcoholics in a general hospital population were noted to develop alcohol withdrawal delirium (American Psychiatric Association, 1980).

The disorder is more likely to develop in the alcoholic patient with an associated medical disorder, for example, an infection, fracture, gastrointestinal hemorrhage. Onset is usually 48–72 hours after the last drink and rarely does it develop after 7 days. The course of the illness runs about 48–72 hours. DSM-III-R criteria are as follows:

1. Delirium developing after cessation of heavy alcohol ingestion or a reduction in the amount of alcohol ingested (usually within one week).
2. Marked autonomic hyperactivity, e.g., tachycardia, sweating.
3. Not due to any other physical or mental disorder. (p. 131)

The DSM-III-R criteria for delirium are given below:

1. Reduced ability to maintain attention to external stimuli (e.g., questions must be repeated because attention wanders) and to appropriately shift attention to new external stimuli (e.g., perseverates answer to a previous question).
2. Disorganized thinking, as indicated by rambling, irrelevant, or incoherent speech.
3. At least two of the following: reduced level of consciousness, e.g., difficulty keeping awake during examination; perceptual disturb-

ances: misinterpretations, illusions, or hallucinations; disturbance of sleep-wake cycle with insomnia or daytime sleepiness; increased or decreased psychomotor activity; disorientation to time, place, or person; memory impairment, e.g., inability to learn new material, such as the names of several unrelated objects after five minutes, or to remember past events, such as history of current episode of illness.

4. Clinical features develop over a short period of time (usually hours to days) and tend to fluctuate over the course of a day.
5. Either (1) or (2):
   (1) evidence from the history, physical examination, or laboratory tests of a specific organic factor (or factors) judged to be etiologically related to the disturbance
   (2) in the absence of such evidence, an etiologic organic factor can be presumed if the disturbance cannot be accounted for by any nonorganic mental disorder, e.g., Manic Episode accounting for agitation and sleep disturbance (p. 103)

Treatment: If a patient develops alcohol withdrawal delirium, transfer to a medical unit is indicated. The search for an underlying medical or surgical illness is essential (Thompson, 1978).

- A calm, quiet, well-lighted room with as much continuity of staff as possible. The presence of a family member remaining with the patient may be helpful. Each procedure should be explained to the patient, for example, taking blood pressure, starting intravenous fluids. Occasionally restraints may be necessary.
- Fluid and electrolyte imbalances must be corrected. Fever, sweating, and excessive motor activity make dehydration a greater risk than occurs with alcohol withdrawal.
- Parenteral vitamins, especially B vitamins, are indicated. Nutritional deficiency can be assumed and the administration of thiamine may help prevent the onset of Wernicke-Korsakoff syndrome.
- A cooling blanket should be available in the case of high fever. Mortality from delirium tremens increases if the temperature suddenly rises to 105 degrees or more (Edwards, 1982). Careful monitoring of vital signs is required.

Sedation with benzodiazepines is the preferred pharmacologic approach. Senay (1983) recommends administration of 10 mg to 20 mg of diazepam or 25 mg to 50 mg of chlordiazepoxide and observation of the effects for 30 minutes. If sedation has not been achieved, double the dose and observe again. Once sedation is obtained, administer that dose every 4 hours over the next 24–48 hours. After that the benzodiazepines usually can be tapered off over 3–5 days.

Alcohol withdrawal delirium or "DTs" is a very serious disorder requiring medical consultation and management. The psychiatrist needs to be prepared to encounter the disorder, recognize delirium, implement a treatment regimen, and obtain consultation from internal medicine.

Alcohol hallucinosis. The DSM-III-R criteria for alcohol hallucinosis are given below:

1. Organic Hallucinosis with vivid and persistent hallucinations (auditory or visual) developing shortly (usually within 48 hours) after cessation of or reduction in heavy ingestion of alcohol in a person who apparently has Alcohol Dependence.
2. No Delirium as in Alcohol Withdrawal Delirium.
3. Not due to any physical or other mental disorder. (p. 132)

The absence of delirium is important in distinguishing this disorder from delirium tremens. The usual age of onset (40 years or older) is later than the typical onset of schizophrenia. Another distinction between this disorder and schizophrenia is the absence of classical schizophrenic thought disorder (Edwards, 1982).

Although this disorder usually subsides within one week, about 10% of cases become chronic (Victor & Hope, 1957).

A 48-year-old baker refused to go to work because of the voices threatening that his life was in danger. Auditory hallucinations had accompanied his alcoholism for several years, but he was now sober for 8 months. After a trial of several major tranquilizers combined with reassurance, thiothixene (Navane) in low doses was effective in curbing the hallucinations and enabled the patient to resume employment.

A more typical case, except for the age of onset, is described below:

After drinking a fifth of whiskey a day for months prior to hospitalization, an 18-year-old male was withdrawn from alcohol without incident, except for brief visual hallucinations. Subsequent auditory hallucinations developed which consisted of voices of his parents criticizing his behavior. These subsided within three days with the use of chlorpromazine (Thorazine). There was no subsequent development of psychotic symptoms.

Alcohol hallucinosis presents the need for careful differential diagnosis. Schizophrenia, alcohol withdrawal delirium, amphetamine delirium, and amphetamine delusional disorder are the major conditions requiring differentiation.

Severe Disorders

Alcohol amnestic disorder. This disorder, also known as Korsakoff's psychosis, is the result of a thiamine deficiency secondary to chronic alcohol use. Studies by Victor, Adams, and Collins (1971) have identified that the memory defect is best correlated with lesions of the dorsal medial nucleus of the thalamus and the mammiliary bodies. The disorder is a continuum involving Wernicke's acute encephalopathy, Korsakoff's psychosis (the amnestic disorder), and cerebellar degeneration.

Typically, the illness presents with the triad of findings of Wernicke's encephalopathy: confusion, ocular movement abnormalities (nystagmas and 6th nerve [abducens] paralysis), and ataxia. Vigorous treatment with thiamine will clear some of Wernicke's symptoms, but then a disorder of memory is typically revealed, i.e., Korsakoff's psychosis. The condition is characterized by: (a) anterograde amnesia—the inability to learn new information or benefit from experience; (b) a retrograde amnesia extending back in a patchy fashion for several years; (c) apathy and indifference; and (d) the loss of the ability to maintain grooming, housekeeping skills, and social amenities (Victor et al., 1971). McEvoy (1982), in a review of the Wernicke-Korsakoff syndrome, points out that nearly 20% of patients have essentially complete recovery over a period of months to years, 60% show some improvement, and 20% require institutionalization.

Confabulation, the tendency to fill in memory gaps with fantastic stories, is not as common as once believed and may be secondary to frontal lobe damage rather than the periventricular lesions of the Wernicke-Korsakoff syndrome (Benson, 1978).

DSM-III-R criteria for alcohol amnestic disorder are as follows:

1. Amnestic Syndrome following prolonged, heavy ingestion of alcohol.
2. Not due to any physical or other mental disorder. (p. 133)

The DSM-III-R criteria for an amnestic syndrome are given below:

1. Demonstrable evidence of impairment in both short- and long-term memory; with regard to long-term memory, very remote events are remembered better than more recent events. Impairment in short-term memory (inability to learn new information) may be indicated by inability to remember three objects after five minutes. Long-term memory impairment (inability to remember information that was known in the past) may be indicated by inability to remember past personal information (e.g., what happened yesterday, birthplace, occupation) or facts of common knowledge (e.g., past Presidents, well-known dates).

2. Not occurring exclusively during the course of Delirium, and does not meet the criteria for Dementia (i.e., no impairment in abstract thinking or judgment, no other disturbances of higher cortical function, and no personality change).
3. There is evidence from the history, physical examination, or laboratory tests of a specific organic factor (or factors) judged to be etiologically related to the disturbance. (p. 109)

The clinician needs to be alert to the possibility of a developing Wernicke-Korsakoff syndrome in the heavy drinking, poorly eating alcoholic patient. The syndrome is clearly underdiagnosed. In a large series, 1.7% of brains examined at autopsy had findings of Wernicke's encephalopathy. However, less than one fifth of the victims had the diagnosis made during their lives (Harper, 1979). The presentation is often not the classical Wernicke triad. An apathetic or confused mental state may be most prominent, or associated symptoms of muscle weakness, ataxia, or peripheral neuropathy may dominate the clinical picture. Since prompt administration of intramuscular thiamine may lessen morbidity, alertness to this syndrome is crucial.

Alcohol amnestic disorder should not be confused with "blackouts." The latter are physiologically induced periods of amnesia, lasting minutes to hours, caused by high blood alcohol levels. "Blackouts" are commonly considered an early sign of alcoholism.

Dementia associated with alcoholism. There is a spectrum of mental impairment in alcoholic patients that cannot be attributed to thiamine deficiency. Alcohol itself is a neurotoxin and may account for the dementia to be described. Other factors which need to be considered include other nutritional deficiencies, hypoglycemia, head trauma, seizures, and alcohol-induced liver disease (Tarter & Edwards, 1986; Tuck, Brew, Britton, & Lowey, 1984).

This disorder is the second most common adult dementia after Alzheimer's disease. About 9% of alcoholics acquire this condition (Eckardt & Martin, 1986).

The DSM-III-R criteria for dementia are as follows:

1. Demonstrable evidence of impairment in short- and long-term memory. Impairment in short-term memory (inability to learn new information) may be indicated by inability to remember three objects after five minutes. Long-term memory impairment (inability to remember information that was known in the past) may be indicated by inability to remember past personal information (e.g., what happened yesterday, birthplace, occupation) or facts of common knowledge (e.g., past Presidents, well-known dates).

2. At least one of the following:
    1) impairment in abstract thinking, as indicated by inability to find similarities and differences between related words, difficulty in defining words and concepts, and other similar tasks
    2) impaired judgment, as indicated by inability to make reasonable plans to deal with interpersonal, family, and job-related problems and issues
    3) other disturbances of higher cortical function, such as aphasia (disorder of language), apraxia (inability to carry out motor activities despite intact comprehension and motor function), agnosia (failure to recognize or identify objects despite intact sensory function), and "constructional difficulty" (e.g., inability to copy three-dimensional figures, assemble blocks, or arrange sticks in specific designs)
    4) personality change, i.e., alteration or accentuation of premorbid traits
3. The disturbance in A and B significantly interferes with work or usual social activities or relationships with others.
4. Not occurring exclusively during the course of Delirium.
5. Either 1) or 2):
    1) there is evidence from the history, physical examination, or laboratory tests of a specific organic factor (or factors) judged to be etiologically related to the disturbance
    2) in the absence of such evidence, an etiologic organic factor can be presumed if the disturbance cannot be accounted for by any nonorganic mental disorder, e.g., Major Depression accounting for cognitive impairment (p. 107)

The DSM-III-R diagnostic criteria for dementia associated with alcoholism are listed below:

1. Dementia following prolonged, heavy ingestion of alcohol and persisting at least three weeks after cessation of alcohol ingestion.
2. Exclusion, by history, physical examination, and laboratory tests, of all causes of Dementia other than prolonged heavy use of alcohol. (p. 134)

When chronic alcoholics are compared with controls from the general population on computerized tomography (CT) and neuropsychological testing, the following generalizations can be made: Brain shrinkage and neuropsychological impairment are more common in alcoholics; evidence of brain damage in alcoholics can be found by the third decade of life; alcohol may have an effect similar to the aging process (Bergman, Borg, Hinchmarsh, Idestrom, & Mutzell, 1980).

In regard to the aging process, Ryan and Butters (1980) have advanced an "accelerated aging" hypothesis of alcohol's effect on brain function.

This hypothesis formulates that the test performance of alcoholics will be inferior to nonalcoholics across the entire adult age span. This formulation differs from an "increased vulnerability" hypothesis (Jones & Parsons, 1971) which postulates performance differences in older alcoholics and the relatively younger alcoholics are protected from deficits. The "accelerated aging" hypothesis is favored in a study by Noonberg, Goldstein, and Page (1985) where brain age quotient differences were found between alcoholics and controls as early as the 30-year-old group.

The neuropsychological deficits found in alcoholics are largely related to nondominant hemisphere functions, and tests of propositional language function remain relatively intact. Nonverbal abstracting, visual-spatial, tactile-spatial, and visual-motor speed are among the performance items commonly impaired (Parsons & Farr, 1981).

On the positive side, it is apparent that improvement in cognitive functioning, as determined by neuropsychological testing, can occur (Goldman, 1983). Repeated CT scans have also documented an improved anatomical picture as evidenced by a lessened degree of brain shrinkage (Carlen & Wilkinson, 1980).

Thus, we have sufficient information to know on the one hand that chronic alcoholism leads to a progressive deterioration in brain function and, on the other, that the decline may be stopped and even partially reversed if the underlying condition of alcohol dependence is successfully treated.

AFFECTIVE DISORDERS AND ALCOHOLISM

Affective disorder will refer to either major depression or dysthymic disorder. The relationship of bipolar disorder to alcoholism will be addressed later in this section. The relationship between alcoholism and affective disorders is complex and is only gradually being understood. On one hand, alcoholism has been seen as an attempt at self-medication for depression, while on the other the depressive consequences of alcohol use have been emphasized (Vaillant, 1984).

The fact that alcoholism and affective disorder commonly coexist is well established. Weissman and Myers (1980), in a community survey using Research Diagnostic Criteria (Spitzer, Endicott, & Robins, 1978), found that 68% of individuals diagnosed as alcoholic also had either major or minor depressive episodes in their lifetimes. This is a substantially higher incidence of depression than occurs in the general population. For example, a recent study of household samples in three urban areas found a 5% lifetime incidence of major depression and a 3.3% lifetime incidence of dysthymic disorder (Robins et al., 1984).

Clinical studies of patients being treated for alcoholism reveal a high incidence of depression. On the basis of Research Diagnostic Criteria, 33% of alcoholics in a rehabilitation center sample were diagnosed as having had an episode of major depression in their lifetimes (women, 43%; men, 29%). Young female alcoholics seemed particularly vulnerable as 60% of women between age 20 and 30 were diagnosed as having met criteria for major depression (Bedi & Halikas, 1985). In a Canadian study of alcoholic inpatients, 22 of 48 (46%) had a history of major depression. In most of these patients it was determined that the alcoholism preceded the affective disorder. The depressed alcoholics, compared to alcoholics with no history of depression, were more likely to be divorced, to have had trouble with the law, to have made more suicidal gestures, to have begun drinking at an earlier age, and to be more irritable and angry (Bowen, Cipywnyk, D'Arcy, & Keegan, 1984).

In a larger study (Hesselbrock, Meyer, & Keener, 1985) of hospitalized alcoholics, major depression was found to precede the alcoholism in one half of the males with a history of major depression and in two thirds of the women with major depression. In this study, 32% of the men and 52% of the women had a lifetime diagnosis of major depression.

At the initiation of treatment, depression is common, but by the completion of brief treatment (about 4 weeks) most alcoholics make considerable improvement. Of 49 alcoholics who met Research Diagnostic Criteria for major depression, only 10 remained depressed after 2 weeks of sobriety (Dackis, Gold, Pottash, & Sweeney, 1986). A private university hospital service found that 45% of 73 alcoholics rated by the Zung Self-Rating Depression Scale were clinically depressed at admission, but only 10% were so rated 4 weeks later (Overall, Reilly, Kelly, & Hollister, 1985). In a Veterans Administration sample only 12 of 84 alcoholics remained depressed after brief treatment (Nakamura, Overall, Hollister, & Radcliffe, 1983). The brief depression observed in recently detoxified alcoholic patients may often best be classified as an organic affective disorder. In each of the latter two studies, persisting depression was related to either disruption of personal relationships as a result of drinking or the threat of loss of relationships as a result of the need to avoid previous activities associated with alcohol use—for example, a social life that centered around bars.

Several studies have looked at the relationship between depression and alcoholism over an extended time period after treatment. Fourteen percent of those AA members who had been abstinent for at least 1 year were found, by Research Diagnostic Criteria, to experience serious depressive symptoms. The depressive symptoms developed after an average of 35 months of sobriety. Males and females were equally affected. This study did not determine whether depression had existed prior to the alcoholism, but did ascertain that the depressed alcoholics had had a prior history of significant drug abuse (Behar, Winokur, & Berg, 1984).

In a mail and telephone survey of alcoholics who had received alcoholism treatment 1 year earlier, 16% of those abstinent were rated as depressed, and 33% of those drinking rated themselves depressed (Hatsukami & Pickens, 1982).

Continuation of depression is related to whether or not abstinence is achieved. In alcoholics treated on an outpatient basis, 59% were depressed at intake and 60% at a one-year follow-up. However, at follow-up, 72% of those still depressed were still drinking, whereas 75% of those not depressed were abstinent (Pottenger et al., 1978). Pettinati et al. (1982) were able to document improved psychological functioning as measured by the MMPI in a careful 4-year follow-up study of alcoholics treated in a private psychiatric hospital. The alcoholics who remained abstinent over the 4-year follow-up period were characterized by an elevated D (depression) score on the initial MMPI (completed during hospitalization). Four years later, the MMPI was entirely within the normal range for the abstinent group. Those who had the worst outcomes had elevated Pd (psychopathic deviation) and Ma (mania) scores initially, and their scores were unchanged 4 years later. An intermittent outcome group, which was characterized by slips over the 4-year period, but not regular drinking, had initially elevated D and Pd scores. By the time of follow-up, this relatively improved group had normal MMPIs.

It is not clear from these data whether those who achieved abstinence did so in part because depression was largely alleviated, or whether depression improved because of continuing abstinence. In practice, both possibilities seem to play a role. The study of Pottenger et al. (1978) emphasized the need to consider specific treatment of depression (for example, the use of antidepressants) in depressed alcoholics. Using multiple criteria they documented depression in alcoholics and ascertained that the depressed alcoholics remained both depressed and drunk when the depression was untreated.

Thus far the literature suggests that the coexistence of alcoholism and depression is common, that the depression is usually secondary in manifestation to the onset of alcoholism, that depression in alcoholics often remits with brief treatment, and that alcoholics remaining depressed are likely to need specific treatment for depression if abstinence is to be gained.

The next question to be addressed is whether those with depression prior to the onset of alcoholism (primary depressives) are at greater risk to develop alcoholism. The commonly held notion that alcoholism occurs secondary to depression does not hold up to close scrutiny. The ubiquity of the assumption may be rooted in the need for alcoholic patients to find an "excuse" for their drinking and in the clinician's underestimation of alcoholism as a primary disorder. On the other hand, the data from Hesselbrock et al. (1985) reopens this question since the majority of their depressed alcoholic patients were ascertained to be depressed prior to the onset of the alcoholism.

When primary depressed patients are studied, an unremarkable incidence of secondary alcoholism is found. For example, Woodruff, Guze, Clayton, and Carr (1973) found that of 39 depressed alcoholics only 3 had a primary depression (that is, depression which preceded the onset of alcoholism). In an affective disorder program only 6.4% of patients were determined to be alcoholics. In this small group of depressed alcoholics (N = 10) 3 were considered primarily depressed while the other 7 alcoholics were diagnosed as having a depression secondary to alcoholism (Spring & Rothgery, 1984). Merikangas, Leckman, Prusoff, Pauls, and Weissman (1985), in a study of patients selected for primary depression, found only 19 alcoholics (14%) in their sample of 133 primary depressives. Similarly, Lewis, Helzer, Cloninger, Crougham, and Whitman (1982), in a study of 37 women hospitalized for primary unipolar depression, found only 3% to be alcoholic. The same authors analyzed data from a large community sample and concluded that 10% of women with primary depression had alcoholism in contrast to 6% of women without primary depression.

Family studies provide further support for the separateness of primary depression and alcoholism. Woodruff et al. (1973) found that, on a variety of behavioral variables such as history of delinquency and antisocial behavior, alcoholics with depression were more similar to nondepressed alcoholics than to depressed patients without alcoholism. In another study (Spring & Rothgery, 1984), the incidence of alcoholism in first degree relatives of bipolar patients was 3%, and in the relatives of patients with major depression alcoholism was 13.6%. By contrast, affective disorder was found in 39.4% and 31.8%, respectively, of first degree relatives of bipolar and major depression patients. Schuckit (1983) found no increase in the incidence of affective disorder in families of alcoholics, but families with no alcoholism had a high incidence of affective disorder.

Available data indicate, therefore, that alcoholism and primary depression are separate disorders. The alcoholic patient is very vulnerable to depression, but the risk of alcoholism for the primary depressed patient is less clear. Clinically, the psychiatrist encounters patients with a history of depressive symptomatology which preceded alcohol abuse or dependence, yet systematic studies (Lewis et al., 1982; Merikangas et al., 1985; Schuckit, 1983; Spring & Rothgery, 1984) fail to document a substantially increased risk of alcoholism in the primary depressed patient. Perhaps, the most useful clinical points to be derived from this information are that the patient who is depressed and alcoholic needs treatment for both conditions and that treatment of only one disorder cannot be expected to resolve the other.

Bipolar Affective Disorder

For some patients an affective disorder includes manic episodes. If a patient has a manic episode, he or she is diagnosed as having bipolar affective disorder even if there has been only one episode of mania and many depressive episodes. It is believed that when a manic episode occurs, a different affective disorder is being expressed from those cases which experience depression only.

The preceding discussion of depression and alcoholism was less than clear because depression associated with bipolar affective disorder was included in many of the studies. However, the large majority of subjects in the above review were in the category of unipolar depressive disorders, that is, depression without a history of manic episodes. This section will summarize the apparent relationship between manic episodes and alcoholism. A manic episode occurs in about 1% of the general population (Robins et al., 1984). In contrast, 3% of hospitalized alcoholics were found to have had a manic episode during their lifetime (Hesselbrock et al., 1985).

An increased rate of alcoholism in manic-depressive patients has been reported (Mayfield & Coleman, 1968), but other studies have failed to support this finding. In a Swedish study, only 4% of male and 0% of female hospitalized manic-depressive patients were alcoholic (Stenstedt, 1952). Spring and Rothgery (1984) found no alcoholism in their bipolar patients, and Dunner, Hensel, and Fieve (1979), in a study of 73 patients with bipolar disorder, found alcohol-related problems in 7 males and none of the females.

The best established relationship is that drinking commonly increases during a manic episode (Winokur, Clayton, & Reich, 1969). The increase in alcohol use is substantial, and a decrease in alcohol use during elation seems to be rare (Mayfield, 1979). The increased use may be an attempt at self-medication and increases the chance of hospitalization (Reich, Davies, & Himmelhoch, 1974).

Reasons the Alcoholic Patient May Be Depressed

There are a number of reasons the alcoholic patient may be depressed or have depressive-like symptoms as treatment is initiated. First, the patient may be in withdrawal or in the immediate post-withdrawal phase. Organic factors such as sleep disturbance, anorexia, anxiety, and fatigue are prominent symptoms which facilitate a dysphoric mood.

Second, to admit to being alcoholic brings one face to face with the stigma of alcoholism, the recognition that one has been "defeated" by alcohol, and/or the realization that one has a chronic illness. Any or all of these factors influence alcoholic patients as they embark on a course of treatment and, understandably, may lead to at least temporary feelings of depression.

Third, perhaps the most potent basis for depression in the early phases of treatment is the feeling of loss. The threat that giving up alcohol poses to the alcohol-dependent person is not to be underestimated. The alcoholic has an attachment to alcohol. The consideration of alcohol as "my best friend" has deeper implications than this cliché implies. In addition to the loss of an "object" (alcohol) upon which one has been dependent, the alcoholic also faces the possibility of many other losses. Some losses may have occurred already, others are potential. A career may have been limited or actually destroyed; divorce may have taken place, or the marriage may be faced with an extended period of uncertainty. The alcoholic patient often faces a relative loss of health because brain damage, cirrhosis, and various GI disorders may remain.

In addition to external losses, the alcoholic also experiences internal losses, e.g., disappointment in self, a keener awareness of personal limitations, and possibly a response to the lessened "utility" of defenses such as self-sufficiency or other manifestations of grandiosity.

In many alcoholics the depressive reaction is self-limiting. Others remain depressed and require treatment specifically for depression. More will be said about this when treatment is discussed.

To return to the common observation of a relatively quick resolution of depressive symptomatology: For some, removal of alcohol, restoration of nutritional status, and improved sleep may account for the improvement. For some others, more appropriate conceptualization of the depressive symptomatology may be that of a grief reaction (Friedman, 1984). As noted, the alcoholic has typically experienced many losses. While one is drinking actively, the losses are unlikely to be adequately acknowledged, grieved, or integrated into one's present status. The process of treatment, with its focus on a lessening of denial, will increase one's awareness of losses, actual or potential. The stages of grief have been categorized by Kubler-Ross (1969) as denial, anger, bargaining, depression, and acceptance. Similar responses are observed when alcoholic patients struggle to accept the facts of their alcoholism.

McGovern (1983) documented that alcoholic patients during the course of inpatient treatment develop an increased awareness of losses, and, further, gradually show a lessening of both depression and grief as determined by independent measures. For many alcoholic patients, recovery from alcoholism seems to parallel the process of mourning, as an emancipation from lost objects, a readjustment to reality, and the establishment of new relationships occur (Parkes, 1972).

Depression and grief obviously overlap, and the distinction remains a methodological problem. Possibly some of the depressive symptomatology, especially that which resolves relatively quickly, could be part of a grief reaction to the loss of alcohol and/or to losses resulting from alcoholism.

Treatment

In a study of relapse, the most frequent reason given for relapse was a depressed or anxious mood (Pickens, Hatsukami, Spicer, and Svikis, 1985). It behooves us, therefore, to be aware of the strong association between alcoholism and depression and to evaluate our patients in regard to manifestations of depression. The following guidelines are offered as a useful approach to depressive symptoms in alcoholic patients.

1. Observe and monitor the intensity of depression during the early weeks after detoxification.
2. If clinically relevant depressive symptoms (see DSM-III-R criteria for major depression) remain or have worsened after 3 weeks, the use of antidepressants as a parallel treatment to the alcoholism should be considered.
3. Avoid initiating pharmacotherapy until the patient is at least 3 weeks post-detoxification.
4. If there is a history of bipolar affective disorder with current evidence of manic or depressive symptoms, the use of lithium carbonate, antidepressants, or other pharmacologic approaches may be warranted sooner than the 3-week period indicated above.
5. Supportive psychotherapy oriented toward facilitating the expression of grief is often appropriate. Assist the patient to identify specific losses; support the patient as he or she experiences an array of emotions—anger, depression, resentment, regret, disappointment, or guilt. Reassure the patient that one's reactions are a normal process (grieving) as one learns to readjust without alcohol.
6. If the facilitation of grief work fails to improve affective status, then an additional diagnosis of major depression, dysthymic disorder or atypical depression will need to be considered and parallel treatment of an affective disorder and alcoholism provided.

ANXIETY DISORDERS

The study of anxiety disorders has been greatly improved by the application of the Schedule for Affective Disorders and Schizophrenia—Life Time Version (SADS-L) (Endicott & Spitzer, 1978); Research Diagnostic Criteria (Spitzer, Endicott, & Robins, 1978); the Structured Clinical Interview for DSM-III (SCID) (Spitzer & Williams, 1983) and the Standard Self-Rating for Phobic Patients (Fear Questionnaire) (Marks & Mathews, 1979).

Recently, general population surveys have determined a high rate of anxiety disorders in nonclinical populations. The Epidemiologic Catchment Area Program (Robins et al., 1984) determined that in three urban areas the lifetime prevalence rate for combined anxiety disorders ranged from 10% to 25% across the three sites. Phobias (simple phobias and agoraphobia) accounted for the majority of the anxiety disorders and were more prevalent in women than men.

Despite advances in diagnosis, the relationship between anxiety disorders and alcoholism has not been studied as extensively as with affective disorders. As with affective disorders, anxiety disorders may be primary or secondary to alcoholism. The degree to which each disorder is primary versus which are secondary remains to be determined.

Weissman, Myers, and Harding (1980), in a community based sample of individuals diagnosed as alcoholic, found that 9% of the alcoholics also had a diagnosis of generalized anxiety disorder and 3% had a diagnosis of a phobia at some time during their life. The figures are surprisingly low in consideration of the Epidemiologic Catchment Area's Study wherein the lifetime incidence of anxiety disorders in nonclinical samples ranged from 10 to 25% (Robins et al., 1984). Recently, Epidemiologic Catchment Area data from five community samples involving over 18,000 interviews found panic disorder to be present in 6 to 12% of alcoholic subjects (Boyd, 1986).

Clinical samples of alcoholics have a much higher prevalence of anxiety disorders. Mulhaney and Trippett (1979), in a study of 102 inpatient alcoholics, found about one-third to be "fully phobic." More recently, Bowen et al. (1984b), in an inpatient sample of alcoholic patients, found that 20.8% met DSM-III criteria for panic disorder, 22.9% for generalized anxiety disorder, and 33% had phobias at some time during their lives (29% currently). In all, 44% of this sample had experienced at least one of the anxiety disorders. In another study (Weiss & Rosenberg, 1985) of alcoholic inpatients, 19 of 84 (22.6%) met DSM-III criteria for anxiety disorder. In the latter two studies the anxiety disorder preceded the alcoholism in the majority of the cases. Hesselbrock et al. (1985) also found a high percentage of hospitalized alcoholic patients to have anxiety disorders: 44% of women and 20% of men in their sample had a history of phobia disorder; 14% women and 8% men, panic disorder. However, the anxiety disorder followed the onset of alcoholism in approximately two-thirds of cases.

Most clinicians encounter patients who drink to control symptoms of a panic disorder, post-traumatic stress disorder, or other form of anxiety disorder. These cases may proceed to the development of alcohol abuse which resolves if the anxiety disorder is successfully treated. An example of the latter is illustrated by the following patient:

> A young engineer, soon after obtaining a job in a distant city, began to have panic attacks. At first he thought they were "flashbacks" from LSD which he had tried on a few occasions in the Army 5 years earlier. His only source of relief was to drink a six-pack of beer rapidly as the symptoms began. This was an unsatisfactory remedy because then he was unable to go to work or function on the job. His consumption of beer had increased dramatically during the months prior to his seeking help. He responded to a brief hospitalization, imipramine, and a brief course of psychotherapy. Alcohol consumption subsided as the panic disorder came under control.

Other cases may be more complex:

> During her early 20s a married woman had been treated for Valium dependence. About 5 years later she had her first child and began to experience bouts of anxiety. Her earlier abuse of Valium had not been related to the presence of an anxiety disorder. Her current symptoms were less intense than panic disorder, but clearly troubling. Alcohol provided relief, and she soon began drinking throughout the day as a "preventive" measure. By the time she presented for treatment, the drinking was out of control and was causing greater difficulty than the anxiety disorder. She refused an alcoholism treatment program and tried a course of carefully controlled benzodiazepines and antidepressants on an outpatient basis. When she stopped drinking, her demand for medication increased greatly. Finally, she resumed drinking and hospitalization became necessary.

In the above case, nonpharmacologic approaches to anxiety eventually proved necessary because of her history of dual addictions. Supportive psychotherapy combined with intense involvement in AA proved to be the most helpful approach.

The next example illustrates the development of an anxiety disorder several years after recovery from alcoholism.

> A man in his early 50s had been sober nearly 4 years. Divorced from his first wife, he had been living with a woman for over 2 years. For the 6 months preceding treatment he noticed severe anxiety if his girlfriend was late for an appointment, and later began to feel anxious if he were kept waiting for any reason. The anxiety led him to seek psychiatric consultation. He was firmly committed to sobriety and wanted to use no medication. Weekly

insight-oriented psychotherapy over a 6-month period led to a full remission of symptoms.

The relationship between alcoholism and anxiety disorders is not well established. The coexistence of both disorders may be more common than has been appreciated, and recent reports in the literature emphasize the need for a closer evaluation of anxiety disorders in alcoholic patients (Hudson & Perkins, 1984).

Treatment for some of the anxiety disorders, most notably panic disorder, has improved considerably with the use of imipramine or MAO inhibitors. On the other hand, the treatment of other anxiety disorders is often more complicated than that of alcoholism and coexisting affective disorder because the benzodiazepines, a major treatment modality, are often contraindicated. The possibility of a cross-addiction is very real and nonpharmacologic approaches to anxiety disorders (excepting panic disorders) are suggested. On the other hand, new nonsedating anxiolytics such as buspirone may hold promise for anxiety-disordered alcoholics if cross-addiction proves to be minimal (Meyer, 1986a).

An outline of treatment for patients with alcoholism and a coexisting anxiety disorder is given below:

Treatment

1. Obtain a careful history of symptoms and observe the patient for at least 3 weeks following detoxification. As with depression, symptoms of anxiety may abate as the irritability and autonomic instability of the withdrawal process subsides. Phobias are common and often not of major clinical importance (Glass & Freedman, 1985).
2. If the criteria for a current diagnosis of panic disorder are met, imipramine or an MAO inhibitor should be considered.
3. The other anxiety disorders (generalized anxiety disorder, simple phobias, social phobia, agoraphobia without panic attacks, obsessive-compulsive disorder and post-traumatic stress disorder) should be evaluated for treatment with psychotherapy and/or behavior techniques.
4. The use of benzodiazepines may be necessary and can be used appropriately in selected cases. The principles which enable benzodiazepines to be used include:
   a. the establishment of a therapeutic alliance
   b. no prior history of abuse of prescription medications
   c. use briefly for specific, discreet symptoms
   d. observe any tendency to request increasing amounts of medication
   e. use agents with a possibly lower abuse potential (for example, alprazolam). Diazepam should be avoided because of its known abuse potential.

The treatment of anxiety disorders in alcoholic patients tests the judgment of the clinician more surely than most other "dual disorders." Severe anxiety facilitates a relapse to alcohol, while sole reliance on pharmacologic approaches may lay the groundwork for drug dependence.

Educating the patient about the possibility of a dual addiction, careful monitoring of clinical progress, cautious prescribing habits, and an emphasis on healing through a therapeutic relationship will minimize the risks of drug abuse and maximize the potential for a favorable outcome.

DELUSIONAL (PARANOID) DISORDER AND SCHIZOPHRENIA

Delusional (Paranoid) Disorder

Delusional (paranoid) disorder is a psychotic condition characterized by the presence of persistent, nonbizarre delusions, but otherwise there is an absence of the prominent hallucinations, incoherence, loosening of associations, or bizarre delusions associated with schizophrenia (APA, 1987).

There has been a condition listed in earlier diagnostic manuals as "alcohol paranoid state," but the term was dropped in DSM-III because ". . . there is no compelling evidence that a paranoid state due to chronic alcohol use is a distinct entity. . . ."

Although not common, clinicians may find an intertwining of "pathological jealousy" and alcoholism in some patients. It is difficult to determine which came first and whether the disorders are dynamically related or coincident.

The following case is an example of a paranoid disorder followed by alcoholism:

> After nearly 20 years of marriage, an engineer became preoccupied with the idea that his wife had been unfaithful and that he was not the father of his firstborn son. To prove his contention, he conducted an elaborate fact-finding mission which included a comparison of pictures of his son and a former neighbor, now suspected to be the actual father. Further, he attempted to determine blood types. Depression over his wife's "unfaithfulness" led to hospitalization. The patient's wife and children were devastated by his illness which remained intractable. Years after the onset of his paranoid disorder he developed alcoholism. Alcohol had become a respite from the obsession which dominated this man's existence.

In another instance, traits of jealousy preceded the development of alcoholism, but became increasingly prominent years after successful recovery from alcoholism.

> During his first marriage, Roger learned of a boyfriend who had been intimate with his wife during her high school years. Rage, depression, and jealousy dominated him affectively for a period of months. This subsided, but years later a full-blown syndrome of alcohol dependence led to divorce. Eventually, Roger was treated successfully for alcoholism, became successful in business, and remarried. His second wife had been sexually active as a former divorcée. Awareness of this from early in the courtship grew into an obsession over his wife's behavior. Intimate details were sought and resentment and jealousy constantly threatened the relationship.

Schizophrenia

The six-month prevalence rates for schizophrenia and alcoholism in the United States are approximately 1% and 5%, respectively (Myers, Weissman, Tischler, et al., 1984).

Early studies of patients being treated for alcoholism report an incidence of schizophrenia ranging from 1% (Gillis & Keet, 1969) to 49% (Tomsovic & Edwards, 1970). A recent review by Gottheil and Waxman (1982) concludes that on average 10 to 15% of hospitalized schizophrenics had "serious drinking problems" and that 10 to 15% of outpatient and hospitalized samples of alcoholics have been diagnosed as schizophrenic. The latter figure is most likely inflated in the light of current stricter criteria for schizophrenia (DSM-III-R). In a study (Alterman, Ayre, & Williford, 1984) from a Veterans Administration hospital, using Research Diagnostic Criteria, patients who had earlier been given diagnoses of both alcoholism and schizophrenia did not meet research criteria for schizophrenia in one-third of the cases. Of 11 patients who had met criteria for both diagnoses, 6 had been schizophrenic first, and 5 had developed alcoholism first.

Other studies have found less overlap between alcoholism and schizophrenia. Schuckit (1982) in a study of 220 male alcoholics found that 43% had a history of psychotic symptoms (transient hallucinations or delusions), but there was no relationship between the symptoms and a personal or familial history of schizophrenia. A study (Rimmer & Jacobsen, 1977) of Danish schizophrenic adoptees found only 3% to be alcoholic. The prevalence of alcoholism in the biological parents of the schizophrenic adoptees was low and did not significantly differ from control families, suggesting that alcoholism and schizophrenia do not share a common genetic diathesis.

Edwards (1982) drawing upon the experience of Maudsley and Bethlem Royal Hospitals reports that "schizophrenia is not a frequent concomitant of alcoholism." He reasons that alcohol is not a particularly useful drug for the unpleasant feelings of schizophrenia.

Two clinical vignettes illustrate this point:

> A chronic paranoid schizophrenic cooperated fully with the recommendation for alcoholism treatment. He reasoned that when he was drinking he "talked too much" and became anxious about having revealed his thoughts to others.

> A young male schizophrenic with religious preoccupations resented his periods of hospitalization. Alcohol abuse made him aggressive and led to a discontinuance of medication and ultimately a return to the hospital. He wished to avoid alcohol, cigarettes, other drugs, and certain foods so that he could follow his religious interests and avoid the disruption of hospitalization.

At times alcoholic hallucinations have been confused with schizophrenia. DSM-III-R criteria help to distinguish between the two: Alcohol hallucinosis bears a close temporal relationship to drinking, is usually brief, and typically has a later age of onset than schizophrenia. When alcoholic hallucinosis becomes chronic, distinction between the two disorders is difficult.

Thus, the relationship between alcoholism and schizophrenia is unclear. Schizophrenia is not found at a markedly higher rate among alcoholic inpatients when current diagnostic criteria are used (Hesselbrock, Meyer, & Keener, 1985). At present there are not sufficient data to determine if a higher than usual prevalence of alcoholism occurs in schizophrenia.

> A schizophrenic male in his mid-twenties acknowledged that his alcoholism led to exacerbations of his psychosis. The patient's anxiety, poor tolerance for confrontation, and undeveloped interpersonal skills precluded transfer to the hospital's substance abuse program. Instead, this patient was able to attend hospital education classes on alcoholism and drug abuse which were nonconfrontive and minimally threatening. Later, AA meetings proved satisfactory because the patient was not "forced" to speak and found an atmosphere of acceptance.

To conclude, the alcoholic psychotic patient need not be approached pessimistically. Obviously, two serious chronic conditions present a challenge and test our capacity to individualize care. As these patients recover from psychosis, they express their appreciation for the chance to learn about alcoholism and other drug problems. Some conceptualize their prior episodes of illness as alcohol or drug-related. Although this conceptualization is technically inaccurate in many cases, it often strengthens their motivation. Treatment staff should appreciate the need to modify the intensity of treatment to avoid overstimulating the psychotic patient.

Finally, aftercare plans need to be built around the alliances that have been formed with the treatment staff. Successful use of aftercare groups, AA, or other modalities depends on the patient's being able to continue the primary therapeutic relationships formed during hospitalization. Routine referral to AA or outpatient groups without the "bridge" of that initial therapeutic alliance substantially increases the likelihood of regression, drinking, and eventually psychosis.

PERSONALITY DISORDERS

The past several decades have seen an evolution in the thinking about the relationship between addictions and personality disorders. The first edition of the American Psychiatric Association's Diagnostic and Statistical Manual of Mental Disorders, DSM-I (APA, 1952), listed alcoholism and other addictions as subtypes of sociopathic personality disorders. In 1968, the second edition, DSM-II (APA, 1968), listed alcoholism as a subtype of personality disorders in general. With the publication of DSM-III (APA, 1980), substance use disorders were no longer a subtype of personality disorders, but were recognized as an entity themselves and were divided into abuse and dependence categories. The change in classification status is important because it acknowledges that alcohol dependence does not necessarily depend on a preexisting personality disorder (Gottheil & Waxman, 1982).

In this section the relationship between alcoholism and personality disorders will be discussed. The forebearance of the reader will be necessary as an attempt is made to simplify a complex and not well-understood interaction. Does alcoholism itself cause a personality disorder? Strictly speaking, it does not; among the criteria for the diagnosis of personality disorder is that the features are apparent by childhood or adolescence, ages that usually precede the onset of alcoholism.

One exception is the development of an organic personality disorder wherein a marked change in behavior or personality occurs and alcohol can be etiologically related to the change. As discussed in Chapter 5, chronic alcohol dependence does produce personality regression, and this facet of alcoholism is nearly identical in presentation to that of a personality disorder in the more strict use of the term. With recovery, however, there is usually sufficient personality growth and ego strengthening so that the features of personality disorders (poor impulse control, poor judgment, egocentricity, suspiciousness, and passivity) dissipate. If such characteristics persist after a year of abstinence, the possibility of a preexisting personality disorder or an organic personality disorder should be considered.

Does a personality disorder cause alcoholism? The etiology of alcoholism is multivariate. A personality disorder can be one variable in the etiologic equation and increases chances for the development of either alcoholism or other forms of drug dependence. The association between personality disorders and substance abuse was recently demonstrated among psychiatric patients at a large medical center. Substance abuse was the diagnosis most highly associated with personality disorders which occurred in 46% of alcoholics and 81% of drug abusers (Koenigsberg, Kaplan, Gilmore, & Cooper, 1985).

Definition

Before proceeding, the definition of a personality disorder is necessary:

> Personality *traits* are enduring patterns of perceiving, relating to, or thinking about the environment and oneself, and are exhibited in a wide range of important social and personal contexts. It is only when *personality traits* are inflexible and maladaptive and cause either significant functional impairment or subjective distress that they constitute *Personality Disorders*. (APA, 1987, p. 335)

A personality disorder, therefore, is a condition manifested by *inflexible, maladaptive traits* which cause *social or occupational consequences* and/or *personal discomfort*. Frequently, the affected individual does not consider these traits undesirable, but he or she is usually distressed by the effect of his or her behavior on others.

DSM-III describes 11 specific personality disorders. These disorders can be grouped into 3 larger categories as listed below (Webb, DiClemente, Johnstone, Sanders, & Perley, 1981, pp. 126–128):

1. *Odd or eccentric behavior*
   Paranoid
   Schizoid
   Schizotypical
2. *Dramatic, emotional, or erratic behavior*
   Histrionic
   Narcissistic
   Antisocial
   Borderline

3. *Anxious or fearful behavior*
   Avoidant
   Dependent
   Compulsive
   Passive-Aggressive

Within the above classification, alcoholism is most likely to be found in association with Group 2. The antisocial and borderline types represent the two most commonly associated personality disorders (Koenigsberg et al., 1985).

Antisocial Personality Disorder

Historically, the personality disorder most frequently associated with alcoholism has been antisocial personality disorder. In a review of studies on antisocial personality disorder and alcoholism, 11 of 14 studies showed a positive association (Grande, Wolfe, Schubert, Patterson, & Brocco, 1984). Schuckit (1973) reported that approximately 20% of male alcoholics and 5% of female alcoholics admitted to public or private treatment centers met criteria for primary antisocial personality disorder with secondary alcoholism. More recently, alcoholics studied in three inpatient settings were found to meet DSM-III criteria for antisocial personality disorder in 49% of males and 20% of females (Hesselbrock, Meyer, & Keener, 1985).

A major difficulty is determining whether antisocial personality disorder is primary or secondary to the alcoholism. Prospective studies (Robins, 1966; Vaillant, 1983b) have demonstrated clearly that alcoholism is common in the primary sociopath. In Robins's study (1966), sociopathy was about three times more common than primary alcoholism and typically preceded alcohol abuse. In the hospital sample referred to above (Hesselbrock, Meyer, & Keener, 1985), antisocial personality disorder was determined to precede alcohol abuse in 98% of the males and 94% of the females.

Vaillant's (1983a) prospective 33-year study of a sample (N=456) selected for nondelinquency found that 71 men became alcoholic and 32 men met criteria for sociopathy. There was an overlap; 21 men met criteria for both diagnoses. Of these 21, 12 developed alcoholism first, and 9 were sociopathic prior to the onset of alcoholism. Of the 32 men who met criteria for sociopathy, 20 were primary sociopaths. Nine (45%) of these men also became alcoholic. In contrast, there were 62 men whose alcoholism was not secondary to sociopathy. Twelve of these 62 (19%) developed criteria for sociopathy after the onset of alcoholism.

Those with antisocial personality disorder are at a high risk for the development of alcoholism. In fact, Lewis, Rice, and Helzer (1983) found that the presence of an antisocial personality disorder increased the risk for alcoholism more than having a family history of alcoholism. In a further refinement, Stabenau (1984) demonstrated that family history of alcoholism and antisocial personality disorder were not interactive, but contributed separate additive effects to the development of alcoholism. Cadoret, Troughton, and Wishmer (1984), in a comparison of primary alcoholics with antisocial alcoholics, found that antisocial alcoholics developed alcoholism at a younger age and reported a significantly greater number of additional psychiatric symptoms (depression, anxiety, drug abuse, and childhood conduct disorder).

Alcoholics with a preexisting antisocial personality disorder should not be considered a homogeneous group. Recently, evidence of manic and depressive symptoms in some antisocial alcoholics has suggested the need to consider lithium and/or antidepressants as part of the treatment regimen (Whitters, Troughton, Cadoret, & Wishmer, 1984), and Woody, McLellan, Luborsky, & O'Brien (1985) demonstrated that antisocial substance-abusing patients with symptoms of an affective disorder have a more favorable treatment outcome.

It can be concluded that the majority of alcoholics are not sociopaths. Those who "appear" sociopathic often have developed sociopathic symptoms as a consequence of alcoholism. On the other hand, the primary sociopathic personality is at very high risk to become alcoholic and may also display a varied picture of other psychiatric symptoms.

Borderline Personality Disorder

Borderline personality disorder is characterized by impulsivity, unpredictability, affective instability, inappropriate anger, feelings of emptiness or boredom, disturbances in identity, and manipulative suicide attempts (APA, 1987).

One study (Koenigsberg et al., 1985) found borderline personality disorders to coexist with substance abuse disorders in 43% of cases. A second study (Johnson & Connelly, 1981) considered 28% of addicted physicians to be borderline. When more precise criteria for the diagnosis of borderline personality disorder are used, a lower incidence is seen. Consecutive alcoholic admissions to an inpatient program were studied (Nace, Saxon, & Shore, 1983) using the Diagnostic Interview for Borderlines (Gunderson, Kolb, & Austin, 1981). When items specific to drinking behavior were eliminated from the scoring, 13% of the alcoholics were found to have a borderline personality disorder. The "borderline" alcoholics did not differ from other alcoholics in their pattern of alcoholism (e.g., years of heavy drinking, binge drinking, blackouts, seizures, etc.). The borderline group did use a significantly greater number of other drugs, made more suicide attempts, had more accidents, and experienced craving more frequently than did the nonborderline alcoholics (Nace, Saxon, & Shore, 1983).

Other Personality Disorders

Alcoholism may be associated with any of the personality disorders, but essentially no data are available regarding the prevalence of the other personality disorders in the alcoholic population. As mentioned, the group of personality disorders characterized by dramatic, emotional, or erratic behavior seems most closely associated with alcoholism. The third grouping of personality disorders, those characterized by anxious or fearful behavior, are also commonly seen in alcoholic patients.

The obsessive compulsive personality disorder may find in alcohol a respite from the restricted ability to express emotion. Preoccupation with detail, work, and perfectionism yields to the disinhibiting effect of alcohol, which provides a regressive experience otherwise unattainable. In a similar vein, the individual with an avoidant personality disorder finds in alcohol the courage to overcome his or her usual hypersensitivity to rejection. The usual shyness and feelings of low self-esteem are briefly dissipated.

The passive aggressive personality disorder presents the same dilemma as the antisocial personality disorder. Which came first? Alcohol dependence is certainly associated with "forgetfulness," inefficiency, and social and occupational ineffectiveness, all of which characterize passive aggressive personality disorder. Clinically, it often appears that alcohol released anger and assertiveness in the passive aggressive individual, sidestepping the usual indirect characterologic expression of affect. In this respect there would also be a similarity with those with dependent personality disorder, who typically allow their lives to revolve around the decisions of others. Resentment and anger seem inevitable, and alcohol often provides the only release available.

Rather than belabor the particular role which the effect of alcohol may have in any of the personality disorders, it may prove more useful to view personality disorders as a generic entity with features that cut across the line between specific diagnoses. From this vantage point, the interaction between temperament, personality disorder, and alcoholism can be presented.

Alcoholism and Temperament

Consideration of temperament and its relationship to alcoholism is well placed in a discussion of personality disorders. In an extensive review, Tarter, Alterman, and Edwards (1985) have documented dimensions of temperament empirically demonstrated to be associated with vulnerability to alcoholism. The potential relationship between temperament and personality disorders is apparent from their definitions of temperament as taken from Allport (1961):

> . . . the characteristic phenomena of an individual's nature, including his susceptibility to emotional stimulation, his customary strength and speed of response, the quality of his prevailing mood, and all the peculiarities of fluctuation and intensity of mood, these being phenomena regarded as dependent on constitutional make-up, and therefore largely hereditary in nature. (p. 34)

The dimensions of temperament empirically related to alcoholism are listed below (Tarter et al., 1985):

- *Activity level*: high activity level or hyperactivity in childhood increases the risk for development of alcoholism.
- *Attention span persistence*: difficulties in concentration, persistence, and attention predate the onset of alcoholism and exist in samples at high risk for alcoholism.
- *Soothability*: low soothability—a diminished facility to be calmed after emotional excitement—is described in young alcoholics.
- *Emotionality*: a propensity to become easily and intensely distressed has been described in offspring of alcoholics.
- *Sociability*: Bold, confident, uninhibited, and impulsive characteristics have been noted in future alcoholics as determined by prospective studies.

Further research from neuropsychology and neurophysiology will be necessary to bridge the gaps in our understanding of the relationship between dimensions of temperament, environmental factors, biochemistry, and the clinical phenomena of alcoholism. Awareness of such gaps is highlighted by the shift in this discussion from the preliminary findings of neuropsychology to characterizations of alcoholic patients derived from clinical experience. The next section summarizes "clinical wisdom" as to the personality and temperament of the alcoholic. As such, it lacks a much-needed empirical underpinning, but, nevertheless, provides clinical descriptors that enrich our understanding of the interaction between alcoholism and personality disorders.

Alcoholism and Personality Disorders: Interaction

From a wide range of written material and experience common to the field of alcoholism rehabilitation, a composite picture of the alcoholic personality can be drawn (Table 12-2). This picture does not answer the question of whether these traits precede or derive from alcohol abuse. The description is useful in clinical settings because it helps patients see

TABLE 12-2
Traits Associated with the Alcoholic Patient*

Self-Centered	*Impulsive*	*Dependency Conflict*
—narcissistic	—cannot delay gratification	—struggle between
—lacks empathy	—overreacts to situations	being defiantly
—stubborn and	—inconsistent level of	independent and
defiant	response	childlike dependence
Isolation	*Lives Life in Extremes*	*Difficulties with Anger*
—withdraws and	—over/under evaluation of	—bottled-up anger,
is distrustful;	self	passive-aggressiveness,
avoids groups	—perfectionism	rebelliousness
—sees self as	—dichotomizes—sees things	—anger turned inward,
unique, lone	as either/or rather than	guilt, depression
wolf image;	shades of gray; can't	—anger held on to
avoids self-	compromise	resentment, self-
revelation		pity, passivity

*This description was provided by Bill McAlpin, Certified Alcohol and Drug Abuse Counselor, Timberlawn Psychiatric Hospital.

aspects of themselves that might interfere with satisfactory personal relationships and/or the attainment of sobriety.

These traits may be the result of chronic alcohol abuse and the subsequent regressive effect on personality structure. This explanation is diagrammed below:

Pharmacologic Effect of Alcohol
—Rapid
—Predictable
—Pleasurable

↓

Immediate gratification with
little behavioral output

↓

Regressed ego state
—Impulsivity
—Decreased frustration tolerance
—Self-centeredness
—Grandiosity
—Passivity
—Affect intolerance
—Emotional/social isolation

Similarly, the above "traits" may serve as components of a generic concept (Lion, 1974) of personality disorders that could exist independent of alcohol use. The interaction between the regressive effect of alcohol dependence and a preexisting personality disorder is summarized by the diagram below:

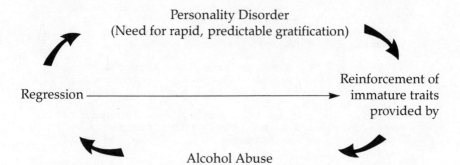

Personality Disorder
(Need for rapid, predictable gratification)

Regression ⟶ Reinforcement of immature traits provided by

Alcohol Abuse

To conclude, data accumulated from the field of neuropsychology, combined with long-standing clinical observations, support the proposition that personality disorders increase the individual's vulnerability to alcoholism (and other forms of substance abuse), which is represented in the above figure by the right half of the circle: Personality disorder→ Alcohol Abuse.

Also, alcohol abuse leads to a clinical presentation similar to the syndrome of personality disorder. The latter is represented in the figure by the left half of the circle: Alcohol Abuse→Personality Disorder.

As with the other psychiatric disorders discussed in this chapter, answering the question of which condition is primary and which secondary requires careful history taking and skilled observation over time.

Treatment Considerations

The treatment of personality disorders would require a discussion beyond the scope of this text. However, the treatment of alcohol dependence (or other addictions) influences personality functioning so that, in parallel, chemical dependence and characterologic pathology are affected. The structure of an alcoholism treatment program as described in Chapter 8 consists of an environment strong in structure, limit-setting, and reality orientation. These functions strengthen the ego. The problem of alcoholism and the emphasis on abstinence provide a paradigm for therapeutic issues beyond that of not drinking. That is, giving up alcohol calls forth major issues in the treatment of character pathology such as frustration tolerance, the development of patience, impulse control, and recognition and tolerance of affect.

Empirical support for the proposition that alcoholism treatment af-

fects character pathology is available in a recent study of alcoholic patients with borderline personality disorder (Nace, Saxon, & Shore,
1986). The patients were treated for four to six weeks in an inpatient
alcoholism program. One year following discharge they were significantly improved in regard to alcohol use and its complications. Of particular
interest, however, were the findings that improvement in other aspects
of their lives had also occurred, such as greater leisure satisfaction, greater family satisfaction, improved health, fewer accidents, and fewer hospitalizations, reflecting, perhaps, some modification in personality functioning.

Alcoholism treatment programs typically emphasize "adaptational
adjustment" (Gordon & Beresin, 1983) wherein modest goals and firm
limits are emphasized and regressive behaviors discouraged. These elements (in contrast to a more permissive approach that is tolerant of
regression) develop ego skills that are essential to obtaining sobriety and
promote personality growth as well.

DRUG ABUSE

The epidemic of drug abuse in American society over the past 20 years
has demonstrated that dependence or abuse typically involves more
than one substance. Multiple substance abuse (rather than abuse of a
single specific substance) is the most frequently occurring pattern (Carroll, Malloy, Hannigan, Santo, & Kenrick, 1977; Kaufman, 1977).

The alcohol-abusing and alcohol-dependent population has followed
suit. The abuse of drugs by alcoholics has been documented extensively.
Grande, Wolfe, Schubert, Patterson, and Brocco (1984) found that of 44
studies investigating an association between alcoholism and drug abuse,
80% found a positive association. A review by Freed (1973) determined
that about 20% of alcoholics had abused another drug. A more recent
review found drug abuse in alcoholics to range from 20 to 80% in various
samples (Malloy, 1981). Typically, younger alcoholics have a greater history of multiple-substance abuse than older alcoholics (Ashley, LeRiche,
Olin, Hatcher, Kornaczewski, Schmidt, & Rankin, 1978).

The 6-month prevalence of drug abuse/dependence in the general
population has been determined to range from 1.8 to 2.2% (Myers,
Weissman, Tischler, et al., 1984). By contrast, hospitalized alcoholics
have a current prevalence of drug abuse of 9%—over four times as great
as the general population (Hesselbrock, Meyer, & Keener, 1985). The
lifetime prevalence of drug abuse in the sample of alcoholic patients was
45% for men and 38% for women.

Which drugs are abused by alcoholics? Most commonly, prescription drugs such as tranquilizers and sedative-hypnotics are abused by older alcoholics, whereas younger alcoholics will show considerable variability. Marijuana, amphetamines, cocaine, and other illicit drugs are commonly used; availability seems to govern the choice.

The interchangeability of use of drugs and alcohol was documented in the Vietnam veteran population. Veterans who were found to be alcoholic several years after discharge from the service were currently using marijuana and amphetamines significantly more often than nonalcoholic veterans. Similarly, the alcoholic veterans had a history of significantly greater use of cocaine, tranquilizers, and inhalants prior to entry into the service. The pattern of usage was largely concurrent multiple drug use and alcohol use (Nace, O'Brien, Mintz, Ream, & Meyer, 1977). A similar pattern has been found in adolescents (Stephenson, Moberg, Daniels, & Robertson, 1984) and regular marijuana users (Weller & Halikas, 1985).

Treatment Implications

The recognition that alcoholism and the various forms of drug abuse/dependence are commonly observed in the same patient has fostered the concept of addiction as a generic process. That is, an addiction, regardless of the substance involved, presents with similar symptoms, pathological defenses, and personality dynamics. This recognition points to the *first* treatment implication: that alcohol and drug abusing patients can be treated with the same program, that is, a program which focuses on the phenomenon of substance abuse. The feasibility of this approach has been well documented (Carroll & Schnoll, 1982) and represents modern treatment planning.

The *second* implication is that treatment is oriented toward a drug-free state. Regardless of the drug of choice or the substance upon which one was dependent, successful recovery depends on elimination of all mind-altering drugs (Kaufman, 1982). The continued use of one intoxicating substance compromises the individual's ability to avoid other forms of substance abuse as well. Thus, the young alcoholic who accepts the need to abstain from alcohol will also need to face the importance of eliminating marijuana and other potential drugs of abuse from his/her lifestyle. Similarly, the middle-aged alcoholic will be best served by learning to cope not only without alcohol but also without resort to diazepam and other dependence-prone drugs.

A *third* implication is the need to observe for multiple withdrawal syndromes. Depending on the patterns of abuse, a given patient may need to be detoxified from a variety of drugs other than alcohol. A description of the procedures for detoxification from drugs other than alcohol is beyond the scope of this text, but can be obtained from references (Welford, 1981; Bourne, 1976; Czechowicz, 1979).

CONCLUSION

Psychiatric disorders are commonly associated with alcoholism. It is usually difficult to unravel which is primary and which secondary, and the etiologic role of one vis-à-vis the other typically remains obscure. Affective disorders, drug abuse, and personality disorders are the three most commonly associated conditions. Any psychiatric disorder is unlikely to be adequately treated if coexisting alcohol abuse or dependence is not also treated. Similarly, to address only a substance abuse disorder without an awareness of or attention to additional psychiatric disorders is a disservice to the patient. Recidivism rates in the alcoholic patient may, in part, reflect a lack of awareness of additional disorders. A careful history combined with an adequate period of skilled observation will enable the diagnoses of "dual disorders" to be made. Parallel treatment of both disorders, with an emphasis on individual needs, is essential for recovery.

CHAPTER 13

Alcoholics Anonymous

If any feel that as psychiatrists directing a hospital for alcoholics we appear somewhat sentimental, let them stand with us a while on the firing line, see the tragedies, the despairing wives, the little children; let the solving of these problems become a part of their daily work, and even of their sleeping moments, and the most cynical will not wonder that we have accepted and encouraged this movement.—William D. Silkworth, M.D., "The Doctor's Opinion" in *Alcoholics Anonymous*, 3rd edition, p. xxvi, 1976.*

Alcoholics Anonymous (AA) officially dates its beginning to June 10, 1935 (Wilson, 1957). Within 4 years there were an estimated 100 members. By the end of 1941, membership was mushrooming, and an estimated 8,000 members could be counted (*Alcoholics Anonymous*, 1955). In 1968 reported membership in the United States and Canada was 170,000; in 1974, 331,000; by 1983, 653,000 (*About AA*, 1984). The spectacular growth of AA testified to its capacity to meet the needs of a great number of alcoholic men and women.

---

*Official AA publications are available from The General Service Office of Alcoholics Anonymous, Box 459, Grand Central Station, New York, NY 10163.

WHAT IS AA?

There is no official definition, but "the AA Preamble," a statement read at many AA meetings, provides a succinct description:

Alcoholics Anonymous is a fellowship of men and women who share their experience, strength, and hope with each other that they may solve their common problem and help others to recover from alcoholism.

The only requirement for membership is a desire to stop drinking. There are no dues or fees to AA membership; we are self-supporting through our own contributions. AA is not allied with any sect, denomination, politics, organization, or institution; does not wish to engage in any controversy, neither endorses nor opposes any causes. Our primary purpose is to stay sober and help other alcoholics to achieve sobriety.*

In his history of the AA movement, Kurtz (1979) describes four "founding moments" of AA. The first moment involved a major twentieth century figure in psychiatry, Carl Jung. One of Jung's patients was an American alcoholic, Rowland H. In 1931 Rowland, a wealthy financier, spent nearly a year in treatment with Jung, hoping to be freed of his chronic alcoholism. Upon his return to America, he resumed drinking. Rowland returned to Zurich to consult once more with Jung. Jung advised this discouraged alcoholic that medical and psychiatric treatment had nothing more to offer, but that there remained the hope, however unlikely, that a spiritual or religious experience might lead to a conversion and, thereby, recovery from alcoholism. Rowland proceeded to join the Oxford Group, a popular nondenominational movement which sought to recapture the essence of First Century Christianity. Jung's influence on Rowland H.'s efforts toward a spiritual conversion is considered the first founding moment.

A successful conversion occurred. In return, Rowland H. influenced an old friend and fellow alcoholic, Edwin T. (nicknamed "Ebby"). Ebby, about to be committed to a state institution, found the Oxford Group and its evangelical efforts sufficient to release him from the compulsion to drink, at least temporarily.

In November, 1934, Ebby called on his friend Bill Wilson. Their conversation would constitute the second founding moment of AA (Kurtz, 1979). William G. Wilson, later to be known as Bill W., was a stockbroker

---

*Reprinted from the *Grapevine*, The AA Grapevine, Inc., New York, NY 10017.

in New York City. A chronic alcoholic, Wilson was at home and drinking when Ebby visited. Ebby refused a drink, explaining "I don't need it anymore. I've got religion" (Kurtz, 1979, p. 7). Ebby soon was drinking again and died of his alcoholism decades later. Bill W. went on, after completing one last binge, to develop the program and fellowship of AA.

Before Bill W. could embark on the remarkable course that led to the development of AA, another psychiatrist, William Silkworth, played a facilitating role. Bill, although disdainful of Ebby's sobriety and religion, decided to investigate the change in his friend a bit further. To do this, he requested admission for detoxification to the Charles B. Towns Hospital in New York City. Bill was admitted on December 11, 1934 (his fourth admission) under the care of Dr. Silkworth, who had treated him previously (Kurtz, 1979).

It was during this admission that Bill W. experienced a deepening of depression followed by a spiritual experience. "I was caught up into an ecstasy which there are no words to describe" (Wilson, 1957a, p. 63).

After being reassured by Dr. Silkworth that his experience was not alcoholic brain damage, Bill attempted to understand what had happened to him. He turned to *The Varieties of Religious Experience* by William James. James's description of "deflation at depth" (Wilson, 1957a, p. 21) struck Bill as the essence of his struggle. He had been considered hopeless in his alcoholism. Both Dr. Silkworth and Ebby had impressed that upon him. Recognition of the utter hopelessness of his drinking combined with the effect of his conversations with Ebby—one alcoholic talking to another—led Bill to envision "a chain reaction among alcoholics, one carrying the message and these principles to the next" (Wilson, 1957a, p. 21).

The third founding moment, therefore, was Wilson's spiritual experience and discovery of William James's writings during the November, 1934, hospitalization.

The fourth and final founding moment came in May, 1935. Bill was in Akron, Ohio on a business trip. The deal had fallen through. It was late Saturday afternoon, the day before Mother's Day. Urges to drink began to mount. In a state of anxiety, Bill, lured toward a hotel bar, quickly turned instead to a church directory. In his panic he had recognized that to stay sober he would have to talk to another alcoholic. He called a minister, identified himself as a member of the Oxford Group and asked to be in touch with other alcoholics. After several false leads, he made contact with Henrietta Sieberling, a devout member of the Oxford Group. She invited Bill to her home and arranged a meeting between Bill and Dr. Bob Smith. "Dr. Bob," as he was later to be known, was a "project" of Mrs. Sieberling, who was a close friend of Smith's wife. Bob Smith was a chronic alcoholic and drug-dependent surgeon with a failing practice and no sense of hope in regard to reversing his decline. Reluctantly, Bob Smith met with Bill Wilson in the Sieberling home. Kurtz (1979) has pieced together the accounts of this historical meeting as follows:

> . . . here was someone who did understand, or perhaps at least could. This stranger from New York didn't ask questions and didn't preach; he offered no "you musts" or even "let's us's." He had simply told the dreary but fascinating facts about himself, about his own drinking. And now, as Wilson moved to stand up to end the conversation, he was actually thanking Dr. Smith for listening. "I called Henrietta because I needed another alcoholic. I needed you, Bob, probably a lot more than you'll ever need me. So, thanks a lot for hearing me out. I know now that I'm not going to take a drink, and I'm grateful to you." While he had been listening to Bill's story, Bob had occasionally nodded his head, muttering "Yes, that's like me, that's just like me." Now he could bear the strain no longer. He'd listened to Bill's story, and now, by God, this "rum hound from New York" was going to listen to him. For the first time in his life, Dr. Bob Smith began to open his heart. (p. 29)

While attending a medical convention in Atlantic City, Dr. Smith was to have his last binge. The date of the last drink of an alcoholic surgeon marks the official founding date of Alcoholics Anonymous: "1935, June 10: Dr. Bob has his last drink. Alcoholics Anonymous founded" (Wilson, 1957).

Bill Wilson and Bob Smith are considered the cofounders of AA. Influenced by the thinking of Jung and encouraged by the counsel of Dr. Silkworth, Bill Wilson went on to develop the fellowship of AA and to provide a remarkable chapter in the social history of 20th Century America. By 1939 the program of AA was well-developed, and its results were sufficiently encouraging (membership was estimated to be about 100) (Alcoholics Anonymous, 1955) to enable the publication of the classic "Big Book"—*Alcoholics Anonymous*. Since then the "Big Book" has gone through three editions and serves as the basic text for AA.

With the publication of the first edition, AA members were enthusiastic about reaching out to the medical community. Thomsen (1975) provides the following description:

> Hank had decided that doctors were the public they should aim for. He wanted to launch a mail-order campaign, send out cards, inundate the medical profession with announcements about the broadcast and the book *Alcoholics Anonymous*, they'd attach an order form to every card. (p. 288)

Twenty thousand mailings were sent to physicians. Two orders for *Alcoholics Anonymous* were received (Thomsen, 1975, p. 289).

Since this inauspicious beginning, physicians have grown aware of and come to value the contributions of AA. By 1975, a survey in Great Britain indicated that 65% of general practitioners felt that AA had something to provide beyond what they could offer (Henry & Robinson, 1978), and The General Service Office of Alcoholics Anonymous reported that in 1977 10% of alcoholics coming into AA were referred by physicians (*About AA*, 1984).

HOW DOES AA WORK?

The answer to this question is necessarily speculative. That AA is an effective force in achieving sobriety has been well documented (Leach & Norris, 1977). The General Service Office of Alcoholics Anonymous in its 1983 survey of 7,600 members determined that of newcomers to AA, 60% were still attending 3 months later. This was an increase from a 1977 survey where the figure was 50% (*About AA*, 1984). The latter statistic did not distinguish between those abstinent or those still drinking.

Although it is a difficult undertaking, efforts have been made to determine length of abstinence in AA members. Leach and Norris (1977) report that a 1968 survey by the General Service Board of AA showed that 60% of those surveyed had been sober for more than a year. A similar survey in 1971 yielded the same result. In two different studies, sobriety greater than 2 years duration was found in 46% of those sampled (Bailey & Leach, 1965; Edwards, Hensman, Haukes, & Williamson, 1967).

An unusual study by an AA member involved records of meeting attendance and a 7-year follow-up of 393 members. It was determined that 70% who stay sober for 1 year will stay sober for 2 years, and that 90% of those sober for 2 years will be sober at the end of 3 years (Leach & Norris, 1977).

Methodological problems are immense when trying to evaluate the effectiveness of AA (or other forms of treatment). Leach and Norris (1977) have reviewed the efforts to conduct such an evaluation and acknowledged the sampling difficulties. Most of their review focuses on studies from the 1940s through the 1960s, a period when relatively few alcoholism rehabilitation programs were available; therefore, more weight can be given to the impact of AA alone. Their conclusion seems appropriate: "Until better quality studies are published, the assertion that AA members by the thousands do remain abstinent for years seems reasonable and modest" (p. 499).

Having established AA's effectiveness, at least for many alcoholics, we are still left with the question: *How does it work?* If evaluation of effectiveness seems a treacherous undertaking, an explanation of why AA works will further magnify our uncertain understanding.

Are there features of brainwashing or religious revivalism that operate? Frank's (1961) classic elucidation of common elements in psychotherapy, thought reform, and religious healing comes to mind. The importance of emotional arousal, hope, and dependence on another for expected relief are common features of symptoms of persuasion and healing, and they may be as operative in AA as in individual and group psychotherapies. Hope is certainly engendered in AA by the presence and testimony of many recovered alcoholics from diverse walks of life. An AA meeting fosters emotional arousal, not by exhortation or threat, but subtly through enthusiasm, acceptance, and humor. The AA speaker's "story" often strikes an emotional chord in the listener. In regard to dependence and expectation for relief, the concept of "Higher Power" and the suggestion to "turn it over" (to a Higher Power) emphasize the relative helplessness of the suffering alcoholic, yet offers him or her a powerful source of assistance.

Just as psychotherapy as practiced in America is distinctively different from brainwashing or religious healing regardless of some common elements, the same can be said of AA. Thought reform or brainwashing relies on total milieu control, interrogation, and emotional arousal secondary to psychological harassment (Frank, 1961). By contrast, AA offers a nonjudgmental setting with no obligations imposed on its visitants. Unlike religious revivalism, AA does not preach or proselytize. The alcoholic is not made to feel guilty, nor threatened with impending doom. The similarity to religious healing in AA would lie less with the format of an AA meeting and more with the condition of the alcoholic. As Frank (1961) describes, the individual susceptible to revivalist religion or miracle cures has suffered ". . . environmental or bodily stresses, internal conflicts and confusion, and a sense of estrangement or isolation from his usual sources of group support. He tends to be fearful and despairing and to be hungry for supportive human contact" (p. 94).

It is no wonder, then, that many alcoholic persons have responded to AA with religious fervor. As identity is restored and self-esteem reestablished, relief, peace, and joy can be expected. Such compelling changes may account for the zeal of some alcoholics in AA. Unfortunately, this same zeal may thwart other alcoholics from becoming involved in AA, as some newcomers associate a fervent attitude with earlier church experiences which are viewed negatively.

My impressions of what makes AA work are from the vantage point of an outsider and would not necessarily correspond with those who experience the fellowship of AA, or, for that matter, with other non-AA observers. The explanations given below are not to be considered original. They are based on therapy with AA members, periodic attendance at open AA meetings (meetings where nonalcoholics are welcome), conversations with AA members, and a reading of AA literature. In addition, Leach and Norris (1977) and Alibrandi (1982) have provided enlightening chapters on the workings of AA.

The first impression of why AA is effective is that of unconditional acceptance. AA is sometimes referred to as "the last house on the street," meaning that the alcoholic will always be welcome even when other institutions have given up or rejected him or her. AA makes no demand that an individual consider himself or herself alcoholic. The basis for membership is "a desire to stop drinking." Emphasis is placed not on what the alcoholic should or should not do, but rather on a sharing of what AA has found helpful. AA meetings are generally characterized by warmth, openness, honesty, and humor.

A second impression is that drinking and denial are quickly faced (see Tables 13-1 and 13-2 of Steps and Traditions). Consider the first step of

TABLE 13-1
The Twelve Steps of Alcoholics Anonymous*

1. We admitted we were powerless over alcohol—that our lives had become unmanageable.
2. Came to believe that a Power greater than ourselves could restore us to sanity.
3. Made a decision to turn our will and our lives over to the care of God *as we understood Him*.
4. Made a searching and fearless moral inventory of ourselves.
5. Admitted to God, to ourselves, and to another human being the exact nature of our wrongs.
6. Were entirely ready to have God remove all these defects of character.
7. Humbly asked Him to remove our shortcomings.
8. Made a list of all persons we had harmed, and became willing to make amends to them all.
9. Made direct amends to such people wherever possible, except when to do so would injure them or others.
10. Continued to take personal inventory and when we were wrong promptly admitted it.
11. Sought through prayer and meditation to improve our conscious contact with God *as we understood Him*, praying only for knowledge of His will for us and the power to carry that out.
12. Having had a spiritual awakening as the result of these steps, we tried to carry this message to alcoholics, and to practice these principles in all our affairs.

*Reprinted with permission of Alcoholics Anonymous World Services, Inc.

TABLE 13-2
The Twelve Traditions of Alcoholics Anonymous*

1. Our common welfare should come first; personal recovery depends upon AA unity.
2. For our group purpose there is but one ultimate authority—a loving God as he may express himself in our group conscience. Our leaders are but trusted servants; they do not govern.
3. The only requirement for AA membership is a desire to stop drinking.
4. Each group should be autonomous except in matters affecting other groups or AA as a whole.
5. Each group has but one primary purpose—to carry its message to the alcoholic who still suffers.
6. An AA group ought never endorse, finance, or lend the AA name to any related facility or outside enterprise, lest problems of money, property, and prestige divert us from our primary purpose.
7. Every AA group ought to be fully self-supporting, declining outside contributions.
8. Alcoholics Anonymous should remain forever nonprofessional, but our service centers may employ special workers.
9. AA, as such, ought never be organized; but we may create service boards or committees directly responsible to those they serve.
10. Alcoholics Anonymous has no opinion on outside issues; hence the AA name ought never be drawn into public controversy.
11. Our public relations policy is based on attraction rather than promotion; we need always maintain personal anonymity at the level of press, radio, and films.
12. Anonymity is the spiritual foundation of all our Traditions, ever reminding us to place principles before personalities.

*Reprinted with permission of Alcoholics Anonymous World Services, Inc.

AA: "We admitted we were powerless over alcohol—that our lives had become unmanageable." The issue of drinking and its effects are succinctly and powerfully stated. At AA meetings each person who speaks or chooses to make a comment identifies himself or herself as "My name is . . . , I'm an alcoholic." The group then responds with a loud and warm "Hi. . . ."

Why do AA members invariably add after their name, "I'm an alcoholic"? Are they bragging about it? No. The identification "I'm an alcoholic" is quickly put forth to counter any possible question, any possible return of denial. It conveys a sense of acceptance, of admission. There is no stigma here. It is interesting that the 12 Steps do not mention abstinence. What is referred to is powerlessness over alcohol (Step 1), and the need for self-examination (Steps 4 and 10). Steps 5, 9 and 12 emphasize the need to share one's experience with others. Thus, drinking and its consequences to oneself and others are addressed and, not unlike the process of psychotherapy, a sharing of these experiences with another is emphasized.

Third, group process is operating. Yalom's (1975) elements of group therapy can be found in the context of AA fellowship. For example, *hope* is provided by the role models of alcoholics who no longer drink. The element of *universality* becomes quickly apparent as AA members share their experiences and break through the isolation of those who have felt alienated from their social environment. *Information* is provided informally as well as through AA publications, and *imitation* of the way sober alcoholics approach their disease facilitates the *learning* of new social skills. The format of a discussion or speaker meeting provides an opportunity for *catharsis*, and the subsequent sense of solidarity and identity reinforces *cohesiveness*. The informal socializing at AA meetings is yet another "therapeutic" element. Members quickly feel useful as they help make coffee, welcome a newcomer, or find that their interest in another alcoholic helps both of them.

A fourth factor at work may be a successful deflation of pathological narcissism. The defenses of grandiosity and self-sufficiency are addressed, albeit subtly in Steps 1, 2 and 11. For example, Step 11 is interpreted by Leach and Norris (1977) as an effort to prevent the reemergence of the old "self-will run riot" (Alcoholics Anonymous, 1955) behavior characteristic of the drinking alcoholic. Acceptance of Step 1 indicates an inability to control alcohol, a loss of control, an admission of defeat as far as use of alcohol is concerned. To acknowledge that one's life has become unmanageable implies, at the least, that one is less than perfect. More likely it also implies the need for assistance.

Step 2 expresses the necessity for the alcoholic to turn to a Power (however that may be understood) which is more capable (greater) than oneself in order to be freed from the insanity of alcoholism. The concept of "Higher Power" is allowed wide conceptual latitude ranging from the orthodox religious concept of God to the AA group itself. Just as the first step undermines grandiosity by admitting powerlessness, the second step wisely offers hope through a source "greater than ourselves." Step 7 contains the phrase "Humbly asked," another effort at countering a defensively inflated ego (Leach & Norris, 1977).

The program of AA, therefore, revolves around the Twelve Steps as formulated by Bill Wilson in 1939. These deceptively simple Steps convey genius in their ability to encapsulate the dynamics of the alcoholic and the process for recovery. AA members would answer the question of how AA works by referring to the 12 Steps. This sentiment is summarized by the opening sentence of the Big Book's chapter on How it works: "Rarely have we seen a person fail who has thoroughly followed our path" (*Alcoholics Anonymous*, 1976).

THE RELATIONSHIP BETWEEN PSYCHIATRY AND AA

How can mental health professionals relate to, work with, and integrate the AA approach into their clinical work with alcoholic patients? Potential conceptual differences need to be understood and an effort made to integrate these differences.

Table 13-3 summarizes potential differences by presenting extreme views (for the purpose of clarification) of AA and traditional psychiatry. The psychiatrist or other mental health professional can maximize his or her effectiveness by understanding AA and by respecting its position in the field of alcoholism treatment. As emphasized in earlier chapters, trying to treat the alcoholic one to one in an office setting is very difficult. AA can be an invaluable ally.

One approach to developing an alliance is to get to know some men and women who are active in local AA chapters. Discuss with them your need to have a support system for your alcohol-dependent patients, and ask if they would be willing to help. Invariably, AA members will be pleased to meet with a patient at your request. Sometimes they can be introduced at the office following an appointment and go out for a cup of coffee. Other times the patient can be taken to an AA meeting. The success of this hinges first on the clinician's firm sense of the value of AA; second, success hinges on the clinician's finding AA members in whom he has confidence. They may be former patients or be known from elsewhere in the community. Just as the professional will need to understand AA, so those AA members working in collaboration with a physician or other therapist will need to understand and respect the value of the patient's treatment program.

A second way to use the resources of AA is to attend some "open" AA meetings. Anyone is welcome at an open meeting, whereas closed meetings are for AA members only. A meeting may be held in a variety of formats: for example, a discussion meeting, a Step meeting, or a speaker's meeting. A discussion meeting focuses on a particular topic, for example, sponsorship. Step meetings concentrate on the meaning and implications of a given Step. The speaker's meeting is the most common format. After the preamble is read, a member tells his or her "story" for about 20 to 30 minutes. Comments are invited after the speaker has finished. The informal mingling over coffee before and after each meeting provides an opportunity to meet others, to develop relationships, and to form a sense of belonging. Direct exposure to meetings can give one a "feel" for what it is like. A supply of directories of scheduled AA meetings can be obtained for distribution to patients. The directory will list time, location, and format for each meeting.

Occasionally, a therapist may feel rivalry from AA. The most extreme

TABLE 13-3
AA and Psychiatry*

Subject	AA (Extreme)	Psychiatric (Extreme)	Resolution
Cause of drinking	Unimportant—therapy leads to intellectualization or denial.	Real change requires understanding of all conflicts and events in growth.	Patient gains an understanding of the reason for his pain, hurt, anger, depression. He knows it is there for reasons. But, ultimately he/she must say, "I choose not to drink."
Complexity of Recovery	Easy—Just follow the Program.	Long, involved therapeutic quest.	Need to look at who taught the person he was unworthy of success or had to fail; explore with the alcoholic why he/she can't attend AA meetings regularly or why he/she can't change people, places or things which facilitate drinking.
AA	It's a divine gift. It saved my life.	It's rigid.	It's both. It gives the alcoholic early in treatment a rigid program to save his life. The alcoholic early in treatment doesn't need a philosophy course, needs rules on how to live without alcohol.

Permissiveness and Pathological Behavior	Alcoholics early in treatment are incapable of decisions. Another bout of pathological behavior may kill them.	Therapy is to help one understand his or her behavior, not to direct the behavior.	The guide to behavior is "Will it threaten sobriety?" If attending a function where alcohol is served stimulates craving and makes drinking likely, avoid such functions at least until sobriety is more secure. During treatment patients will need to be exposed to their usual environment. They may then appreciate the need for changes and that it isn't as easy as they had hoped.
Social Drinking	A myth which kills.	"I know an alcoholic who . . . "	This alcoholic may have been in the early stages. It rarely occurs in those who reach health care facilities.
Abstinence	Only goal.	Abstinence is deviance in Western Society.	Should an alcoholic be deviant by being drunk or being sober?
Medication	It's bad.	Good—corrects biochemical defects.	Benzodiazepines have a place during detoxification. The schizophrenic alcoholic who ends up psychotic or the alcoholic who becomes depressed or manic may need medication.
Psychopathology	Alcoholics are like everyone else.	All alcoholics have specific conflicts which predate their alcoholism.	Alcoholics are like everyone else. Some are very impaired. Some are well-integrated personalities when sober.

(continued)

TABLE 13-3 (continued)

Subject	AA (Extreme)	Psychiatric (Extreme)	Resolution
Disease Model	A disease, not a moral failing.	"Sure isn't like pneumonia."	That's right. It isn't like pneumonia, but most other diseases aren't either. Alcoholics have a disease and should receive the same care from psychiatrists and other physicians that other sick people receive.
Treatment	The Twelve Steps.	Medical and psychological procedures.	The two are not contradictory, but can be utilized effectively by most alcoholics, with one receiving more emphasis at certain times.
Basis for Treatment	Personal experience of other alcoholics.	Scientifically based and empirically validated procedures.	These sources of understanding are divergent, but enable the experience of many sources to bear on a complex disease.

*This table is modified from a presentation by Dr. Ivan Cohen at the 137th Annual Meeting of the American Psychiatric Association, Los Angeles, May, 1984. I am indebted to his thoughtful efforts to bridge the potential gap between AA and psychiatry.

example is when a patient is encouraged by another AA member to discontinue medication. For example, a schizophrenic on phenothiazines or an alcoholic using disulfiram may be warned that medication is a "crutch" or that it can lead back to drinking. It is my impression that this occurs much more rarely today than 10 or 15 years ago. Many AA members have received psychiatric help, including medications, and understand the role of therapy and pharmacotherapy in the management of alcoholism or other disorders. It should be remembered that conflicting advice received from fellow AA members is not AA speaking (see the Twelve Traditions) but reflects a misguided attempt to offer assistance by an individual member.

Some patients after beginning AA no longer feel the need for psychotherapy or find contradictions between what they are learning in AA and therapy. For example, a young woman had made considerable gains through therapy. When she began AA, she was distressed to find some women who, when angry at their husbands, dealt with their anger by "turning it over" to a Higher Power. She had learned to deal with her emotions in a direct, assertive manner and found such an approach helpful. In this instance, therapy could address some particular benefits of AA for her as well as acceptance of others' styles of coping. If a patient terminates therapy because his or her needs are being met through AA, I feel it is important to respect that decision and remain available for the future.

There are circumstances for which I believe psychotherapy, medication, or other forms of treatment are necessarily inadequate. When this condition or circumstance exists, I do all I can to encourage and nurture involvement in AA. I am referring to the individual steeped in deep regret and remorse. Years have been lost. Relationships, career, and family may have been destroyed, or, if not, one's keen sense of personal disappointment is very poignant. Meaning is lost as one stands between a regrettable past and an empty future. I think a therapeutic relationship is vital at this time, but often it is not enough. The spiritual core needs to be addressed (Frankl, 1975). Here AA can be very helpful because it is in many respects a program of spiritual enrichment. By the same token, pastoral counseling or a renewal of ties to a religious denomination may be sustaining. Observing this cutting edge, this ultimate limitation of our clinical work has deepened my respect for the spiritual side of the recovery process.

In summary, our patients' needs are likely to be met better if we draw clinical psychiatry and AA together. By this I do not suggest an affiliation of sorts, as that contradicts the traditions of AA. The issue is one of mutual respect and improved understanding. A mutual need is suggested by AA survey data which reveal more and more members who are also drug dependent. Also, younger people are entering AA. In 1971, 6% of AA members were under 31; by 1983 20% were under 31 years of age, and 3% of those were under 21 years (*About AA*, 1984).

A younger population with a complicated pattern of substance abuse warrants medical evaluation, including a careful psychiatric assessment. As severity of alcoholism is greater in those with early onset (Goodwin, 1985), the input of psychiatrists trained in the field of alcoholism and other forms of substance abuse is essential. Similarly, the use of a well-established, effective support system such as AA is a necessity.

References

Abbott, J. A., Goldberg, G. A., and Becker, E. B. The role of a medical audit in assessing management of alcoholics with acute pancreatitis. *Q. J. Stud. Alcohol*, 35: 272–276, 1974.

Abel, E. L. Consumption of alcohol during pregnancy: A review of effects on growth and development of offspring. *Human Biology*, 54: 421–453, 1982.

Abou-Saleh, M. T., Merny, J., and Coppen, A. Dexamethasone suppression test in alcoholism. *Acta. Psychiatr. Scand.*, 69: 112–116, 1984.

About AA: A Newsletter for Professional Men and Women. Fall, 1984.

Alcoholics Anonymous, Foreword to the Second Edition, p. xviii. New York, Alcoholics Anonymous World Services, Inc., 1955.

Alcoholics Anonymous, 2nd Edition. New York, Alcoholics Anonymous World Services, Inc., 1955.

Alcoholics Anonymous, 3rd Edition. New York, Alcoholics Anonymous World Services, Inc., 1976.

Alibrandi, L. A. The fellowship of Alcoholics Anonymous. In: Pattison, E. M., and Kaufman, E. (eds.), *Encyclopedic Handbook of Alcoholism*. New York, Gardner Press, 1982, pp. 979–986.

Allport, G. *Patterns and Growth in Personality*. New York, Holt, Rinehart and Winston, 1961, p. 34.

Alterman, A. I., Ayre, F. R., and Williford, W. O. Diagnostic validation of conjoint schizophrenia and alcoholism. *J. Clin. Psychiatry*, 45(7): 300–303, 1984.

Alterman, A. I., and Erdlen, D. L. Illicit substance abuse in hospitalized psychiatric patients: Clinical observations. *J. of Psychiatric Treatment and Evaluation*, 5: 377–380, 1983.

American Psychiatric Association, *Diagnostic and Statistical Manual* (1st edition). Washington, DC, American Psychiatric Press, 1952.

American Psychiatric Association, *Diagnostic and Statistical Manual* (2nd edition). Washington, DC, American Psychiatric Press, 1968.

American Psychiatric Association, *Diagnostic and Statistical Manual* (3rd edition). Washington, DC, American Psychiatric Press, 1980.

American Psychiatric Association, *Diagnostic and Statistical Manual* (3rd edition revised). Washington, DC, American Psychiatric Press, 1987.

American Psychiatric Press. *Psychiatric Glossary.* Washington, DC, Author, 1984.

Andreasen, N. C., and Winokur, G. Secondary depression: Familial, clinical and research perspective. *American Journal of Psychiatry*, 136(11): 62–66, 1979.

Armor, D. J., Polich, J. M., and Stanbul, H. B. *Alcoholism and Treatment.* Santa Monica, CA, Rand Corporation, June, 1976.

Ashley, M. J., LeRiche, W. H., Olin, J. S., Hatcher, J., Kornaczewski, A., Schmidt, W., and Rankin, J. G. "Mixed" (drug-abusing) and "pure" alcoholics: A socio-medical comparison. *Br. J. Addict.*, 73: 19–34, 1978.

Bailey, M. B. Alcoholism and marriage: A review of research and professional literature. *Q. J. Stud. Alc.*, 22: 81–97, 1961.

Bailey, M. B., Haberman, P., and Alksne, H. Outcomes of alcoholic marriages: Endurance, termination, or recovery. *Q. J. Stud. Alc.*, 23: 610–623, 1962.

Bailey, M. B., and Leach, B. Alcoholics Anonymous: Pathway to recovery, a study of 1,058 members of the AA fellowship in New York City. New York, National Council on Alcoholism, 1965 (cited in Leach and Norris, 1977, p. 496).

Barcha, R., Stewart, M. A., and Guze, S. B. The prevalence of alcoholism among general hospital ward patients. *Am. J. Psychiatry*, 125(5): 681–684, 1968.

Bean, M. H. Denial and the psychological complications of alcoholism. In: Bean, M. H., and Zinberg, N. E. (eds.), *Dynamic Approaches to the Understanding and Treatment of Alcoholism.* New York, The Free Press, pp. 55–96, 1981.

Becker, C. E. Pharmacotherapy in the treatment of alcoholism. In: Mendelson, J. H., and Mello, N. K. (eds.), *The Diagnosis and Treatment of Alcoholism.* New York, McGraw-Hill, pp. 283–303, 1979.

Bedi, A. R., and Halikas, J. A. Alcoholism and affective disorder. *Alcoholism: Clin. and Exp. Research*, 9(2): 133–134, 1985.

Begleiter, H. Brain potentials in boys at risk for alcoholism. Presented at the American Psychiatric Association Annual Meeting, Los Angeles, CA, May 5–11, 1984.

Begleiter, H., and Porjesz, B. Persistence of a "subacute withdrawal syndrome" following chronic ethanol intake. *Drug Alcohol Dependence*, 4: 353–357, 1979.

Behar, D., Winokur, G., and Berg, C. J. Depression in the abstinent alcoholic. *Am. J. Psychiatry*, 141(9): 1105–1107, 1984.

Benson, D. F. Amnesia. *Southern Med. J.*, 71: 1221–1231, 1978.

Bergler, E. *Unhappy Marriage and Divorce: A Study of Neurotic Choice of Marriage Partners.* New York, International Universities Press, 1946.

Bergman, H., Borg, S., Hinchmarsh, T., Idestrom, C. M., and Mutzell, S. Computerized tomography of the brain and neuropsychological assessment of male alcoholic patients and a random sample from the general male population. *Acta. Psychiatr. Scand.*, 65: 77–88, 1980.

Bernat, J. L., and Victor, M. The neurological complications of alcohol and alcoholism. *Alcohol Use and Its Medical Consequences: Unit 7.* Timonium, MD, Project Cork of Dartmouth Medical School, Milner-Fenwick, 1982.

Blane, H. J. *The Personality of the Alcoholic: Guises of Dependency.* New York, Harper and Row, 1968.

Bliven, F. E. The skeletal system: Alcohol as a factor. In Pattison, E. M., and Kaufman, E. (eds.), *Encyclopedic Handbook of Alcoholism.* New York, Gardner Press, pp. 215–224, 1982.

Blouin, A., Bornstein, R., and Trites, R. Teenage alcohol use among hyperactive children: A five-year follow-up study. *J. Pediatric Psychology*, 3: 188–194, 1978.

Blume, S. B. Psychodrama in the treatment of alcoholism. In: Estes, N., and Heinemann, E. (eds.), *Alcoholism: Development, Consequences, and Interventions*. St. Louis, C. V. Mosby, 1977.

Bohman, M., Sigvardsson, S., and Cloninger, C. R. Maternal inheritance of alcohol abuse. Cross-fostering analysis of adopted women. *Archives of General Psychiatry*, 38: 965–969, 1981.

Bonkowsky, H. L., and Anderson, P. B. Alcohol: The alimentary tract and pancreas. *Alcohol Use and Its Medical Consequences: Unit 4*. Timonium, MD, Project Cork of Dartmouth Medical School, Milner-Fenwick, Inc., 1981.

Boroman, E. N., and Thimann, J. Treatment of alcoholism in the subacute stage. *Dis. Nerv. System*, 27: 342–346, 1966.

Bourne, P. G. (ed.) *Acute Drug Abuse Emergencies: A Treatment Manual*. New York, Academic Press, 1976.

Bowen, M. Alcoholism and the family. In: Bowen, M. (ed.), *Family Therapy in Clinical Practice*. New York, Jason Aronson, pp. 259–268, 1978.

Bowen, M. *Family Therapy in Clinical Practice*. New York, Jason Aronson, pp. 259–268, 1978.

Bowen, R. C., Cipywnyk, D., D'Arcy, C., and Keegan, D. Types of depression in alcoholic patients. *Can. Med. Assoc. J.*, 130: 869–874, 1984a.

Bowen, R. C., Cipywnyk, D., D'Arcy, C., and Keegan, D. Alcoholism, anxiety disorders and agoraphobia. *Alcoholism: Clin. and Exp. Research*, 8(1): 48–50, 1984b.

Boyd, J. H. Use of mental health services for the treatment of panic disorder. *Am. J. Psychiatry*, 143(12): 1569–1574, 1986.

Brown, K. Alcoholism education for physicians and medical students: Overview. *Alcohol Health and Research World*, National Institute on Alcohol Abuse and Alcoholism, Spring, 1979, pp. 2–9.

Bullock, S. C., and Mudd, E. H. The interaction of alcoholic husbands and their nonalcoholic wives during counseling. *Am. J. Orthopsychiatry*, 29: 519–527, 1959.

Busch, H., Kormendy, E., and Feuerlein, W. Partners of female alcoholics. *Br. J. Addict.*, 68: 179–184, 1973.

Butts, S. V., and Chotlas, J. Closed mindedness in alcoholics. *J. Stud. Alcohol*, 35: 906–910, 1979.

Caddy, G. R., and Gottheil, E. Contributions to behavioral treatment from studies on programmed access to alcohol. In: Galanter, M. (ed.), *Recent Developments in Alcoholism*, Vol. I. New York, Plenum Press, pp. 195–232, 1983.

Cadoret, R., Troughton, E., and Wishmer, R. Clinical differences between antisocial and primary alcoholics. *Comprehensive Psychiatry*, 25(1): 1–8, 1984.

Cahalan, D. Epidemiology: Alcohol use in American society. In: Gomberg, E. L., White, H. R., and Carpenter, J. D. (eds.), *Alcohol, Science and Society Revisited*. Ann Arbor, MI, Univ. Mich. Press, pp. 96–118, 1982.

Cahalan, D., Cisin, H., and Crossley, H. M. *American Drinking Practices: A National Study of Drinking Behavior and Attitudes*. New Brunswick, NJ, Rutgers Center of Alcohol Studies, 1969.

Cantwell, D. P. Psychiatric illness in the families of hyperactive children. *Arch. Gen. Psychiatry*, 27: 414–417, 1972.

Carlen, P. L., and Wilkinson, D. A. Alcoholic brain damage and reversible deficits. *Acta. Psychiatr. Scand.*, 62 (Suppl. 286): 103–118, 1980.

Carroll, J. F. X., Malloy, T. E., Hannigan, P. C., Santo, Y., and Kenrick, F. M. The meaning and evolution of the term "multiple-substance abuse." *Contemporary Drug Problems*, 6: 101–134, 1977.

Carroll, J. F. X., and Schnoll, S. H. Mixed drug and alcohol populations. In: Pattison, E. M., and Kaufman, E. (eds.), *Encyclopedic Handbook of Alcoholism*. New York, Gardner Press, 1982, pp. 742–758.

Cassell, E. J. *The Healer's Art: A New Approach to the Doctor-Patient Relationship*. Philadelphia, J. B. Lippincott, 1976, pp. 47–83.

Cermak, T. L. Children of alcoholics and the case for a new diagnostic category of codependency. *Alcohol Health and Research World*, 8(4): 38–42, 1984.

Chafetz, M. E. Research in the alcohol clinic and around-the-clock psychiatric service of the Massachusetts General Hospital. *Amer. J. Psychiatry*, 124: 1674–1679, 1968.

Chafetz, M. E. *The Alcoholic Patient: Diagnosis and Management*. Oradell, NJ, Medical Economics Books, 1983.

Chanarin, I. Effects of alcohol on the hematopoietic system. In: Pattison, E. M., and Kaufman, E. (eds.), *Encyclopedic Handbook of Alcoholism*. New York, Gardner Press, pp. 281–292, 1982.

Chaney, E. P., O'Leary, M. R., and Marlatt, G. A. Skill training with alcoholics. *J. of Consulting and Clinical Psychology*, 46(5): 1092–1104, 1979.

Chappel, J. N. Physician attitudes and the treatment of alcohol and drug dependent patients. *J. Psychedelic Drugs*, 10(1): 27–34, 1978.

Chappel, J. N., Veach, T. L., and Krug, R. S. The substance abuse attitude survey. An instrument for measuring attitudes. *Journal of Stud. Alcohol*, 46(1): 48–52, 1985.

Chappel, J. N., Jordan, R. D., Treadway, B. J., and Miller, P. R. Substance abuse attitude changes in medical students. *Am. J. Psychiatry*, 134(4): 379–384, 1977.

Clark, W., and Midanik, L. Alcohol use and alcohol problems among U.S. adults: Results of the 1979 National Survey. In: *National Institute on Alcohol Abuse and Alcoholism: Alcohol Consumption and Related Problems* (Alcohol and Health Monograph No. 1), pp. 3–54, DHHS Publ. No. (ADM) 82-1190, Washington, DC, USGPO, 1982.

Clifford, B. J. A study of the wives of rehabilitated and unrehabilitated alcoholics. *Social Casework*, 41: 457–460, 1960.

Cloninger, C. R., Bohman, M., and Sigvardsson, S. Inheritance of alcohol abuse. Cross-fostering analysis of adopted men. *Archives of General Psychiatry*, 38: 861–868, 1981.

Cohen, M., Liebson, I. A., Faillace, L. A., and Allen, R. P. Moderate drinking by chronic alcoholics. *J. of Nerv. and Mental Disease*, 153: 434–444, 1971.

Cohen, S. Drugs in the workplace. *J. Clinical Psychiatry*, 45(12): 4–8, 1984.

Connell, L. J., and Berlin, R. M. Withdrawal after substitution of a short-acting for a long-acting benzodiazepine. *JAMA*, 250(20): 2838–2840, 1983.

Coppen, A., Montgomery, S. A., Gupta, R. K., and Bailey, J. E. A double-blind comparison of lithium carbonate and maprotiline in the prophylaxis of the affective disorders. *Br. J. Psychiatry*, 128: 479–485, 1976.

Coppen, A., Noguera, R., and Bailey, J. Prophylactic lithium in affective disorders. Controlled trial. *Lancet*, 2: 275–279, 1971.

Corder, B. F., Hendricks, A., and Corder, R. F. An MMPI study of a group of wives of alcoholics. *Q. J. Stud. Alc.*, 25: 551–554, 1964.

Cork, R. M. The forgotten children: A study of children with alcoholic parents. *Alcoholism and Drug Addiction Research*. Toronto, Foundation of Ontario, 1969.

Cornwell, G. G. III. Hematologic complications of alcohol use. *Alcohol Use and Its Medical Consequences: Unit 3.* Timonium, MD, Project Cork of Dartmouth Medical School, Milner-Fenwick, Inc., 1981.

Corwin, H. A. Therapeutic confrontation from routine to heroic. In: Adler, G., and Myerson, P. G. (eds.), *Confrontation in Psychotherapy.* New York, Science House, 1973.

Costello, R. M., Biever, P., and Baillargeon, J. G. Alcoholism treatment programming: Historical trends and modern approaches. *Alcoholism: Clin. and Exp. Research,* 1(4): 311–318, 1977.

Cotton, N. S. The familial incidence of alcoholism. *Journal of Studies on Alcohol,* 40: 89–116, 1979.

Criteria Committee, National Council on Alcoholism. Criteria for the Diagnosis of Alcoholism. *Amer. J. Psychiatry,* 129(2): 127–135, 1972.

Cutter, H. S. G., Schwaab, E. L., Jr., and Nathan, P. E. Effects of alcohol and its utility for alcoholics and nonalcoholics. *Q. J. Stud. Alc.,* 31: 369–378, 1970.

Czechowicz, D. *Detoxification Treatment Manual,* Treatment Program Monograph Series, No. 6, National Institute on Drug Abuse, DHEW Publications, No. (ADM) 79-738, 1979.

Dackis, C. A., Gold, M. S., Pottash, A. L. C., and Sweeney, D. R. Evaluating depression in alcoholics. *Psychiatric Research,* 17(2): 105–109, 1986.

DeLuca, J. R. (ed.) *Fourth Special Report to the US Congress on Alcohol and Health* from the Secretary of Health and Human Services, DHHS Publication No. (ADM) 81-1080, printed 1981, Washington, DC, USGPO.

Ditman, K. S. Review and evaluation of current drug therapies in alcoholism. *Psychosom. Med.,* 28: 667–677, 1966.

Dixon, K., Exon, P. D., and Malins, J. M. Third National Cancer Survey: Data from the U.S. *Q. J. Med.,* 44: 343, 1975.

Docherty, J. P., and Fiester, S. J. The therapeutic alliance and compliance with psychopharmacology. In: Hales, R. E., and Frances, A. J. (eds.), *Psychiatry Update,* Volume 4. Washington, DC, American Psychiatric Association, 1985.

Dodes, L. M. Abstinence from alcohol in long-term individual psychotherapy with alcoholics. *Am. J. Psychotherapy,* 38(2): 248–256, 1984.

Dreiling, D. A., and Bordalo, O. A toxic-metabolic hypothesis of pathogenesis of alcoholic pancreatitis. *Alcoholism: Clin. and Exp. Res.,* 1: 293–299, 1977.

Dunner, D. L., Hensel, B. M., and Fieve, R. R. Bipolar illness: Factors in drinking behavior. *Am. J. Psychiatry,* 136(4B): 583–585, 1979.

Dupont, R. L., Jr. *Getting Tough on Gateway Drugs: A Guide for the Family.* Washington, DC, American Psychiatric Press, 1984.

Eckardt, M. J., and Martin, P. R. Clinical assessment of cognition in alcoholism. *Alcoholism: Clin. Exp. Res.,* 10(2): 128–137, 1986.

Eckert, E. D., Goldberg, S. C., Halmi, K. A., Casper, R. C., and Davis, J. M. Alcoholism in anorexia nervosa. In: Pickens, R. W., and Heston, L. L. (eds.), *Psychiatric Factors in Drug Abuse.* New York, Grune & Stratton, 1979, pp. 267–283.

Eddy, N. B., Halbach, H., Isbell, H., and Seevers, M. H. Drug dependence: Its significance and characteristics. *Bulletin of the World Health Organization,* No. 32, 1965, pp. 721–733.

Edwards, G. *The Treatment of Drinking Problems.* New York, McGraw Hill, 1982.

Edwards, G., Hensman, C., Haukes, A., and Williamson, V. Alcoholics Anonymous: The anatomy of a self-help group. *Social Psychiatry,* 1: 195, 1967.

Edwards, G., Orford, J., Egert, S., Guthrie, S., Hawker, A., Hensman, C.,

Mitcheson, M., Oppenheimer, E., and Taylor, C. Alcoholism: A controlled trial of 'treatment' and 'advice'. *J. Stud. on Alc.*, 38(5): 1004–1031, 1977.

Elmasian, R., Neville, H., Woods, D., Schuckit, M. A., and Bloom, F. Event-related brain potentials are different in individuals at high and low risk for developing alcoholism. *Proc. Natl. Acad. Sci. USA*, 79: 7900–7903, 1982.

Emrick, C. D. A review of psychologically oriented treatment of alcoholism. I. The use and interrelationships of outcome criteria and drinking behavior following treatment. *Q. J. Stud. Alc.*, 35: 523–549, 1974.

Emrick, C. D. A review of psychologically oriented treatment of alcoholism. II. The relative effectiveness of different treatment approaches and the effectiveness of treatment versus no treatment. *J. of Stud. Alc.*, 36(1): 88–108, 1975.

Endicott, J., and Spitzer, R. L. A diagnostic interview. The schedule for affective disorders and schizophrenia. *Arch. Gen. Psychiatry*, 35: 837–844, 1978.

Ends, E. J., and Page, C. W. A study of three types of group psychotherapy with hospitalized male inebriates. *J. Stud. Alcohol*, 18: 267–277, 1957.

Ewing, J. A. Disulfiram and other deterrent drugs. In: Pattison, E. M., and Kaufman, E. (eds.), *Encyclopedic Handbook of Alcoholism*. New York, Gardner Press, 1982, pp. 1033–1042.

Ewing, J. A. Detecting alcoholism, the CAGE questionnaire. *JAMA*, 252(14): 1905–1907, 1984.

Ewing, J. A., and Rouse, B. A. Failure of an experimental treatment program to inculcate controlled drinking in alcoholics. *Brit. J. Addict.*, 71: 123–134, 1976.

Fazekas, I. G. Hydrocortisone content of human blood, and alcohol content of blood and urine, after wine consumption. *Q. J. Stud. Alc.*, 27: 439–446, 1966.

Feldman, L. B. Marital conflict and marital intimacy: An integrative psychodynamic-behavioral-systematic model. *Family Process*, 18(1): 69–78, 1979.

Fifth Special Report to the US Congress on Alcohol and Health from the Secretary of Health and Human Services, DHHS Publ. No. (ADM) 84-1291, Washington, DC, USGPO, 1983.

Fillmore, K. M., and Midanik, L. Chronicity of drinking problems among men: A longitudinal study. *J. Stud. Alc.*, 45(3): 228–236, 1984.

Fisher, J. C., Mason, R. L., Keeley, K. A., and Fisher, J. V. Physicians and alcoholics. The effect of medical training on attitudes toward alcoholics. *J. Stud. Alc.*, 36(7): 949–955, 1975.

Fisher, J. V., Fisher, J. C., and Mason, R. L. Physicians and alcoholics, modifying behavior and attitudes of family-practice residents. *J. Stud. Alc.*, 37(11): 1686–1693, 1976.

Fourth Special Report to the U.S. Congress on Alcohol and Health, U.S. Department of Health and Human Services, Washington, DC, January, 1981.

Frank, J. D. *Persuasion and Healing*. New York, Schocken Books, 1961.

Frankl, V. *The Unconscious God*. New York, Simon & Schuster, 1975.

Freed, E. X. Drug abuse by alcoholics: A review. *International J. of the Addictions*, 8: 451–473, 1973.

Freed, E. X. Mental hospitals: Hospitalization and treatment of the alcoholic. In: Pattison, E. M., and Kaufman, E. (eds.), *Encyclopedic Handbook of Alcoholism*. New York, Gardner Press, 1982, pp. 848–855.

Freud, A. *The Ego and the Mechanisms of Defense*. New York, International Universities Press, 1946.

Friedman, M. A. Grief reactions: Implications for treatment of alcoholic clients. *Alcoholism Treatment Quarterly*, 1(1): 55–69, 1984.

Fries, H. Experience with lithium carbonate treatment at a psychiatric department in the period 1964–1967. *Acta. Psychiatr.*, Suppl. 207, pp. 41–43, 1969.

Futterman, S. Personality trends in wives of alcoholics. *J. Psychiat. Social Work*, 37–41, 1953.

Galanter, M. The use of social networks in office management of the substance abuser. In: Galanter, M., and Pattison, E. M. (eds.) *Advances in the Psychosocial Treatment of Alcoholism*. Washington, DC, American Psychiatric Press, 1984, pp. 98–114.

Galanter, M., and Pattison, E. M. (eds.) *Advances in the Psychosocial Treatment of Alcoholism*. Washington, DC, American Psychiatric Press, 1984, pp. 19–20.

Galanter, M., and Sperber, J. General hospitals in the alcoholism treatment system. In: Pattison, E. M., and Kaufman, E. (eds.), *Encyclopedic Handbook of Alcoholism*. New York, Gardner Press, 1982, pp. 828–836.

Galanter, M., Karasu, T. B., and Wilder, J. F. Initiating alcoholism treatment on medical services. In: Seixas, F. A. (ed.), *Currents in Alcoholism*, Volume 1. New York, Grune & Stratton, 1977.

Gallant, D. M., Rich, A., Bay, E., and Terranova, L. Psychotherapy with married couples: A successful technique in New Orleans alcoholic clinic patients. *J. LA State Med. Soc.*, 122: 41, 1970.

Gallup, G. *Alcohol Abuse: A Problem in One of Three American Families*. Princeton, NJ, The Gallup Poll, November 15, 1982.

Gavaler, J. S. Effects of alcohol on endocrine function in post-menopausal women: A review. *J. Stud. Alcohol*, 46(6): 495–516, 1985.

Gelles, R. J., and Straus, M. A. Determinants of violence in the family: Toward a theoretical integration. In: Burr, R. W., Hill, R., Nye, F. D., and Reiss, D. L. (eds.), *Contemporary Theories About the Family*. New York, The Free Press, 1979, pp. 549–581.

Gillis, L. S., and Keet, M. Prognostic factors and treatment results in hospitalized alcoholics. *Q. J. Stud. Alc.*, 30: 426–437, 1969.

Glass, R. M., and Freedman, D. X. Contempo 85: Psychiatry. *JAMA*, 254(16): 2280–2283, 1985.

Glatt, M. M. The question of moderate drinking despite loss of control. *Brit. J. Addict.*, 62: 267–274, 1967.

Goldfrank, L., Bresnitz, E., Melinek, M., and Weisman, R. S. Antabuse. *Hospital Physician*, December, 1980, p. 36.

Goldman, M. S. Cognitive impairment in chronic alcoholics: Some cause for optimism. *American Psychologist*, October, 1983, pp. 1045–1054.

Goodwin, D. W. Familial and non-familial alcoholism. Presented at the Ninth Annual Conference on Alcoholism, El Paso, TX, February 14, 1985.

Goodwin, D. W., and Guze, S. B. *Psychiatric Diagnosis*, 2nd edition. New York, Oxford University Press, 1979, pp. 118–144.

Goodwin, D. W., Schulsinger, F., Hermansen, L., Guze, S. B., and Winokur, G. Alcohol problems in adoptees raised apart from alcoholic biological parents. *Archives of General Psychiatry*, 28: 238–243, 1973.

Goodwin, D. W., Schulsinger, F., Hermansen, L., Guze, S. B., and Winokur, G. Alcoholism and the hyperactive child syndrome. *Journal of Nervous and Mental Disease*, 160: 349–353, 1975.

Goodwin, D. W., Schulsinger, F., Moller, N., Hermansen, L., Winokur, G., and Guze, S. B. Drinking problems in adopted and nonadopted sons of alcoholics. *Archives of General Psychiatry*, 31: 164–169, 1974.

Gordon, C., and Beresin, E. Conflicting treatment models for the inpatient management of borderline patients. *Am. J. Psychiatry*, 140(8): 979–983, 1983.

Gottheil, E., Crawford, H., and Cornelison, F. S. The alcoholics' ability to resist available alcohol. *Disease of the Nervous Systems*, 34: 80–84, 1973.

Gottheil, E., and Waxman, H. M. Alcoholism and schizophrenia. In: Pattison, E. M., and Kaufman, E. (eds.), *Encyclopedic Handbook of Alcoholism*. New York, Gardner Press, pp. 636–646, 1982.

Gough, H. G. Diagnostic patterns on the MMPI. *J. Clin. Psychology*, 2: 23–37, 1947.

Grande, T. P., Wolfe, A. W., Schubert, D. S. P., Patterson, M. B., and Brocco, K. Associations among alcoholism, drug abuse, and anti-social personality: A review of the literature. *Psychological Reports*, 55: 455–474, 1984.

Greenblatt, D. J., Shader, R. I., and Abernathy, D. R. Drug therapy: Current status of benzodiazepines. *New England Journal of Medicine*, August 18, 1983, pp. 410–416.

Griffiths, R., Bigelow, G., and Liebson, I. Suppression of ethanol self-administration in alcoholics by contingent time-out from social interactions. *Behavioral Research and Therapy*, 12: 327–334, 1974.

Gruchow, H. W., Sobocinski, K. A., and Barboriak, J. J. Alcohol, nutrient intake, and hypertension in U.S. adults. *JAMA*, 253(11): 1567–1570, 1985.

Gunderson, J. G., Kolb, J. E., and Austin, V. The diagnostic interview for borderline patients. *Am. J. Psychiatry*, 138(7): 896–903, 1981.

Haberman, P. W. Psychological test score changes for wives of alcoholics during periods of drinking and sobriety. *J. Clin. Psychology*, 20: 230–232, 1964.

Hamilton, C. J., and Collins, J. J., Jr. The role of alcohol in wife beating and child abuse: A review of the literature. In: Collins, J. J., Jr. (ed.), *Drinking and Crime: Perspective on the Relationship Between Alcohol Consumption and Criminal Behavior*. New York, Guilford Press, 1981, pp. 253–287.

Hanks, S., and Rosenbaum, P. Battered women: A study of women who live with violent alcohol-abusing men. *Amer. J. Orthopsychiatry*, 47(2): 291–306, 1977.

Harper, C. Wernicke's encephalopathy: A more common disease than realized. A neuropathological study of 51 cases. *J. of Neurology, Neurosurgery and Psychiatry*, 42: 226–231, 1979.

Harwood, H. J., Napcitano, D. M., Kristiansen, P. L., and Collins, J. L. Economic costs to society of alcohol and drug abuse and mental illness: 1980. Research Triangle Institute; report submitted to the Alcohol, Drug Abuse, and Mental Health Administration, Rockville, MD, June, 1984.

Hatsukami, D., and Pickens, R. W. Post-treatment depression in an alcohol and drug abuse population. *Am. J. Psychiatry*, 139(12): 1563–1566, 1982.

Havens, L. L. Taking a history from a difficult patient. *Lancet*, 1: 138–140, 1978.

Haynes, R. B., Davis, D. A., McKibbon, A., and Tugwell, P. A critical appraisal of the efficacy of continuing medical education. *JAMA*, 251(1): 61–64, 1984.

Helzer, J. E., Robins, L. N., Taylor, J. R., Carey, K., Miller, R. H., et al. The extent of long-term moderate drinking among alcoholics discharged from medical and psychiatric treatment facilities. *N. England J. Med.*, 312: 1678–1682, 1985.

Henry, S., and Robinson, D. Understanding Alcoholics Anonymous. *Lancet*, 2: 372–375, 1978.

Hesselbrock, M. N., Meyer, R. E., and Keener, J. J. Psychopathology in hospitalized alcoholics. *Arch. Gen. Psychiatry*, 42: 1050–1055, 1985.

Howland, R. W., and Howland, J. W. 200 years of drinking in the United States:

Evolution of the disease concept. In: Ewing, J. A., and Rouse, B. A. (eds.), *Drinking: Alcohol in American Society—Issues and Current Research*. Chicago, Nelson-Hall, pp. 39–60, 1978.

Hudson, C. J., and Perkins, S. H. Panic disorder and alcohol misuse. *J. Studies on Alcohol*, 45(5): 462–464, 1984.

Igersheimer, W. W. Group psychotherapy for nonalcoholic wives of alcoholics. *Q. J. Stud. Alc.*, 20: 77–85, 1959.

Imber, S., Schultz, E., Funderburk, F., Allen, R., and Flamer, R. The fate of the untreated alcoholic. *J. Nerv. and Mental Disease*, 162: 238–247, 1976.

Inui, T. S., Yourtee, E. L., and Williamson, J. W. Improved outcomes in hypertension after physician tutorials: A controlled trial. *Annals of Internal Medicine*, 84: 645–651, 1975.

Isbell, J. Craving for alcohol. *Q. J. Stud. Alcohol*, 16: 38–42, 1955.

Jackson, J. A. The adjustment of the family to the crisis of alcoholism. *Q. J. Study Alcohol*, 15: 562–586, 1954.

Jacob, T., and Seilhamer, R. The impact on spouses and how they cope. In: Orford, J., and Harwin, J. (eds.), *Alcohol and the Family*. New York, St. Martin's Press, 1982, pp. 114–126.

James, J. E., and Goldman, M. Behavior trends of wives of alcoholics. *Q. J. Stud. Alcohol*, 32: 373–381, 1971.

Jellinek, E. M. Phases in the drinking history of alcoholics: Analysis of a survey conducted by the official organ of Alcoholics Anonymous. *Q. J. Stud. Alcohol*, 7: 1–88, 1946.

Jellinek, E. M. Phases of alcohol addiction. *Q. J. Stud. Alcohol*, 13: 673–684, 1952.

Jellinek, E. M. *The Disease Concept of Alcoholism*. New Haven, College and University Press, 1980.

Jensen, S. B. Sexual function and dysfunction in younger married alcoholics. *Acta. Psychiatr. Scand.*, 69: 543–549, 1984.

Johnson, R. P., and Connelly, J. C. Addicted physicians: A closer look. *JAMA*, 245: 253–257, 1981.

Johnson, V. E. *I'll Quit Tomorrow*. New York, Harper & Row, 1973.

Jones, B., and Parsons, O. A. Impaired abstracting ability in chronic alcoholics. *Arch. Gen. Psychiatry*, 24: 71–75, 1971.

Judd, L. L., Hubbard, B., Janowsky, D. S., Huey, L. Y., Abrams, A. A., Riney, W. B., and Pendery, M. M. Ethanol-lithium interactions in alcoholics. In: Goodwin, D. W., and Erickson, C. K. (eds.), *Alcoholism and Affective Disorders: Clinical, Genetic and Bio-Chemical Studies*. Jamaica, NY, Spectrum Publications, 1979, pp. 109–136.

Judd, L. L., and Huey, L. Y. Lithium antagonizes ethanol intoxication in alcoholics. *Am. J. Psychiatry*, 141(12): 1517–1521, 1984.

Kalashian, M. M. Working with the wives of alcoholics in an outpatient clinic setting. *Marriage and Family Living*, 21: 130–133, 1959.

Kamerow, D. B., Pincus, H. A., and Macdonald, D. I. Alcohol abuse, other drug abuse, and mental disorders in medical practice: Prevalence, costs, recognition, and treatment. *JAMA*, 255(15): 2054–2057, 1986.

Kanas, N. Alcoholism and group psychotherapy. In: Pattison, E. M., and Kaufman, E. (eds.), *Encyclopedic Handbook of Alcoholism*. New York, Gardner Press, pp. 1011–1021, 1982.

Karacan, I., and Hanusa, T. L. The effects of alcohol relative to sexual dysfunctions. In: Pattison, E. M., and Kaufman, E. (eds.), *Encyclopedic Handbook of Alcoholism*. New York, Gardner Press, pp. 686–695, 1982.

Kaufman, E. Polydrug abuse or multi-drug use: It's here to stay. *Br. J. Addict.*, 72: 339–347, 1977.

Kaufman, E. Alcoholism and the use of other drugs. In: Pattison, E. M., and Kaufman, E. (eds.), *Encyclopedic Handbook of Alcoholism*. New York, Gardner Press, pp. 696–705, 1982.

Kaufman, E. Family system variables in alcoholism. *Alcoholism: Clin. and Exp. Research*, 8(1): 4–8, 1984.

Kaufman, E., and Pattison, E. M. Differential methods of family therapy in the treatment of alcoholism. *J. Stud. Alcohol*, 42(11): 951–971, 1981.

Keane, A., and Roche, D. Developmental disorders in the children of male alcoholics. In: Papers presented at the 20th International Institute on the Prevention and Treatment of Alcoholism, Manchester, England, 1974, pp. 82–89.

Keeley, K. A. Emergency room treatment of alcohol abuse and alcoholism. In: Pattison, E. M., and Kaufman, E. (eds.), *Encyclopedic Handbook of Alcoholism*. New York, Gardner Press, pp. 837–847, 1982.

Keller, M. On the loss-of-control phenomenon in alcoholism. *Br. J. Addict.*, 67: 153–166, 1972.

Kernberg, O. F. *Borderline Conditions and Pathological Narcissism*. New York, Jason Aronson, 1975.

Khantzian, E. J. Some treatment implications of the ego and self-disturbances in alcoholism. In: Bean, M. H., and Zinberg, N. E. (eds.), *Dynamic Approaches to the Understanding and Treatment of Alcoholism*. New York, The Free Press, pp. 163–188, 1981.

Khantzian, E. J. The injured self, addiction and our call to medicine. *JAMA*, 254: 2, 249–252, 1985.

Kissin, B. Medical management of the alcoholic patient. In: Kissin, B., and Begleiter, H. (eds.), *Biology of Alcoholism*, Volume 5. New York, Plenum Press, 1977.

Kissin, B. Biological investigations in alcohol research. *J. Stud. Alcohol*, 8 (Suppl.): 146–181, 1979.

Kissin, B., Platz, A., and Su, W. H. Social and psychological factors in the treatment of chronic alcoholism. *J. Psychiatr. Res.*, 8: 13–27, 1970.

Kleinman, A., Eisenberg, L., and Good, B. Culture, illness and care: Clinical lessons from anthropologic and cross-cultured research. *Annals of Internal Medicine*, 88: 251–258, 1978.

Kline, N. S., Wren, J. C., Cooper, T. B., Varga, E., and Cord, O. Evaluation of lithium therapy in chronic and periodic alcoholism. *Amer. J. of Medical Sciences*, 268(1): 15–22, 1974.

Knott, D. H., and Beard, J. D. Effects of alcohol ingestion on the cardiovascular system. In: Pattison, E. M., and Kaufman, E. (eds.), *Encyclopedic Handbook of Alcoholism*. New York, Gardner Press, pp. 332–342, 1982.

Koenigsberg, H. W., Kaplan, R. D., Gilmore, M. M., and Cooper, A. M. The relationship between syndrome and personality disorder in DSM-III: Experience with 2,462 patients. *Am. J. Psychiatry*, 142(2): 207–212, 1985.

Kogan, K. L., Fordyce, W. E., and Jackson, J. K. Personality disturbance in wives of alcoholics. *Q. J. Stud. Alcohol*, 24: 227–238, 1963.

Kohl, R. N. Pathological reactions of marital partners to improvement of patients. *Am. J. Psychiatry*, 118: 1036–1041, 1962.

Kohut, H. *The Analysis of Self*. New York, International Universities Press, 1971.

Korsten, M. A., and Lieber, C. S. Liver and Pancreas. In: Pattison, E. M., and

Kaufman, E. (eds.), *Encyclopedic Handbook of Alcoholism*. New York, Gardner Press, pp. 225–244, 1982.

Kramer, J. F., and Cameron, D. C. (eds.) *A Manual on Drug Dependence*. Geneva, World Health Organization, 1974, p. 7.

Kroll, P., Palmer, C., and Greden, J. F. The dexamethasone suppression test in patients with alcoholism. *Biological Psychiatry*, 18(4): 441–450, 1983.

Kubler-Ross, E. *On Death and Dying*. New York, MacMillan, 1969.

Kurtz, E. *Not-God: A History of Alcoholics Anonymous*. Center City, MN, Hazelden, 1979.

Kwentus, J., and Major, L. F. Disulfiram in the treatment of alcoholism. *J. Stud. Alcohol*, 40(5): 428–446, 1979.

Lader, M. Dependence on benzodiazepines. *J. Clinical Psychiatry*, 44: 121–127, 1983.

Lanyon, R. I. Development and validation of a psychological screening inventory. *J. Consult. Clin. Psychology*, Psychology Monograph 35, 1970.

Leach, B., and Norris, J. L. Factors in the development of Alcoholics Anonymous (AA). In: Kissin, B., and Begleiter, H. *The Biology of Alcoholism, Vol. 5: Treatment and Rehabilitation of the Chronic Alcoholic*. New York, Plenum Press, pp. 441–543, 1977.

Lemert, E. M. The occurrence and sequence of events in the adjustment of families to alcoholism. *Q. J. Stud. Alcohol*, 21: 679–697, 1960.

Levine, J. The sexual adjustment of alcoholics. A clinical study of a selected sample. *Q. J. Stud. Alcohol*, 16: 675–680, 1955.

Lewis, C., Rice, J., and Helzer, J. Diagnostic interactions, alcoholism and antisocial personality. *J. Nerv. Ment. Disease*, 171: 105–113, 1983.

Lewis, C. E., Helzer, J., Cloninger, C. R., Crougham, J., and Whitman, B. Y. Psychiatric diagnostic predispositions to alcoholism. *Comprehensive Psychiatry*, 23(5): 451–461, 1982.

Lewis, J. M. *To Be a Therapist: The Teaching and Learning*. New York, Brunner/Mazel, 1978.

Lewis, J. M. *The Chronically Ill Child and Family*. In: Looney, J. G. (ed.), *Chronic Mental Illness in Children and Adolescents*. Washington, DC, American Psychiatric Press, 1987.

Lewis, J. M. Family structure and stress. *Family Process*, Volume 25, 235–247, 1986.

Lewis, M. L. The initial contact with wives of alcoholics. *Social Casework*, 35: 8–14, 1954.

Lieber, C. S. Alcohol and the liver: Overview. In: Galanter, M. (ed.), *Recent Developments in Alcoholism*, Volume 2. New York, Plenum Press, pp. 93–102, 1984.

Lieberman, M. A., Yalom, I. D., and Mills, M. B. *Encounter Groups: First Facts*. New York, Basic Books, 1973.

Lion, J. R. *Personality Disorders: Diagnosis and Management*. Baltimore, Williams & Wilkins, 1974.

Lisansky, E. S. Alcoholism in women: Social and psychological concomitants. I. Social history data. *Q. J. Stud. Alcohol*, 18: 588–623, 1957.

Lisansky, E. T. Why physicians avoid early diagnosis of alcoholism. *New York State Journal of Medicine*, September, 1975, pp. 1788–1792.

Litman, G. K. Relapse in alcoholism: Traditional and current approaches. In: Edwards, G., and Grant, M. (eds.), *Alcoholism Treatment in Transition*. Baltimore, University Park Press, pp. 294–303, 1980.

Litman, G. K., and Topham, A. Outcome studies on techniques in alcoholism treatment. In: Galanter, M. (ed.), *Recent Developments in Alcoholism*, Volume 1. New York, Plenum Press, pp. 167–194, 1983.

Ludwig, A. M., Bendfeldt, F., Wikler, A., and Cain, R. B. "Loss of control" in alcoholics. *Arch. Gen. Psychiatry*, 35: 370–373, 1978.

Ludwig, A. M., and Wikler, A. "Craving" and relapse to drink. *Q. J. Stud. Alcohol*, 35: 108–130, 1974.

Ludwig, A. M., Wikler, A., and Stark, L. H. The First Drink. Psychobiological aspects of craving. *Arch. Gen. Psychiatry*, 30: 539–547, 1974.

Lundberg, G. D. Ethyl alcohol—ancient plague and modern poison: Editorial. *JAMA*, 252(14): 1911–1912, 1984.

Lundwall, L., and Baekland, F. Disulfiram treatment of alcoholism. *J. Nerv. Ment. Disease*, 153(6): 381–394, 1971.

MacDonald, D. E. Mental disorders in wives of alcoholics. *Q. J. Stud. Alcohol*, 17: 282–287, 1956.

MacGregor, R. R. Scientific evidence of the effects of alcohol on the immune system. Summary of a workshop to provide policy and research recommendations to the National Institute on Alcohol Abuse and Alcoholism, Bethesda, MD, November 4–5, 1985.

MacLeod, L. D. The craving for alcohol. A symposium by members of the WHO Expert Committee on Mental Health and Alcoholism. *Q. J. Stud. Alcohol*, 16: 54–62, 1955.

Macy Foundation. *Medical Education and Drug Abuse: Report of a Joint Conference on Instruction in the Problems of Drug Abuse*. New York, William F. Fell Company, 1973.

Malloy, T. E. Toward a generic concept of alcoholism. *Am. J. of Orthopsychiatry*, 51: 489–492, 1981.

Malzberg, B. First admissions with alcoholic psychoses in New York State, year ended March 31, 1948. With a note on first admissions for alcoholism with psychosis. *Q. J. Stud. Alcohol*, 10: 461–470, 1949.

Mandell, W. Types and phases of alcohol dependence illness. In: Galanter, M. (ed.), *Recent Developments in Alcoholism*, Volume 1. New York, Plenum Press, pp. 415–447, 1983.

Marconi, J. T. The concept of alcoholism. *Q. J. Stud. Alcohol*, 20: 216–235, 1959.

Marconi, J., Poblete, M., Palestine, M., Moga, L., and Bahomondes, A. Role of the dorsomedial nucleus in "loss of control and inability to abstain" during ethanol ingestion. In: Popham, R. A. (ed.), *Alcohol and Alcoholism*. Toronto, University of Toronto Press, 1970.

Marks, I. M., and Mathews, A. M. Brief standard self-rating for phobic patients. *Behav. Res. Ther.*, 17: 263–267, 1979.

Marlatt, G. A. Craving for alcohol, loss of control and relapse: A cognitive-behavioral analysis. In: Nathan, P. E., Marlatt, G. A., and Lobert, T. (eds.), *Alcoholism: New Directions in Behavioral Research*. New York, Plenum Press, pp. 271–314, 1978.

Marlatt, G. A., Demming, B., and Reid, J. B. Loss of control drinking in alcoholics: An experimental analogue. *J. Abnorm. Psychology*, 81(3): 233–241, 1973.

Mathew, R. M., Claghorn, J. L., and Largen, J. Craving for alcohol in sober alcoholics. *Am. J. Psychiatry*, 136(4B): 603–606, 1979.

Mayer, J., and Filstead, W. J. The adolescent alcohol involvement scale: An instrument for measuring adolescents' use and misuse of alcohol. *J. Stud. Alcohol*, 40(3): 291–300, 1979.

Mayer, J., and Myerson, D. J. Characteristics of outpatient alcoholics in relation to change in drinking, work and marital status during treatment. *Q. J. Stud. Alcohol*, 31: 889–897, 1970.

Mayer, R. F., and Khurana, R. K. Peripheral and Autonomic Nervous System. In: Pattison, E. M., and Kaufman, E. (eds.), *Encyclopedic Handbook of Alcoholism*. New York, Gardner Press, pp. 194–203, 1982.

Mayfield, D. G. Alcohol and affects: Experimental studies. In: Goodwin, D. W., and Erickson, C. K. (eds.), *Alcoholism and Affective Disorders: Clinical, Genetic and Biomedical Studies*. Jamaica, NY, Spectrum Publications, pp. 99–108, 1979.

Mayfield, D., McLeod, G., and Hall, P. The CAGE questionnaire: Validation of a new alcoholism screening instrument. *Am. J. Psychiatry*, 131(10): 1121–1123, 1974.

Mayfield, D. G., and Coleman, L. L. Alcohol use and affective disorder. *Dis. Nerv. System*, 29: 467–474, 1968.

McClelland, D. C., Davis, W. N., Kalin, R., and Wanner, E. *The Drinking Man*. New York, The Free Press, 1972.

McCord, W., and McCord, J. *Origins of Alcoholism*. Stanford, Stanford University Press, 1960.

McCreery, M. J., and Hunt, W. A. Physiochemical correlates of alcohol intoxication. *Neuropharmacology*, 17: 451–461, 1978.

McEvoy, J. P. The chronic neuropsychiatric disorders associated with alcoholism. In: Pattison, E. M., and Kaufman, E. (eds.), *Encyclopedic Handbook of Alcoholism*. New York, Gardner Press, pp. 167–179, 1982.

McGovern, T. F. The effects of an inpatient alcoholism treatment program with two variations on measurements of depression, hopelessness, loss, and grief. Unpublished doctoral dissertation, Texas Tech University, Lubbock, TX, 1983.

Mello, N. K. Behavioral studies of alcoholism. In: Kissin, B., and Begleiter, H. (eds.), *Biology of Alcoholism*, Volume II. New York, Plenum Press, pp. 219–291, 1972.

Mendelson, W., Johnson, N., and Stewart, M. A. Hyperactive children as teenagers: A follow-up study. *J. Nerv. Disease*, 153: 273–279, 1971.

Merikangas, K. R., Leckman, J. F., Prusoff, B. A., Pauls, D. L., and Weissman, M. M. Family transmission of depression and alcoholism. *Arch. Gen. Psychiatry*, 42: 367–372, 1985.

Merry, J. The "loss of control" myth. *Lancet*, 1: 1257–1258, 1966.

Merry, J., Reynolds, C. M., Bailey, J., and Coppen, A. Prophylactic treatment of alcoholism by lithium carbonate. *Lancet*, 2: 481–482, 1976.

Meyer, R. E. Anxiolytics and the alcoholic patient. *J. Stud. Alcohol*, 47(4): 269–273, 1986a.

Meyer, R. E. How to understand the relationship between psychopathology and addictive disorders: Another example of the chicken and the egg. In: Meyer, R. E. (ed.), *Psychopathology and Addictive Disorders*. New York, The Guilford Press, pp. 3–16, 1986b.

Mezey, E. Alcoholic liver disease. In: Popper, H., and Schaffner, F. (eds.), *Progress in Liver Disease*, Volume 7. New York, Grune & Stratton, 1982.

Mitchell, H. E., and Mudd, E. H. The development of a research methodology for achieving the cooperation of alcoholics and their nonalcoholic wives. *Q. J. Stud. Alcohol*, 17: 649–657, 1957.

Modlin, H. C. A study of the MMPI in clinical practice, with notes on the Cornell Index. *Am. J. Psychiatry*, 103: 758–769, 1947.

Moore, R. A. The prevalence of alcoholism in a community general hospital. *Am. J. Psychiatry*, 128(5): 638–639, 1971.

Moore, R. A. The diagnosis of alcoholism in a psychiatric hospital: A trial of the Michigan Alcoholism Screening Test (MAST). *Am. J. Psychiatry*, 128(12): 1565–1569, 1972.

Moore, R. A. The involvement of private psychiatric hospitals in alcoholism treatment. In: Pattison, E. M., and Kaufman, E. (eds.), *Encyclopedic Handbook of Alcoholism*. New York, Gardner Press, pp. 856–864, 1982.

Moos, R. H., Bromet, E., Tsu, V., and Moos, B. Family characteristics and the outcome of treatment for alcoholism. *J. Stud. Alcohol*, 40(1): 78–88, 1979.

Morrison, J. Adult psychiatric disorders in parents of hyperactive children. *Am. J. Psychiatry*, 137(7): 825–827, 1980.

Morrison, J. R., and Stewart, M. A. A family study of the hyperactive child syndrome. *Biological Psychiatry*, 3: 189–195, 1971.

Morse, R. M., Mitchell, M. M., and Martin, M. A. Physician attitudes toward alcoholism: A positive trend? In: Seixas, F. (ed.), *Currents in Alcoholism*, Volume II. New York, Grune & Stratton, pp. 207–224, 1977.

Moser, J. *Prevention of Alcohol-Related Problems*. Toronto, Alcoholism and Drug Addiction Research Foundation, 1980.

Mulhaney, J. A., and Trippett, C. J. Alcohol dependence and phobias: Clinical description and relevance. *Br. J. Psychiatry*, 135: 565–573, 1979.

Munjack, D. J., and Moss, H. B. Affective disorder and alcoholism in families of agoraphobics. *Arch. Gen. Psychiatry*, 38: 869–871, 1981.

Myers, J. K., Weissman, M. M., Tischler, J. L., Holzer, C. E., Leaf, P. J., Orvaschel, H., Anthony, J. C., Boyd, J. H., Burke, J. K., Kramer, M., and Stoltzman, R. Six month prevalence of psychiatric disorders in three communities. *Arch. Gen. Psychiatry*, 41(10): 959–967, 1984.

Nace, E. P. Training the psychiatry resident in alcoholism: An evaluation. *J. Psychiatric Education*, 5(3): 248–255, 1981.

Nace, E. P. The role of craving in the treatment of alcoholism. *National Association of Private Psychiatric Hospitals Journal*, 13(1): 27–31, 1982.

Nace, E. P. Understanding the disease in alcoholism. *Texas Medicine*, 79: 36–39, 1983.

Nace, E. P. Epidemiology of alcoholism and prospects for treatment. *Annual Rev. Med.*, 35: 293–309, 1984.

Nace, E. P., DePhoure, M., Goldberg, M., and Cammarota, C. C. Treatment priorities in a family-oriented alcoholism program. *J. Marital and Family Therapy*, pp. 143–150, January, 1982.

Nace, E. P., O'Brien, C. P., Mintz, J., Ream, N., and Meyer, A. L. Drinking problems among Vietnam veterans. In: Seixas, F. A. (ed.), *Currents in Alcoholism*, Volume II. New York, Grune & Stratton, pp. 315–324, 1977.

Nace, E. P., Saxon, J. J., and Shore, N. A. A comparison of borderline and non-borderline alcoholic patients. *Arch. Gen. Psychiatry*, 40: 54–56, 1983.

Nace, E. P., Saxon, J. J., and Shore, N. A. Borderline personality disorder and the treatment of alcoholism: A follow-up study. *J. Stud. Alcohol*, 47(3): 196–200, 1986.

Nakamura, M. M., Overall, J. E., Hollister, L. E., and Radcliffe, E. Factors affecting outcome of depressive symptoms in alcoholics. *Alcoholism: Clin. Exp. Res.*, 7(2): 188–193, 1983.

Nathan, P. E., and Lisman, S. A. Behavioral and motivational patterns of chronic alcoholics. In: Tarter, R. E., and Sugerman, A. A. (eds.), *Alcoholism: Interdisciplinary Approaches to an Enduring Problem*. Reading, PA, Addison-Wesley, pp. 479–522, 1976.

Nelson, W. H., Sullivan, P., Khan, A., and Tamragouri, R. N. The effect of age on dexatheasone suppression test results in alcoholic patients. *Am. J. Psychiatry,* 143: 237–279, 1986.

Neubuerger, O. W., Miller, S. I., Schmitz, R. E., Matarazzo, J. D., Pratt, H., and Hasha, N. Replicable abstinence rates in an alcoholism treatment program. *JAMA,* 248(8): 960–963, 1982.

Nielsen, J. Mental disorders in married couples (assortative mating). *Br. J. Psychiatry,* 110: 683–697, 1964.

Noble, E. P. (ed.) *Third Special Report to the U.S. Congress on Alcohol and Health,* DHEW Publ. No. (ADM) 79-832, Washington, DC, USGPO, 1978.

Noonberg, A., Goldstein, G., and Page, H. A. Premature aging in male alcoholics: "Accelerated aging" or "increased vulnerability"? *Alcoholism: Clin. Exp. Res.,* 9(4): 334–338, 1985.

Novick, D. M. Major medical problems and detoxification treatment of parenteral drug-abusing alcoholics. *Advances in Alcohol and Substance Abuse,* 3(4): 87–105, 1984.

Olegard, R., Sabel, K. G., Anderson, M., Sandin, B., Johansson, P. R., Carlsson, C., Kyllerman, M., Iversen, K., and Hrbek, A. Effects of the child of alcohol abuse. *Acta. Paedicrica. Scandinavies,* (Suppl. 275): 112–121, 1979.

Orford, J. Alcoholism and marriage. The argument against specialism. *J. Stud. Alcohol,* 36(11): 1537–1563, 1975.

Orford, J., Guthrie, S., Nicholls, P., Oppenheimer, E., Egert, S., and Hensman, C. Self-reported coping behavior of wives of alcoholics and its association with drinking outcome. *J. Stud. Alcohol,* 36(9): 1254–1267, 1975.

Orford, J., Oppenheimer, E., and Edwards, G. Abstinence or control: The outcome for excessive drinkers two years after consultation. *Behav. Research & Therapy,* 14: 409–418, 1976.

Orne, M. T. On the social psychology of the psychological experiment: With particular reference to demand characteristics and their implications. *Amer. Psychologist,* 17: 776–783, 1962.

Overall, J. E., Brown, D., Williams, J. D., and Neill, L. T. Drug treatment of anxiety and depression in detoxified alcoholic patients. *Arch. Gen. Psychiatry,* 29: 218–221, 1973.

Overall, J. E., Reilly, E. L., Kelly, J. T., and Hollister, L. E. Persistence of depression in detoxified alcoholics. *Alcohol: Clin. Exp. Res.,* 9(4): 331–333, 1985.

Paige, P. E., LaPointe, W., and Krueger, A. The marital dyad as a diagnostic and treatment variable in alcohol addiction. *Psychology,* 8: 64–73, 1971.

Paolino, T. J., and McCrady, B. S. *The Alcoholic Marriage: Alternative Perspectives.* New York, Grune & Stratton, 1977.

Paolino, T. J., McCrady, B. S., Diamond, S., and Longabaugh, R. Psychological disturbances in spouses of alcoholics. An empirical assessment. *J. Stud. Alcohol,* 37(11): 1600–1608, 1976.

Park, P. Developmental ordering of experiences in alcoholism. *Q. J. Stud. Alcohol,* 34: 473–488, 1973.

Parkes, C. M. *Bereavement: Studies of Grief in Adult Life.* New York, International Universities Press, 1972.

Parsons, O. A., and Farr, S. P. The neuropsychology of alcohol and drug use. In: Filshov, S. B., and Boll, T. J. (eds.), *Handbook of Clinical Neuropsychology.* New York, Wiley, 1981.

Paternoster, L. *Dallas Morning News,* March 19, 1984.

Pattison, E. M. The selection of treatment modalities for the alcoholic patient. In:

Mendelson, J. H., and Mello, N. K. (eds.), *The Diagnosis and Treatment of Alcoholism*. New York, McGraw-Hill, pp. 125–227, 1979.

Pattison, E. M. A systems approach to alcoholism treatment. In: Pattison, E. M., and Kaufman, E. (eds.), *Encyclopedic Handbook of Alcoholism*. New York, Gardner Press, pp. 1089–1108, 1982.

Pattison, E. M., and Kaufman, E. The alcohol syndrome: Definitions and models. In: Pattison, E. M., and Kaufman, E. (eds.), *Encyclopedic Handbook of Alcoholism*. New York, Gardner Press, pp. 3–30, 1982.

Peele, S. The implications and limitations of genetic models of alcoholism and other addictions. *J. Stud. Alcohol*, 47(1): 63–73, 1986.

Pendery, M., Maltzman, I. M., and West, L. J. Controlled drinking by alcoholics? Refutation of a major affirmative study. *Science*, 217: 169, 1982.

Penrose, L. S. Mental illness in husband and wife: A contribution to the study of assortative mating in man. *Psychiat. Q. Suppl.*, 18: 161–171, 1944.

Pettinati, H. M., Sugerman, A. A., DiDonato, N., and Maurer, H. S. The natural history of alcoholism over four years after treatment. *J. Stud. Alcohol*, 43(3): 201–215, 1982.

Pettinati, H. M., Sugerman, A. A., and Maurer, H. S. Four year MMPI changes in abstinent and drinking alcoholics. *Alcohol: Clin. Exp. Res.*, 6(4): 487–494, 1982.

Pickens, R. W., Hatsukami, D. K., Spicer, J. W., and Svikis, D. S. Relapse by alcohol abusers. *Alcohol: Clin. Exp. Res.*, 9(3): 244–247, 1985.

Pinkerton, R. E., Tinanoff, N., Willms, J. L., and Tapp, J. T. Resident physician performance in a continuing education format. Does newly acquired knowledge improve patient care? *JAMA*, 244(19): 2183–2185, 1980.

Pokorny, A. D., and Kanas, T. E. Stages in the development of alcoholism. In: Farr, W. E., Karacan, I., Pokorny, A. D., and Williams, R. L. (eds.), *Phenomenology and Treatment of Alcoholism*. New York, SP Medical and Scientific Books, p. 62, 1980.

Pokorny, A., Putnam, P., and Fryer, J. Drug abuse and alcoholism teaching in U.S. medical and osteopathic schools. *J. of Medical Education*, 53: 816–824, 1978.

Pokorny, A. D., and Solomon, J. A follow-up survey of drug abuse and alcoholism teaching in medical schools. *J. of Medical Education*, 58: 316–321, 1983.

Pollock, V. E., Volavka, J., Goodwin, D. W., Mednick, S. A., Gabrielli, W. F., Knop, J., and Schulsinger, F. The EEG after alcohol administration in men at risk for alcoholism. *Arch. Gen. Psychiatry*, 40: 857–864, 1983.

Pophan, R., Schmidt, W., and deLint, J. Government control measures to prevent hazardous drinking. In: Ewing, J. A., and Rouse, B. A. (eds.), *Drinking: Alcohol in American Society—Issues and Current Research*. Chicago, Nelson-Hall, 1978.

Pottenger, M., McKernon, J., Patrice, L. E., Weissman, M. M., Ruben, H. L., and Newberry, P. The frequency and persistence of depressive symptoms in the alcohol abuser. *J. Nerv. Ment. Disease*, 166(8): 562–570, 1978.

Powell, W. J., and Klatshim, G. Duration of survival in patients with Laennec's Cirrhosis. *Am. J. Med.*, 44: 402–420, 1968.

Price, G. M. A study of the wives of 20 alcoholics. *Q. J. Stud. Alcohol*, 5: 620–627, 1945.

Product Profile: Antabuse (Disulfiram) in Alcoholism. New York, Ayerst Laboratories, 1979.

Purtilo, D. T., and Gottlieb, L. S. Cirrhosis and hepatoma occurring in Boston City Hospital (1917-1968). *Cancer*, 32(2): 458-462, 1973.

Rado, S. The psychoanalysis of pharmacothymia (drug addiction). *Psychoanalytic Quarterly*, 2: 1-23, 1933.

Rae, J. B. The influence of the wives on the treatment outcome of alcoholics: A follow-up study at two years. *Br. J. Psychiatry*, 120: 601-613, 1972.

Rae, J. B., and Forbes, A. R. Clinical and psychometric characteristics of the wives of alcoholics. *Br. J. Psychiatry*, 112: 197-200, 1966.

Rand, C. S. W., Kulchan, J. M., and Roblins, L. Surgery for obesity and marriage quality. *JAMA*, 247: 1419-1422, 1982.

Reich, L. H., Davies, R. K., and Himmelhoch, J. M. Excessive alcohol use in manic-depressive illness. *Am. J. Psychiatry*, 131(1): 83-86, 1974.

Reiss, D. *The Family's Construction of Reality.* Cambridge, MA, Harvard University Press, 1981.

Reynolds, C. M., Merry, J., and Coppen, A. Prophylactic treatment of alcoholism by lithium carbonate: An initial report. In: Goodwin, D. W., and Erickson, C. K. (eds.), *Alcoholism and Affective Disorders.* New York, Spectrum Publishers, pp. 31-37, 1979.

Rezler, A. G. Attitude changes during medical school: A review of the literature. *J. Medical Education*, 49: 1023-1030, 1974.

Rimmer, J. Psychiatric illness in husbands of alcoholics. *Q. J. Stud. Alcohol*, 35: 281-283, 1974.

Rimmer, J., and Jacobsen, B. Alcoholism in schizophrenics and their relatives. *J. Stud. Alcohol*, 38(9): 1781-1784, 1977.

Rimmer, J., and Winokur, G. The spouses of alcoholics: An example of assortative mating. *Dis. Nerv. System*, 509-511, 1972.

Ritchie, J. M. *Pharmacological Basis of Therapeutics* (4th ed.). New York, Macmillan, 1975.

Robins, L. N. *Deviant Children Grow Up: A Sociological and Psychiatric Study of Sociopathic Personality.* Baltimore, Williams & Wilkins, 1966.

Robins, L. N., Helzer, J. E., Weissman, M. M., Orvaschel, H., Gruenberg, E., Burke, J. D., Jr., and Regier, D. A. Lifetime prevalence of specific psychiatric disorders in three sites. *Arch. Gen. Psychiatry*, 41: 949-958, 1984.

Robinson, L. H., and Podnos, B. Resistance of psychiatrists in treatment of alcoholism. *J. Nerv. Ment. Disease*, 143(3): 220-225, 1966.

Rogers, P. D. Viewpoints. *Dallas Morning News*, July 7, 1985.

Rosenbaum, B. Married women alcoholics at the Washingtonian Hospital. *Q. J. Stud. Alcohol*, 19: 79-89, 1958.

Rosenberg, C. M. Drug maintenance in the outpatient treatment of chronic alcoholism. *Arch. Gen. Psychiatry*, 30: 373-377, 1974.

Rosett, H. L., Snyder, P., Sander, L. W., Lee, A., Cook, P., Weiner, L., and Gould, J. Effects of maternal drinking on neonate state regulation. *Developmental Medicine and Child Neurology*, 21: 464-473, 1979.

Rosett, H. L., Weiner, L., and Edelin, K. D. Strategies for prevention of fetal alcohol effects. *Obstet. Gynecol.*, 57: 1-7, 1981.

Rosett, H. L., Weiner, L., Zuckerman, B., McKinley, S., and Edelin, K. Reduction of alcohol consumption during pregnancy with benefits to newborn. *Alcohol: Clin. Exp. Res.*, 4: 178-184, 1980.

Rounsaville, B. J., Spitzer, R. L., and Williams, J. B. W. Proposed changes in DSM-III substance use disorders: Description and rationale. *Am. J. Psychiatry*, 143(4): 463-468, 1986.

Rubin, E. Alcoholic myopathy in heart and muscle. *N. England J. Med.*, 301: 28–33, 1979.

Rush, B. Inquiry into the effects of ardent spirits upon the human body and mind. In: *Aspects of Alcoholism*. New York, J. P. Lippincott, pp. 39–44, 1966.

Ryan, C., and Butters, N. Learning and memory impairments in young and old alcoholics: Evidence for the premature aging hypothesis. *Alcohol: Clin. Exp. Res.*, 4: 288–293, 1980.

Ryan, C., and Butters, N. Cognitive deficits in alcoholics. In: Kissin, B., and Begleiter, H. (eds.), *The Biology of Alcoholism*, Volume 7. New York, Plenum, 1983.

Saxon, J. J., Nace, E. P., and Cammarota, C. A low-cost evaluation of alcoholism treatment in a private psychiatric hospital program. *The Psychiatric Hospital*, 14(2): 114–118, 1983.

Schuckit, M. A. Alcoholism and sociopathy: Diagnostic confusion. *Q. J. Stud. Alcohol*, 34: 157–164, 1973.

Schuckit, M. A. Inpatient and residential approaches to the treatment of alcoholism. In: Mendelson, J. H., and Mello, N. K. (eds.), *The Diagnosis and Treatment of Alcoholism*. New York, McGraw-Hill, pp. 257–282, 1979.

Schuckit, M. A. The history of psychotic symptoms in alcoholics. *J. Clin. Psychiatry*, 43(2): 53–57, 1982.

Schuckit, M. A. Alcoholic men with no alcoholic first-degree relatives. *Am. J. Psychiatry*, 140: 439–443, 1983.

Schuckit, M. A. Genetics and the risk for alcoholism. *JAMA*, 254(18): 2614–2617, 1985.

Schuckit, M. A., Li, T. K., Cloninger, C. R., and Deitrich, R. A. Genetics of alcoholism. *Alcohol: Clin. Exp. Res.*, 9(6): 475–492, 1985.

Schuckit, M. A., and Morrissey, E. R. Alcoholism in women: Some clinical and social perspectives with an emphasis on possible subtypes. In: Greenblatt, M., and Schuckit, M. A. (eds.), *The Diagnosis and Treatment of Alcoholism*. New York, Grune & Stratton, pp. 5–35, 1976.

Schuckit, M. A., and Rayses, V. Ethanol ingestion: Differences in blood acetaldehyde concentrations in relatives of alcoholics and controls. *Science*, 230: 54–55, 1979.

Schuckit, M. A., and Russell, J. W. Clinical importance of age at first drink in a group of young men. *Am. J. Psychiatry*, 140(9): 1221–1222, 1983.

Seixas, F. A. Assessing "emerging concepts" editorial comment. *Alcohol: Clin. Exp. Res.*, 4: 281–282, 1977.

Sellers, E. M., and Kalant, H. Alcohol intoxication and withdrawal. *New England Journal of Medicine*, 294: 757–762, 1976.

Selzer, M. L. The Michigan Alcoholism Screening Test: The quest for a new diagnostic instrument. *Am. J. Psychiatry*, 127: 89–94, 1971.

Senay, E. C. *Substance Abuse Disorders in Clinical Practice*. Littleton, MA, John Wright-PSG, pp. 42–43, 1983.

Shaffer, J. W., Freinek, W. R., Wolf, S., Foxwell, N. H., and Kurland, A. A. A controlled evaluation of chlordiazepozide (lithium) in the treatment of convalescing alcoholics. *J. Nerv. Ment. Disease*, 137: 494–507, 1963.

Shapiro, R. J. A family therapy approach to alcoholism. *Journal of Marriage and Family Counseling*, 39: 71–78, 1977.

Shaywitz, S. E., Cohen, D. J., and Shaywitz, B. A. Behavior and learning difficulties in children of normal intelligence born to alcoholic mothers. *J. of Pediatrics*, 96: 978–982, 1980.

Sheehan, J. J., Wieman, R. J., and Bechtel, J. E. Follow-up of a twelve-month treatment program for chronic alcoholics. *International J. of Addictions*, 16(2): 233–241, 1981.

Skuja, A. T., Wood, D., and Bucky, S. F. Reported drinking among post-treatment alcohol abusers: A preliminary report. *American J. of Drug and Alcohol Abuse*, 3(3): 472–483, 1976.

Sobell, M. B., and Sobell, L. C. Individualized behavior therapy for alcoholics. *Behavioral Therapy*, 4: 49, 1973.

Solberg, R. J. *The Dry Drunk Syndrome Revisited.* Center City, MN, Hazelden Foundation, 1983.

Solomon, J. The role of drug therapies in the context of alcoholism. In: Pattison, E. M., and Kaufman, E. (eds.), *Encyclopedic Handbook of Alcoholism.* New York, Gardner Press, pp. 1043–1053, 1982.

Solomon, J., Vanga, N., Morgan, J. P., and Joseph, P. Emergency room physicians' recognition of alcohol misuse. *J. Stud. Alcohol*, 41(5): 583–586, 1980.

Solomon, S. D. *Tailoring Alcoholism Therapy to Client Needs.* DHHS Publication No. (ADM) 81-1129, p. 24, 1981.

Spitzer, R. L., Endicott, J., and Robins, E. Research diagnostic criteria. Rationale and reliability. *Arch. Gen. Psychiatry*, 35: 773–782, 1978.

Spitzer, R. L., and Williams, J. B. Structured Clinical Interviews for DSM-III (SCID 3/15/86). New York, New York State Psychiatric Institute, Biometrics Research Department, 1983.

Spring, G. K., and Rothgery, J. M. The link between alcoholism and affective disorders. *Hospital and Community Psychiatry*, 35(8): 820–823, 1984.

Stabenau, J. R. Implications of family history of alcoholism, antisocial personality, and sex differences in alcohol dependence. *Am. J. Psychiatry*, 141(10): 1178–1182, 1984.

Steinglass, P. A life history model of the alcoholic family. *Family Process*, 19: 211–226, 1980.

Steinglass, P. The alcoholic family at home. Patterns of interaction in dry, wet, and transitional stages of alcoholism. *Arch. Gen. Psychiatry*, 38: 578–584, 1981.

Steinglass, P., Weiner, S., and Mendelson, J. Interactional issues as determinants of alcoholism. *Am. J. Psychiatry*, 128: 275–280, 1971.

Steinmetz, S. K., and Straus, M. A. *Violence in the Family.* New York, Harper & Row, 1974.

Stenstedt, A. A study in manic-depressive psychosis. *Acta. Psychiat. Neurol. Scand.*, Suppl. 79, 3–111, 1952.

Stephenson, J. N., Moberg, P., Daniels, B. J., and Robertson, J. F. Treating the intoxicated adolescent. A need for comprehensive services. *JAMA*, 252(14): 1884–1888, 1984.

Stewart, R. P. Building an alliance between the families of patients and the hospital: Model and process. *National Association of Private Psychiatric Hospitals Journal*, 12(2): 63–68, 1981.

Stimmel, B., Cohen, M., Sturiano, V., Hanbury, R., Korts, D., and Jackson, G. Is treatment for alcoholism effective in persons on methadone maintenance? *Am. J. Psychiatry*, 140: 862–866, 1983.

Stockwell, T., Hodgson, R., Edwards, G., Taylor, C., and Rankin, H. The development of a questionnaire to measure severity of alcohol dependence. *Br. J. Addict.*, 74: 79–87, 1979.

Stokes, P. E. Endocrine disturbances associated with alcohol and alcoholism. In:

Pattison, E. M., and Kaufman, E. (eds.), *Encyclopedic Handbook of Alcoholism*. New York, Gardner Press, pp. 311–324, 1982.

Streissguth, A. P. *American Medical News*, March 8, 1985.

Streissguth, A. P., Herman, C. S., and Smith, D. W. Intelligence, behavior, and dysmorphogenesis in the fetal alcohol syndrome: A report on 20 patients. *J. of Pediatrics*, 92: 363–367, 1978.

Stuckey, R. F., and Harrison, J. S. The alcoholism rehabilitation center. In: Pattison, E. M., and Kaufman, E. (eds.), *Encyclopedic Handbook of Alcoholism*. New York, Gardner Press, pp. 865–873, 1982.

Sudnow, D. *Dead on Arrival, Passing On: The Social Organization of Dying*. Englewood Cliffs, NJ, Prentice-Hall, 1967.

Swartz, C. M., and Dunner, F. J. Dexamethasone suppression testing of alcoholics. *Arch. Gen. Psychiatry*, 39: 1309–1312, 1982.

Tarter, R. E., Alterman, A. I., and Edwards, K. L. Vulnerability to alcoholism in men: A behavior-genetic perspective. *J. Stud. Alcohol*, 46(4): 329–356, 1985.

Tarter, R. E., and Edwards, K. L. Multifactorial etiology of neuropsychological impairment in alcoholics. *Alcohol: Clin. Exp. Res.*, 10(2): 128–135, 1986.

Tarter, R. E., McBride, H., Buonpane, N., and Schneider, D. U. Differentiation of alcoholics: Childhood history of minimal brain dysfunction, family history, and drinking pattern. *Arch. Gen. Psychiatry*, 34: 761–768, 1977.

Thompson, W. L. Management of alcohol withdrawal syndromes. *Arch. Internal Medicine*, 138: 278–283, 1978.

Thomsen, R. *Bill W.* New York, Harper & Row, 1975.

Tiebout, H. M. The act of surrender in the therapeutic process: With special reference to alcoholism. *Q. J. Stud. Alcohol*, 10: 48–58, 1949. (As distributed by The National Council on Alcoholism, Inc. in pamphlet L66, "The act of surrender in the therapeutic process," pp. 2–15.)

Tiebout, H. M. Surrender versus compliance in therapy. *Q. J. Stud. Alcohol*, 14: 58–68, 1953.

Tiebout, H. M. The ego factors in surrender in alcoholism. *Q. J. Stud. Alcohol*, 15: 610–621, 1954.

Tiebout, H. M. Intervention in psychotherapy. *Am. J. Psychoanal.*, 22(1): 3, 1963.

Tiebout, H. M. Direct treatment of a symptom. Center City, MN, Hazelden Foundation, 1973.

Tiebout, H. M. Intervention in psychotherapy. *Am. J. Psychoanal.*, 33: 1–6, 1982.

Tomsovic, M., and Edwards, R. V. Lysergide treatment of schizophrenic and nonschizophrenic alcoholics: A controlled evaluation. *Q. J. Stud. Alcohol*, 31: 932–949, 1970.

Towle, L. W. Alcoholism treatment outcome in different populations. Proceedings from the Fourth Annual Conference of the NIPAA, April, 1974.

Tuck, R. R., Brew, B. J., Britton, A. M., and Lowey, J. Alcohol and brain damage. *Brit. J. Addict.*, 79: 251–259, 1984.

Vaillant, G. E. Theoretical hierarchy of adaptive ego mechanisms. *Arch. Gen. Psychiatry*, 24: 107–118, 1971.

Vaillant, G. E. Dangers of psychotherapy in the treatment of alcoholism. In: Bean, M. H., and Zinberg, N. E. (eds.), *Dynamic Approaches to the Understanding and Treatment of Alcoholism*. New York, The Free Press, pp. 36–54, 1981.

Vaillant, G. E. *The Natural History of Alcoholism*. Cambridge, MA, Harvard University Press, 1983a.

Vaillant, G. E. Natural history of male alcoholism: Is alcoholism the cart or the horse to sociopathy? *Br. J. Addict.*, 78: 317–326, 1983b.

Vaillant, G. E. The course of alcoholism and lessons for treatment. In: Grinspoon, L. (ed.), *Psychiatry Update*, 3: 311–319, 1984.

Vaillant, G. E. Personal communication, March 20, 1985.

Van Thiel, D. H., Cobb, C. F., Herman, G. B., Perez, H. A., Estes, L., and Gavaler, J. S. An examination of various mechanisms for ethanol-induced testicular injury: Studies utilizing the isolated perfused rot tests. *Endocrinology*, 109: 2004–2015, 1981.

Van Thiel, D. H., Gavaler, S. S., Lester, R., and Goodman, M. D. Alcohol-induced testicular atrophy: An experimental model for hypogonadism occurring in chronic alcoholic men. *Gastroenterology*, 69: 326–332, 1975.

Van Thiel, D. H., Lester, R., and Vartukaitis, J. Evidence for a defect in pituitary secretion of luteinizing hormone in chronic alcoholic men. *J. Clin. Endocrinology and Metabolism*, 47: 499–507, 1978.

Viamontes, J. A. Review of drug effectiveness in the treatment of alcoholism. *American J. Psychoanal.*, 128: 1570–1571, 1972.

Victor, M. The role of hypomagnesemia and respiratory alkalosis in the genesis of alcohol withdrawal symptoms. *Annals New York Acad. Sci.*, 215: 235–248, 1973.

Victor, M., Adams, R. D., and Collins, G. N. *The Wernicke-Korsakoff Syndrome*. Philadelphia, F. A. Davis, 1971.

Victor, M., and Hope, J. M. The phenomenon of auditory hallucinosis in chronic alcoholism. *J. Nerv. Ment. Disease*, 128: 451–481, 1957.

Voegtlin, W. L., and Broz, W. R. The conditioned reflex treatment of chronic alcoholism. X. An analysis of 3,125 admissions over a period of ten and a half years. *Annals of Internal Medicine*, 30: 580–597, 1949.

Wallerstein, R. S., Chotles, J. W., Friend, M. B., Hammersley, D. W., Perlswig, E. D., and Winship, G. M. *Hospital Treatment of Alcoholism: A Comparative Experimental Study*. New York, Basic Books, 1957.

Webb, L. J., DiClemente, C. C., Johnstone, E. E., Sanders, J. L., and Perley, R. A. *DSM-III Training Guide*. New York, Brunner/Mazel, pp. 126–128, 1981.

Wegscheider, S. Co-dependency: The therapeutic void. *Focus on Family and Chemical Dependency*, 6(6): 5, U.S. Journal of Drug and Alcohol Dependence, 1983.

Weiss, K. J., and Rosenberg, D. J. Prevalence of anxiety disorder among alcoholics. *J. Clin. Psychiatry*, 46(1): 3–5, 1985.

Weissman, M., Myers, J., and Harding, P. Prevalence and psychiatric heterogeneity of alcoholism in a United States urban community. *Q. J. Stud. Alcohol*, 41(7): 672–681, 1980.

Weissman, M. M., and Myers, J. K. Clinical depression in alcoholism. *Am. J. Psychiatry*, 137: 372–373, 1980.

Welford, B. B. *Drug Abuse: A Guide for the Primary Care Physician*. Chicago, American Medical Association, 1981.

Weller, R. A., and Halikas, J. A. Marijuana use and psychiatric illness: A follow-up study. *Am. J. Psychiatry*, 142(7): 848–850, 1985.

Wellman, W. M., Maxwell, M. A., and O'Holloren, P. Private hospital alcoholic patients and the changing conception of the "typical" alcoholic. *Q. J. Stud. Alcohol*, 18: 388–404, 1957.

Welsh, G. W. An anxiety index and an internalization ratio for the MMPI. *J. Consult. Psychol.*, 16: 65–72, 1952.

Whalen, T. Wives of alcoholics: Four types observed in a family service agency. *Q. J. Stud. Alcohol*, 14: 632–641, 1953.

Whalley, L. J. Sexual adjustment of male alcoholics. *Acta. Psychiat. Scand.*, 58: 281–298, 1978.

Whitters, A., Troughton, E., Cadoret, R. J., and Wishmer, R. Evidence for clinical heterogeneity in antisocial alcoholics. *Comp. Psychiatry*, 25(2): 158–164, 1984.

Wilsnack, S. C. Femininity by the bottle. *Psychology Today*, p. 39, April, 1973.

Wilsnack, S. C., Klassen, A. D., and Wilsnack, R. W. Drinking and reproductive dysfunction among women in a 1981 national survey. *Alcohol Clin. Exp. Res.*, 8(5): 451–458, 1984.

Wilson, C., and Orford, J. Children of alcoholics. Report of a preliminary study and comments on the literature, *J. Stud. Alcohol*, 39(1): 121–142, 1978.

Wilson, G. T. Effects of alcohol on human sexual behavior. In: Mello, N. K. (ed.), *Advances in Substance Abuse: Behavioral and Biological Research*, Volume 2. Greenwich, CT, JAI Press, pp. 1–40, 1981.

Wilson, W. G. *Alcoholics Anonymous Comes of Age: A Brief History of AA*. New York, AA Publishing, p. vii, 1957a.

Wilson, W. G. *Twelve Steps and Twelve Traditions*. New York, Harper & Row, 1957b.

Winokur, G. Alcoholism and depression in the family. In: Goodwin, D. W., and Erickson, C. K. (eds.), *Alcoholism and Affective Disorders: Clinical, Genetic and Biochemical Studies*. Jamaica, NY, Spectrum Publications, pp. 49–56, 1979.

Winokur, G., Clayton, P. J., and Reich, T. *Manic-Depressive Illness*. St. Louis, Mosby, 1969.

Wolf, I. Alcoholism and marriage. *Q. J. Stud. Alcohol.*, 19: 511–513, 1958.

Wolf, I., Chafetz, M. E., Blane, H. T., and Hill, M. J. Social factors in the diagnosis of alcoholism, II. Attitudes of physicians. *Q. J. Stud. Alcohol*, 26: 72–79, 1965.

Wolin, S. J., Bennett, L. A., Noonan, D. L., and Teitelbaum, M. A. Disrupted family rituals. A factor in the intergenerational transmission of alcoholism. *J. Stud. Alcohol*, 41(3): 199–214, 1980.

Wood, D., Wender, P. H., and Reimherr, F. W. The prevalence of attention deficit disorder, residual type, or minimal brain dysfunction, in a population of male alcoholic patients. *Am. J. Psychiatry*, 140: 95–98, 1983.

Wood, H. P., and Duffy, E. L. Psychological factors in alcoholic women. *Am. J. Psychiatry*, 123: 341–345, 1966.

Woodruff, R. A., Guze, S. B., Clayton, P. J., and Carr, D. Alcoholism and depression. *Arch. Gen. Psychiatry*, 28: 97–100, 1973.

Woody, G. E., McLellan, A. T., Luborsky, L., and O'Brien, C. P. Sociopathy and psychotherapy outcome. *Arch. Gen. Psychiatry*, 42: 1081–1086, 1985.

Wurmser, L. Personality disorders and drug dependency. In: Lion, J. R. (ed.), *Personality Disorders: Diagnosis and Management*. Baltimore, Williams & Wilkins, pp. 113–142, 1974.

Yalom, I. D. *The Theory and Practice of Group Psychotherapy*, 2nd edition. New York, Basic Books, 1975.

Yalom, I. D., Bloch, S., Bond, G., Zimmerman, E., and Qualls, B. Alcoholics in interactional group therapy: An outcome study. *Arch. Gen. Psychiatry*, 35: 419–425, 1978.

Young, L. D., and Keeler, M. H. Sobriety data on lithium in alcoholism. *Lancet*, 1: 144, 1977.

Zimberg, S. New York State Task Force on Alcohol Problems, Position Paper on Treatment. *N. Y. State J. Med.*, 75: 1794–1798, 1975.

Zimberg, S. Psychotherapy in the treatment of alcoholism. In: Pattison, E. M., and Kaufman, E. (eds.), *Encyclopedic Handbook of Alcoholism*. New York, Gardner Press, pp. 999–1010, 1982.

Zimberg, S. *The Clinical Management of Alcoholism*. New York, Brunner/Mazel, pp. 81–87, 1982.

Index